LATE ROMAN STUDIES

LATE

ROMAN

STUDIES

by
Charles Henry Coster

HARVARD UNIVERSITY PRESS
CAMBRIDGE, MASSACHUSETTS
1968

IN MEMORY OF BERNARD BERENSON

AND THEODOR E. MOMMSEN

PREFACE

M<small>ANY OF THESE PAPERS</small> are by no means new and are scattered through periodicals and *Festschriften* not always easily available. Insofar as they are of interest at all, then, it may be convenient to reprint them in a more readily accessible form. There is the further advantage that most of the new matter in this book is so closely connected with the old that the argument may be clearer if both can be read together.

Two papers in this series are perhaps not altogether correctly included in a volume called *Late Roman Studies:* "The Economic Position of Cyrenaica in Classical Times," and my review of "Medieval and Renaissance Studies" by the late Professor Theodor E. Mommsen. Inclusion of the former article, though, is possibly justifiable as background for the articles about Synesius, and the latter does at least call attention to an exceptionally interesting book. There is further sentimental justification. This book is dedicated to two old friends of the author: Bernard Berenson and Theodor E. Mommsen. It was a trip to Cyrenaica with Mr. Berenson — see Mary Berenson, *A Vicarious Trip to the Barbary Coast* (London: Constable, 1938) — that first aroused my interest in that region and in Synesius. It likewise seems fitting to include my tribute to Professor Mommsen in a book dedicated to his memory.

I wish to thank the *Byzantinische Zeitschrift*, the *Annuaire de l'Institut de Philologie et d'Histoire Orientales et Slaves, Speculum*, Professor P. R. Coleman-Norton and the Princeton University Press, *Byzantion*, and the *Classical Journal* for permission to reprint articles and reviews which first appeared in their pages. I am also grateful for permission to use plate 63 (1. Lieferung) and plate 7 (2. Lieferung) from R. Delbrück, *Die Consulardiptychen und verwandte Denkmäler* (Berlin: Walter de Gruyter & Co., 1929) as illustrations for this volume, and for permission to use for the same purpose the magnificent illustration of a gorgon's head that is shown on plate 84 of R. Beny, *Thrones of Earth and Heaven* (New York: Harry N. Abrams, Inc., 1958). It is with sadness that I must acknowledge the kindness of the late Professor Gino Chierici, who some years ago sent me the photograph of a capital from the Edicola di S. Felice at Cimitile. This was intended to illustrate my article on St. Paulinus of Nola when it was first published. It arrived too late for that purpose, and since then Professor Chierici has died. It is the more fitting that the photograph should embellish the reprinting; I am therefore most grateful to Professor Umberto Chierici, Superintendent of the Monuments of Piedmont and son of the late Professor Gino Chierici, for his kind permission to reproduce it here.

My sincere thanks to the Harvard University Press for their assistance, their excellent advice, and great patience. Above all, I am most grateful to Professor Giles Constable for his unfailing and most valuable encouragement and help.

Charles Henry Coster

Warwick, New York

CONTENTS

ILLUSTRATIONS

LATE ROMAN STUDIES

ABBREVIATIONS

BZ	*Byzantinische Zeitschrift*
CAH	*The Cambridge Ancient History*
CMH	*The Cambridge Medieval History,* old series
DS	Daremberg-Saglio, *Dictionnaire des antiquités grecques et romaines*
Iud. Quinq.	C. H. Coster, *The Iudicium Quinquevirale,* Monograph No. 10 of the Mediaeval Academy of America (Cambridge, Mass. 1935)
Jones *LRE*	A. H. M. Jones, *The Later Roman Empire* (Oxford 1964)
MGHAA	Monumenta Germaniae Historica, *Auctores Antiquissimi*
RE	Pauly-Wissowa, *Real-Encyclopädie der classischen Altertumswissenschaft* (References are in every case to volumes, rather than half volumes, and to column numbers.)
SEHHW	M. Rostovtzeff, *The Social and Economic History of the Hellenistic World* (Oxford 1941, 2nd ed. 1953)
SEHRE	—— *The Social and Economic History of the Roman Empire* (Oxford 1926, 2nd ed. 1957)
Stein I	Ernst Stein, *Geschichte des spätrömischen Reiches,* I (Vienna 1928)
Stein II	—— *Histoire du Bas-Empire,* II (Paris, Brussels, Amsterdam 1949)

CHAPTER I

THE IUDICIUM QUINQUEVIRALE
IN CONSTANTINOPLE

᠍᠍᠍

M AX RADIN writes that the *iudicium quinquevirale* (a tribunal of late Roman times, consisting of the prefect of the City and five senators chosen by lot, which was formed under some circumstances to determine whether senators were guilty of capital offenses) may have "thrown . . . a prognostic shadow on the developing *iudicium parium* of the Feudal law." [1] He adds, however, that if this was so the connection "must" have been through Constantinople, since "In Rome, as the well-known lament of Gregory shows, the senate had practically disappeared by 600."

The chief evidence of a connection, it seems to me, is the inclusion of *Cod. Theod.* 2.1.12 (a statute of Honorius dealing with the *iudicium quinquevirale*) in the Breviary of Alaric, and the addition to it of an *interpretatio* which points in the direction of the medieval practice.[2] The Breviary was promulgated in 506 and was law for the Roman

---

This article is reprinted from the *Byzantinische Zeitschrift* 38 (1938) 119–32.

[1] In his review of *The Iudicium Quinquevirale* in *American Journal of Philology* 57 (1936) 489–94. Subsequent quotations from and citations of Radin in this article are from the same source. For a similar view, see C. H. Coster, *The Iudicium Quinquevirale* (The Mediaeval Academy of America [Cambridge, Mass. 1935] 82 n. 216), hereafter referred to as *Iud. Quinq.*

[2] *Lex Romana Wisigotorum* 2.1.12.

subjects of the Visigothic king — that is, it was not law in the Empire but in parts of western Europe outside the Empire,[3] and this at a time when the *iudicium quinquevirale* was still a living institution in Italy.[4] In view of the text in the Breviary and its repetition in various forms in the epitomes,[5] it seems difficult to agree that the *iudicium quinquevirale* "must" have influenced western law solely through Constantinople.

But the *iudicium,* if it ever existed in Constantinople, may have influenced later western institutions from the East as well as from the West. Radin believes, of course, that it did exist there. He argues that the use of the word *licebit* in *Cod. Theod.* 9.1.13 (the statute providing for the setting up of the *iudicium quinquevirale*) shows that "the Emperor reserves to himself an alternative jurisdiction" to the *iudicium* and therefore that "the practice of setting up the *iudicium* may have continued sporadically and have survived in tradition." He would not, that is, expect to find much evidence of its existence. But some evidence he believes he does find: the trial of Theodore Santabarenus in Constantinople in the reign of Leo VI (886–912).

But *licebit,* in this context, will not bear the construction suggested. Nor can it be construed, as proposed by M. L. W. Laistner,[6] to mean that the prefect of the City, hearing cases under the statute, had the choice of sitting alone or with five associate judges. The word occurs only once in the

---

[3] See Berger in *RE* XII 2407ff, art. "Lex Romana Wisigotorum."

[4] Cass. *Var.* 4.22–23. In Mommsen's ed. (*MGHAA* XII 123–24), these letters are dated a. 510/11.

[5] See *Lex Romana Visigotorum,* ed. Gustavus Haenel (Leipzig 1849) 34–35.

[6] In his review of *Iud. Quinq.* in *American Historical Review* 42 (1936–37) 284–85. Subsequent citations of Laistner in this chapter are from the same source.

statute, in the last sentence. This reads: "Sed praefecto urbis cognoscenti de capite senatorum spectatorum maxime virorum iudicium quinquevirale sociabitur et de praesentibus et administratorum honore functis licebit adiungere sorte ductos, non sponte delectos." The sentence makes no reservation in favor of the emperor. The first half states that when cases are brought before the prefect of the City under the terms of the statute, he is to try them with the assistance of five senators[7] as associate judges. It is not permissive, but mandatory; the decisive word is *sociabitur*. The second half tells how the five associate judges are to be chosen. They may (*licebit*) be chosen from present and past holders of administrative offices,[8] but they must be chosen by lot, not selected as the prefect of the City may please. Nor is there any other passage in the statute which should be construed as reserving an alternative jurisdiction for the emperor[9] or

---

[7] A. H. Campbell, in his review of *Iud. Quinq.* in *Classical Review* 50 (1936) 152, is inclined to think that this construction strains the Latin word order. In this he is followed by Radin and Laistner. The point is well taken. Cassiodorus, however, in a letter (*Var.* 4.22) to Argolicus, prefect of the City, wrote: "Sed nos, qui nescimus a legibus discrepare, . . . praesenti auctoritate decernimus, ut quinque senatoribus, id est magnificis et patriciis viris Symmacho Decio Volusiano atque Caeliano nec non illustri viro Maximiano, hanc causam legitima examinatione pensetis." The emphasis on *senatoribus* is striking in view of his insistence on literal compliance with the law.

[8] I am glad to accept the correction suggested by Radin, Laistner, and McGuire (see the review of *Iud. Quinq.* by Martin R. P. McGuire in *Catholic Historical Review* 23 (1937–38) 255–56.

[9] I formerly took the contrary view. See *Ind. Quinq.* 3, 24–25, 32. I had construed the *vel* in a phrase ("referat ad scientiam nostram vel ad inclytas potestates") of *Cod. Theod.* 9.1.13 as disjunctive. It is conjunctive: all cases are to be referred to the emperor and the prefects; certain ones to the prefect of the City, *all* others (*de ceteris*) to the praetorian prefect. The statute then prescribes how cases coming before the prefect of the City are to be heard. It is evident that the emperor wished to have direct information, but that the trials took place before the prefects. If *Cod. Theod.* 9.1.13 is to be read, as probably it ought to be, in conjunction with *Cod. Theod.* 9.40.10, it follows that the emperor reserves the right to determine the sentence to be imposed if the accused has been found

as allowing the prefect of the City to hear cases under the statute without the assistance of the associate judges.

But even so, one could not deny the existence of the tribunal in Constantinople if the trial of Theodore Santabarenus in that city had in fact taken place before it, as Lécrivain, citing Georgius Monachus, believed.[10] Radin is under the impression that I wrote that I could not find an account of the trial in the text of this chronicler as published in the Migne collection, and he points out quite rightly that it is to be found in Migne, *Patr. Gr.* CX 1089, and also in the Bonn *Corpus Script. Hist. Byz.* XLV 850. He adds that both versions tell us of five judges, and that in the Bonn version all five are named. (In this he is mistaken: the text as printed in either of these two collections tells us of four judges only, and names four only — Stephen the *magister,* Andreas Craterus the *domesticus,* the patrician Gouver or Goumer, and John Hagiopolites.) He further suggests that, since Leo VI was "the Leo of the *Basilica,*" that monarch may well have revived the *iudicium quinquevirale* in Constantinople, if indeed it had not always existed there.

In fact, I had discussed Lécrivain's contention on the page of my monograph cited by Radin[11] and had written not that I could not find an account of the trial but that the account did not appear to support Lécrivain's position. My objection

---

guilty. Cf. the reservations in *Cod. Iust.* 3.24.3, and also Otto Karlowa, *Römische Rechtsgeschichte* (Leipzig 1885) I 867. But see also McGuire (above, n. 8), who believes that the provincial governors determined the guilt of the accused and that the *iudicium quinquevirale* (in cases coming before it) was limited to the fixing of the penalty to be imposed.

[10] Charles Lécrivain, *Le Sénat romain depuis Dioclétien à Rome et à Constantinople,* in Bibliothèque des Ecoles françaises d'Athènes et de Rome, fasc. 52 (Paris 1888) 230 n. 9.

[11] *Iud. Quinq.* 8.

was that only four judges were mentioned, not six, and that even these four did not appear to have been chosen by lot. I must now modify my position to the extent of saying that we are here dealing only with various versions of the text of the Logothete, and that in the best of these, cited neither by me in *The Iudicium Quinquevirale* nor by Radin in his review,[12] five judges are named: Stephen the *magister,* Andreas the *domesticus,* the patricians Craterus and Gouver or Goumer, and John Hagiopolites. *Gouver* or *Goumer* is evidently an attempt to deal with some barbarian name such as Cunibert or Gower or Gumoar, so that it is suspicious that we find only Craterus unnamed, with nothing but an epithet and his rank. Nevertheless, the best texts of the Logothete do mention five judges, not four, in this passage.

But that is not enough. When a case was tried before the *iudicium quinquevirale,* it was tried neither by four judges nor by five, but by six: the prefect of the City, who sat *ex officio,* and five associate judges, who were chosen by lot. The words of *Cod. Theod.* 9.1.13 are definite: ". . . Sed praefecto urbis cognoscenti de capite senatorum spectatorum maxime virorum iudicium quinquevirale sociabitur . . ." This is made clear also in the letter of Cassiodorus to Argolicus, prefect of the City, concerning the trial of Basilius and Praetextatus. He writes: ". . . praesenti auctoritate decernimus, ut quinque senatoribus, id est magnificis et patriciis viris Symmacho Decio Volusiano atque Caeliano nec non

---

[12] Cf. Vatican MS. 153, reproduced in V. M. Istrin, *Khronika Georgiia Amartola* 2 (Petrograd 1922) 25; also Theodosius Melitenus, *Chronographia,* ed. Tafel (in *Monumenta Saecularia,* K. Bayr. Akad. d. Wiss., Munich 1859) 184. I am indebted to S. H. Cross for the former reference and to F. Dölger for the latter. Professor Dölger has further referred me to the article by Ostrogorsky in *Seminarium Kondakovianum* 5 (1932) 17–37 for a discussion of the text of the Logothete.

illustri viro Maximiano, hanc causam legitima examinatione pensetis." [13] From both texts, we learn that the prefect of the City sat not merely as president, but as one of the six actual judges (*sociabitur, pensetis*).

Nor is there anything in the law to encourage us to look for the *iudicium quinquevirale* in Constantinople during the reign of Leo VI. Whether or not *Cod. Theod.* 9.1.13 and *Cod. Theod.* 2.1.12 were applied in Constantinople (a question which we shall shortly take up), they were not incorporated in the Code of Justinian, and although Leo VI was indeed, as Radin points out, "the Leo of the *Basilica*," yet that seems no reason for supposing that Leo, in the matter of the trial of capital charges against senators, ceased to follow the Justinian Code and subsequent legislation, upon which the *Basilica* was based, in order to return to the Theodosian Code.

Not only Radin, however, but also W. Ensslin has suggested [14] that the *iudicium quinquevirale* may have existed in Constantinople. Ensslin has rightly pointed out that the inclusion of Gratian's law in the Theodosian Code as *Cod. Theod.* 9.1.13 creates a presumption that, from then on at least, it was valid in the Empire as a whole, not in the western provinces only. Cases within the category covered by the law would, if they arose in the eastern provinces, be referred to the praetorian prefects; if they arose in Constantinople itself, they would be heard by the *iudicium quinquevirale* sitting in that city. He has further suggested that the trial of

[13] *Var.* 4.22 (cf. above, n. 7).
[14] In his review of *Iud. Quinq.* in *BZ* 36 (1936) 438–41. Subsequent quotations from and citations of Ensslin in this chapter are from this review unless otherwise specified.

the *vir quaestorius* Isocasius in Constantinople in the reign of Leo I may well have taken place before the *iudicium quinquevirale*. He observes that if indeed *Cod. Theod.* 9.1.13 was law in the East at any time, it must have been at least much limited by the reforms of Zeno (*Cod. Iust.* 3.24.3), and if it retained any validity after those reforms, it must finally have been abrogated through its exclusion from the Code of Justinian.

The inclusion of Gratian's law[15] in the Theodosian Code does indeed create a presumption that this law thus obtained validity in the Empire as a whole, but it creates nothing more than a presumption. Discussing *Cod. Theod.* 1.1.6, the law in which Theodosius II prescribes the manner in which the Code is to be compiled, Krüger well says: "Hervorgehoben wird noch, was der erste Auftrag stillschweigend enthielt, auch diejenigen Leges generales seien aufzunehmen, welche nur für bestimmte Provinzen oder Gemeinden eingeführt waren." [16] It follows that we cannot assume from the inclusion of Gratian's law in the Theodosian Code that it was necessarily applied in the East as well as in the West.

I summarize various reasons mentioned elsewhere[17] which have caused me to accept Mommsen's opinion[18] that our law was applied only in the western portion of the Empire: the law was part of an oration to the Roman senate; it makes

---

[15] The same is true of the law of Honorius, *Cod. Theod.* 2.1.12. But since that law merely confirms *Cod. Theod.* 9.1.13 and places special emphasis on the selection of the associate judges by lot, it is not necessary to refer to it at every point in the argument.

[16] Paul Krüger, *Geschichte der Quellen und Literatur des römischen Rechts* (2nd ed., Munich and Leipzig 1912) 325.

[17] *Iud. Quinq.* 7–8.

[18] Theodor Mommsen, *Römisches Strafrecht* (Leipzig 1899) 287. This passage was cited in *Iud. Quinq.* 7.

specific provision for the setting up of the *iudicium quinquevirale* to hear cases arising in the suburban provinces but
says nothing of the setting up of such a tribunal to hear
cases arising elsewhere; the only certain case which has come
down to us of a trial before the *iudicium quinquevirale*
arose in the West; the few other cases where there is at least
some evidence that they may have been tried before that
tribunal (with the exception of the trial of Isocasius, of
which we shall write presently) also arose in the West.

But that is not all: a law concerning our tribunal was, as
we have seen, incorporated in the Breviary of Alaric; we
find no such law in the Code of Justinian. On the other
hand, the law of Constantine, *Cod. Theod.* 9.1.1, which provided that all *clarissimi* accused of crimes were to be tried
before the provincial authorities of the place where the crime
had been committed, was incorporated in the Code of Justinian as *Cod. Iust.* 3.24.1. It was modified to bring it into
harmony with Zeno's reforms (*Cod. Iust.* 3.24.3), but its
wording in the Code of Justinian bears not the slightest trace
of its ever having been modified by *Cod. Theod.* 9.1.13 or
Cod. Theod. 2.1.12. This tempts us to conclude that Constantine's statute remained law in the East without substantial modification until the reforms of Zeno — unless, perhaps, by laws now lost to us, but of the same general tendency as Zeno's laws and superseded by them.

The political conditions which led to the promulgation of
Cod. Theod. 9.1.13, and also the political and social develop-
ments during the next century, point toward the same conclusion. If in the West, as I wrote elsewhere,[19] "The only

[19] *Iud. Quinq.* 10.

class having sufficient education to administer it [the later Empire] was the great landed aristocracy," it is also true, as Ensslin has most courteously pointed out, that my statement, even with the restrictions added in the context, was too broad in that it was not specifically restricted to the West, "denn mindestens im Osten war die Entwicklung wesentlich anders." This distinction is well brought out by E. Stein.[20] He states that even the highest offices of the imperial bureaucracy in the East were almost exclusively held by persons of obscure origin, with the result that this bureaucracy remained a powerful tool against aristocratic tendencies. In the West, on the other hand, he points out that the higher offices of the bureaucracy became the perquisites of the great landed families of Italy and Gaul and that they used most effectively the control which they thus secured, to further their own interests at the expense of the state. Now Gratian's law, promulgated shortly after his accession, was one of the chief measures marking his reversal of Valentinian's policy of hostility to the aristocracy.[21] But Valens in the East had always ruled in full harmony with the policies of Valentinian, and there is no reason to suppose that he suddenly reversed himself to follow the lead of his young nephew. Nor, as the power of the senatorial aristocracy in the West became more marked, would the later emperors in the East be inclined to extend too freely to their own magnates the privileges which those in the West abused.

The reforms of Zeno (*Cod. Iust.* 3.24.3), to which we have already referred, constitute, it may be, an exception to the

---

[20] *Geschichte des spätrömischen Reiches,* I (Vienna 1928) 101, 342, hereafter referred to as Stein I. The earlier of these references is cited by Ensslin.

[21] See *Iud. Quinq.* 20–25, 71 (n. 93).

general anti-aristocratic tendency in the East, or perhaps merely a modification or a codification of practices that had already been followed for some time. Among other things, they provided that persons of what we should call cabinet rank should, if accused of crimes requiring their personal appearance, be tried only before the emperor or his deputy; if before a deputy, then with great respect to the accused. Further, the deputy, even if the accused was found guilty, was to refer the matter to the emperor for imposition of sentence. *Viri illustres* who had acquired their rank through honorary patent instead of by holding a cabinet position, were, if they resided in Constantinople, to answer similar charges before the praetorian prefect, the prefect of the City, or in cases especially remitted to him, before the *magister officiorum*. Again, the emperor reserved the right of sentence.

We notice that nothing in Zeno's law specifically repeals *Cod. Theod.* 9.1.13. We notice, too, the unmistakable words used by the emperor when he wants to reserve the right of jurisdiction: *nullius alterius iudicis nisi nostrae pietatis,* or again, *non hi tamen, quorum cognitio ad nostram maiestatem vel ad vice nostri numinis auditurum pertineat.* We notice the reservation by the emperor of the right of sentencing the accused if found guilty.[22] Finally, the express provisions made in Zeno's law for the trial of patricians and other *viri illustres* who had held positions of cabinet rank leave no doubt that these were not heard before the *iudicium quinquevirale.*

But under some circumstances *viri illustres* who had ac-

[22] Cf. above, n. 9.

quired their rank through honorary patents were tried before the prefect of the City. Now, these men were members of the senate.[23] If, then, one of these was brought before the prefect of the City on a capital charge under Zeno's law, he would, if *Cod. Theod.* 9.1.13 had been in force in the East before the promulgation of Zeno's law, still be entitled to trial before the *iudicium quinquevirale* under the old statute. That statute had not been repealed but, if it had been law in the East at all, was superseded only insofar as it was inconsistent with the later law. It provided that when capital charges against senators were brought before the prefect of the City, they should be tried before the *iudicium quinquevirale*. Now, there can be no doubt that a senator accused of a capital offense would run less risk of unfair trial if his guilt were to be determined by a tribunal composed of the president of the senate and five senators chosen by lot, than if it were to be determined by an emperor possibly hostile to the accused or by a deputy possibly anxious to please such an emperor. If, then, *Cod. Theod.* 9.1.13 was in force until the promulgation of Zeno's law, we have to assume the absurdity that, after the promulgation of that law, *viri illustres* of the second category secured, under some circumstances, more privileged treatment than their superiors of the first category.

Because, then, of the circumstances which led to the promulgation of Gratian's law, because of the result of a somewhat legalistic examination of the texts in the Codes, and because of the historical trend during the fifth century, we incline to the conclusion that *Cod. Theod.* 9.1.13 and *Cod.*

---

[23] *Dig.* I 9.12.2. The use of *omnes* precludes any distinction between *viri illustres* who have attained their rank through office and those who have received honorary patents.

Theod. 2.1.12 must have been applied only in the West, and
that the *iudicium quinquevirale* never existed in Constantinople. But all these arguments must fall if we can find clear
proof that the *vir quaestorius* Isocasius was tried in Constantinople before the *iudicium quinquevirale*. The case for
this explanation cannot be expressed better than in Ensslin's
own words:

> Außerdem hätte C. auf den Fall des Quästors Isokasios unter
> Leo I. eingehen sollen; denn nach Johannes Malalas (XIV 370
> Bonn.–II 76 Oxford.) setzte sich der Comes Iacobus, der Arzt
> des Kaisers, mit Erfolg dafür ein, daß der wegen seines
> Heidentums angeklagte Isokasios eben als Quästor, nicht von
> dem Consularis Bithyniae Theophilos (vgl. RE V A 2167, 31),
> dem Leo den Prozeß zugewiesen hatte, sondern in Kon-
> stantinopel von dem Senat und dem Praefectus Praetorio ab-
> geurteilt wurde. Hier will es nun scheinen, daß der Chronist,
> der den Pusaios, der zweimal Prätorianerpräfekt war, als Ver-
> handlungsleiter nennt, ihn auch in diesem Falle versehentlich
> als ἔπαρχος τῶν πραιτωρίων einführte; denn daß Pusaios etwa
> wie Kyros (RE XII 189.21ff) unter Theodosius II. beide Ämter
> vereint habe, wird man nicht annehmen wollen. Da als Ver-
> handlungsort der Zeuxipposmarkt, also das Augustaion, an dem
> die Senatshalle lag, erwähnt wird, wird man um so mehr an den
> Stadtpräfekten als Verhandlungsleiter denken müssen.

This interpretation of the trial, however, presents some
difficulties. According to our chronicler, Count Jacobus did
not say that Isocasius should be heard before a commission
of the senate and the prefect, but παρὰ τῆς συγκλήτου καὶ
τοῦ ἐπάρχου . . . Now, although παρὰ τῆς συγκλήτου may
very well be taken to mean "before the senate" (the more
so because, only a few lines above, Malalas used ἡ σύγκλητος
in that sense when describing the popularity of Jacobus and

the erection of a monument to him by the senate), yet that may not be the meaning here. Since writing his review, Ensslin has noticed several passages in the text of that portion of the Chronicle of Malalas which deals with the post-Constantinian period, in which σύγκλητος is used, not of the senate, but as designating a group of the most distinguished members of the imperial suite — an informal consistory or *comitativa*. He has most generously given me the following references. Julian, just before his death, contemplates an attack on Babylon: καὶ βουλομένου μετὰ τῆς ἰδίας συγκλήτου καὶ τοῦ στρατοῦ αὐτοῦ ἄχρι τῆς βαβυλῶνος τῇ ἑξῆς ὁρμῆσαι . . . (II 22 Oxford; in the Bonn ed., at 332, 16ff). And in a passage, unfortunately too long to quote, telling of the trial of the patrician Probus before Justinian (II 171 Oxford; in the Bonn ed., at 438, 20ff), the word is used twice in the sense indicated. Ensslin also draws my attention to the analogous use of συγκλητικὴ 'Ρώμης in Malalas (II 95 Oxford; in the Bonn ed., at 384, 5ff). To these instances one may add the passage (II 19 Oxford; in the Bonn ed., at 330, 20ff) in which Malalas writes of δύο συγκλητικοὺς of the king of Persia. Perhaps, then, Count Jacobus meant, not that Isocasius should be tried before the senate and the prefect, but before a commission of magnates and the prefect.

Nor is it certain that Malalas was mistaken in writing that Count Jacobus wished the case referred to the praetorian prefect, and in writing of Pusaeus as praetorian prefect, not as prefect of the City. The *Chronicon Paschale,* in the passage telling of this trial,[24] speaks of Pusaeus as praetorian

---

[24] Under A.D. 467; vol. I 595–96 in Dindorf's ed. of 1832 (*Corpus Script. Hist. Byz.*).

prefect and consul; it does not say that he ever held the office of prefect of the City. In fact, Pusaeus was consul and praetorian prefect, but there is no reliable evidence that he was prefect of the City too.[25] He may very well have been, but in the absence of further evidence, we should try to avoid altering our best authorities to make them conform even to a very plausible theory rather than to known facts.

Further, when Malalas writes that Isocasius was led εἰς τὸν Ζεύξιππον for trial and later taken ἀπὸ τοῦ Ζευξίππου, he may have been referring to the Augustaeum, as Ensslin supposes, but it seems more likely that he meant the Baths of Zeuxippus. In his description of Constantinople,[26] the chronicler distinguishes clearly between the Baths of Zeuxippus, the Augustaeum, and the senate house. More, in his account of the trial of Isocasius, he tells us that the senate, in recognition of the eminence of Count Jacobus as philosopher and physician, erected a statue to him ἐν τῷ Ζευξίππῳ. A more suitable place for such a statue could hardly have been found than the great Baths of Zeuxippus.

Although, then, one cannot deny that the attractive theory of Ensslin may ultimately prove to be the right one, we should look for an explanation that would avoid these

[25] Authorities supporting the view that Pusaeus was praetorian prefect are: Malalas and the *Chronicon Paschale* and Theophanes (5960; I 115 de Boor). Zonaras (14.1; III 251 Dindorf) merely writes of "the prefect." Manasses (2864ff; 124 Bonn) says that the trial took place before the prefect of the City. Cedrenus (P, 349; I 612, 21ff Bonn) writes that the trial took place before the prefect of Constantinople and names Pusaeus, though misspelling the name. Malalas and the *Chronicon Paschale*, both because of their dates and the detail of their accounts, possess a value which none of the other versions even approaches, and if we are to suppose that Pusaeus was prefect of Constantinople, we must do so for the reasons given by Ensslin, not on the strength of the passages in Manasses and Cedrenus.

[26] II 7 Oxford; at p. 321 in the Bonn ed.

difficulties. Leo had remitted the case to Theophilus, governor of Bithynia, ὅστις καὶ τὰς φωνὰς αὐτοῦ ἔλαβεν. The Governor went no further, remitting it to the praetorian prefect Pusaeus. This sounds in accord with *Cod. Theod.* 9.1.13, once we know why the case originally came before Theophilus. We are told the reason in the account of the trial in the *Chronicon Paschale:* διὰ τὴν τότε γενομένην ἀταξίαν ἐν Κωνσταντινουπόλει . . . But this theory encounters a fatal obstacle in the intervention of Count Jacobus. According to our law, once the Governor had undertaken the preliminary investigations, the final trial would have taken place before the praetorian prefect Pusaeus without any intervention whatever. But our accounts leave us no doubt that the activity of Count Jacobus was the decisive factor; the procedure was not being governed by *Cod. Theod.* 9.1.13.

There seems a simpler explanation if we may assume that, as we have argued, *Cod. Theod.* 9.1.13 and *Cod. Theod.* 2.1.12 were not applied in the East. Mommsen well writes of the agelong attempt of the senatorial class to free itself from imperial jurisdiction in criminal matters "und die Kriminalgerichtsbarkeit über dessen Angehörige im Wege des Pairsgerichts dem Senat vorzubehalten." [27] *Cod. Theod.* 9.1.13 — a statute which, as we have pointed out, does seem substantially to have impaired the emperor's jurisdiction — was of course a product of this tendency. And even if we agree with Mommsen[28] in believing that *Cod. Theod.* 9.1.1 remained in force in the East unmodified by *Cod. Theod.*

[27] *Römisches Strafrecht* 286–87.
[28] *Ibid.*

9.1.13 and *Cod. Theod.* 2.1.12, still it does not follow that the eastern magnates secured no modification of the law in the East at all until the reforms of Zeno. As the *viri clarissimi* increased in numbers, as *viri clarissimi et spectabiles* and *viri clarissimi et illustres* came to be raised above the lower ranks of the clarissimate, at least these higher dignitaries must have felt that they deserved different treatment from the less distinguished members of the group.

We have evidence that this was the case. In the West, it is apparent from the trials of Julius Festus Hymetius[29] and of Lollianus[30] that the strict prohibitions of Constantine's law had been modified even before the promulgation of *Cod. Theod.* 9.1.13. In the East, we have evidence tending to show that the trials of Tatianus and Proculus in the reign of Theodosius I, and of Timasius in the reign of Arcadius took place before judicial commissions not unlike that before which, as I believe, Isocasius may have been heard. (I am once more indebted to the kindness of Professor Ensslin for this illuminating comparison.)

Of the trial of Tatianus, Zosimus writes: . . . ἤγετο [Tatianus] εἰς κρίσιν, ὑπάρχου τῆς αὐλῆς ἀποδεδειγμένου Ῥουφίνου. καὶ τῷ μὲν φαινομένῳ κοινωνεῖν ἐτάχθησαν ἕτεροι Ῥουφίνῳ τῆς κρίσεως, ἐκεῖνος δὲ μόνος εἶχε τῆς ψήφου τὸ κῦρος.[31]

The last phrase means not that the associates of Rufinus were appointed in a consultative capacity only, but merely that they were completely dominated by Rufinus. Proculus was not condemned by Rufinus alone, but by the court as

---

[29] See Seeck in *RE* VI 2256, art. "Festus" 9, and authorities there cited.
[30] Ammianus Marcellinus 28.1.26.
[31] 4.52 (in the Bonn ed. of 1837 — *Corpus Script. Hist. Byz.* — at pp. 236–37).

a whole, the other judges acting in accordance with their private agreement with Rufinus.[32] The point is made even clearer by the words used by Zosimus in describing the trial of Timasius: καὶ ὁ μὲν βασιλεὺς προυκάθητο δικαστής, Εὐτρόπιος δὲ παρεστώς, ἐπειδὴ καὶ τὴν ἡγεμονίαν πάντων τῶν βασιλικῶν εἶχε κοιτώνων, τῆς πάσης ψήφου κύριος ἦν.[33] The authority of Eutropius is described in almost the very words that have been used to describe that of Rufinus. Yet the notorious eunuch cannot have had an authority technically superior to that of the emperor Arcadius himself at a trial at which Arcadius presided.

In the trial of Tatianus and Proculus, other judges than Rufinus are mentioned. In that of Timasius, it is not clear whether Eutropius was an associate judge as well as actually the dominating figure. But there seems to have been a formal tribunal, not, apparently, the consistory, since the Emperor later withdrew, turning his functions over to Saturninus and Procopius. The former was distinguished by age and by the offices he had held, the latter was the son-in-law of the emperor Valens; the tribunal of which they were members might well have been described by Malalas as σύγκλητος in the less technical sense of the word.

These trials, and that of the patrician Probus under Justinian, which we have already cited, seem to establish a different usage from that which apparently prevailed in the West after the promulgation of *Cod. Theod.* 9.1.13. The provisions of *Cod. Theod.* 9.1.1 seem in part to have been superseded in the East as well as in the West: in the

[32] *Ibid.*
[33] 5.9 (Bonn ed., p. 257)

East, state trials of great magnates apparently took place before tribunals composed of the highest dignitaries headed by the emperor, or by some great official especially designated by him. As in the West, the accused is now heard not by his inferiors in rank but by his equals. Nevertheless, the eastern institution differs fundamentally from the western one, from the *iudicium quinquevirale:* the former represents the imperial jurisdiction; the latter, a modification of the old senatorial jurisdiction. And for practical purposes, a court selected by the emperor and headed by him or his delegate must have been far less independent than one composed of the prefect of the City (the president of the senate) and five senators chosen by lot. The western procedure seems definitely to have restricted imperial authority in theory and probably to a considerable extent in practice; the eastern procedure did not. Finally, we may notice that the reforms of Zeno appear now not in the light of radical innovations but rather as the codification of existing practices, perhaps as modifications of practices authorized by statutes which have not come down to us.

But how do these theories tally with the account of the trial of Isocasius? As a former *quaestor,* he was a *vir illustris*. A resident of Constantinople, he was charged with paganism, stripped of his dignities, and sent before Theophilus, governor of Bithynia. Through the intervention of Count Jacobus, the case was transferred to Constantinople and heard by the praetorian prefect Pusaeus. Isocasius, naked and with bound hands, was led before his judge.

In the West, a few years later,[34] Arvandus on trial before,

---

[34] Seeck in *RE* I 2367, art. "Anthemius" 3, gives 469 as the date of the banishment of Arvandus. Ensslin in *RE* XII 1961, art. "Leo" 3, gives 467 as the date

in all probability, the *iudicium quinquevirale*,[35] availed himself of his rank before his trial and during it, his insolent behavior and foppish appearance shocking even his supporters. But *after* his conviction, "confestim privilegiis geminae praefecturae . . . exauguratus et, plebeiae familiae non ut additus sed ut redditus, publico carceri adiudicatus est."[36] Evidently Isocasius had not received the treatment which would have been accorded to him if the laws of Zeno (*Cod. Iust.* 3.24.3), so careful of the dignity of the defendant, had been in force, and even after the intervention of Count Jacobus, he was not restored to his rank. Even more clearly, he had not received the treatment which would have been accorded to him in the West, where *Cod. Theod.* 9.1.13 and *Cod. Theod.* 2.1.12 were in force. His treatment, though, was entirely consonant with *Cod. Theod.* 9.1.1, the law of Constantine already referred to. If we believe this law to have been modified, even in the East, so as to afford the accused, if he was a great magnate, trial before a panel of judges of illustrious rank, it does not follow that it was modified in other particulars. And in it we find the words, "Omnem enim honorem reatus excludit, cum criminalis causa et non civilis res vel pecuniaria moveatur."

We deduce, then, that Jacobus was probably not asking that Isocasius should be tried before the *iudicium quinquevirale*, but merely that the usual eastern procedure should

---

of the trial of Isocasius. The *Chronicon Paschale* puts this trial under the consulate of Pusaeus and Johannes (see above, n. 24), and this was 467. It is more probable, perhaps, that it took place in 465, the year in which Pusaeus was certainly praetorian prefect, or in 473, when he seems to have held that office again. For these dates, see Otto Seeck, *Regesten der Kaiser und Päpste* (Stuttgart 1919) 137–38, 414, 461

[35] See *Iud. Quinq.* 34–36.

[36] Sidonius Apollinaris *Epist.* 1.7 (in *MGHAA* VIII 12).

be followed, that Isocasius should be tried before the praetorian prefect and a panel of judges of high rank. (We
remember that Rufinus, who had been appointed praetorian
prefect, presided at the trial of Tatianus and Proculus. We
remember the use of σύγκλητος in the text of Malalas and
the creation of tribunals of persons of high rank to try
Tatianus, Proculus, Timasius, and — though the trial is of
far later date — the patriarch Photius and Theodore Santabarenus.) The protest was successful, and although nothing
is said of the appointment of associate judges to assist
Pusaeus, yet if the meaning suggested for the word σύγκλητος
can be accepted, they had been requested, and it would be
very rash to assume that none had been appointed. The
intervention of Count Jacobus is explained by the fact
(which we learn from the account in the *Chronicon
Paschale*) that he, like Isocasius, was a Cilician; he was
probably the close friend of his fellow provincial. His
eagerness to have the trial take place before the praetorian
prefect is explained by the fact that the prefect was Pusaeus,
the former colleague of Isocasius. That the trial was held
in the magnificent Baths of Zeuxippus and that the accused
was treated with the greatest harshness possible even under
the law of Constantine — these details were to lend point
to the jeer of Pusaeus, and that jeer was deliberately made
to arouse popular sympathy for the accused. (We remember
that Leo, afraid of riots in Constantinople, originally wished
the trial to be in Chalcedon.) The jeer of Pusaeus and the
sublime reply of Isocasius produced their intended effect
(perhaps there were friends in the crowd, ready to direct
its impulses): Isocasius was carried off to baptism, the heart

was taken out of the prosecution, and the matter ended with the banishment of Isocasius to his estates.

If this explanation can stand, we need not suppose that Malalas twice wrote of a praetorian prefect when he meant a prefect of the City. Nor need we overcome the legal and historical difficulties involved in supposing that *Cod. Theod.* 9.1.13 and *Cod. Theod.* 2.1.12 were accepted in the East. Further, we find a rational explanation of the contrast between the humiliations to which Isocasius was subjected before his conviction and the extreme deference shown Arvandus until his conviction. Again, the protest of Count Jacobus is accounted for satisfactorily enough, though the explanation is certainly less brilliant than that suggested by Ensslin. Finally, we acquire a background for the reforms of Zeno: the trial of Isocasius may have called attention to the need of defining or modifying practices which had grown up in the East, and thus have started a movement destined to bear fruit in Zeno's reign.

But if Isocasius was not tried before the *iudicium quinquevirale,* then the last reason vanishes which has been advanced in favor of assuming the existence of that tribunal in Constantinople. And, if we are not to suppose that the *iudicium quinquevirale* existed in Constantinople, we cannot assume that it influenced western law from there; much less, that it influenced western law from there exclusively. We are coming more and more to realize the importance of the influence of the Byzantine Empire upon the history and institutions of western Europe; it seems probable, however, that we should not be justified in assuming the existence of that influence in the present instance.

CHAPTER II

THE IUDICIUM QUINQUEVIRALE
RECONSIDERED

𒀸𒀸𒀸𒀸𒀸𒀸𒀸𒀸𒀸𒀸𒀸𒀸𒀸𒀸𒀸𒀸𒀸𒀸𒀸𒀸𒀸𒀸𒀸𒀸𒀸𒀸𒀸𒀸

SINCE my paper, "The Iudicium Quinquevirale in Constantinople," is republished above as Chapter I, it seems necessary to discuss points concerning which others have disagreed with it and also to explain various changes of opinion on my part since the article first appeared.

The late Ernst Stein[1] felt that the prefect of the City was not obliged to draw five senators by lot under the terms of *Cod. Theod.* 9.1.13 of February 11, 376; he believed that this practice was merely permissive, only becoming mandatory by virtue of *Cod. Theod.* 2.1.12 of August 6, 423. He added that the words "de praesentibus et administratorum honore functis" used in the statute to describe the group from whom the associate judges were to be chosen by lot, should not be translated "from present and past holders of administrative offices." Rather, the phrase meant, "l'ensemble des sénateurs siégeant effectivement au sénat, c'est-à-dire se trouvant à Rome (*praesentes*) et n'étant pas *in actu positi* mais *administratorum honore functi,* car en générale les *in actu positi* ne siégeaient pas alors au sénat." He further held that during the last years of the Empire in the West and in

---

[1] Ernst Stein, *Histoire du Bas-Empire,* II (Paris, Brussels, Amsterdam 1949, hereafter referred to as Stein II) 70ff, 257f, and notes.

the dominions of Odovacar and Theodoric important cases not originating in the urban prefecture were delegated to this tribunal by the ruler as a special mark of his deference to the senate, the trials of Arvandus and of Boethius being examples of this extension of the jurisdiction of the tribunal. Analogously, that trials of prominent people other than senators were sometimes delegated to the *iudicium quinquevirale* at this period; the trial of Basilius and Praetextatus seemed to him an instance of this practice. He also thought it possible that in that trial the associate judges were named by the king, not selected by lot. In this connection, he pointed out that the magician Basilius could not have been the Basilius who later figured as an accuser of Boethius, since we learn from the *Dialogues* of Gregory that Basilius the magician was burnt long before the fall of Boethius. Finally, although he agreed that the two relevant statutes were not accepted in the East, and that consequently the *iudicium quinquevirale* did not exist there, he felt that I was mistaken in supposing that Malalas might have used σύγκλητος loosely to mean a committee of magnates, not necessarily the senate as a whole.

Some of these criticisms seem to me entirely sound, others more doubtful, and some unacceptable, so that it becomes necessary to consider them in detail. First, it seems to me clear that under the terms of *Cod. Theod.* 9.1.13, the prefect of the City was *obliged,* in hearing cases brought before him in accordance with the terms of the statute, to select five associate judges by lot from the categories of persons specified in the statute. To repeat the relevant portion: "Sed praefecto urbi cognoscenti de capite senatorum spectatorum maxime virorum iudicium quinquevirale sociabitur et de praesentibus et administratorum honore functis licebit adiungere sorte ductos, non sponte delectos." It is impossible to find anything permissive in the first half of this sentence: a panel of five associate judges will be joined (*sociabitur*) to the prefect of the City in trying cases under the statute. In the next phrase, the prefect is told from what categories the associate judges are to be drawn. The final words of the statute tell him that he may draw them by lot but is not to select them as he may please. The *licet,* then, does not tell the prefect that he may associate five judges with him if he wishes (he has already been told that he *must* associate them), but merely tells him how he is to select them. In the second statute, *Cod. Theod.* 2.1.12, the emperor again emphasizes that the associate judges are to be selected by lot. The prefect must often have been tempted to pick a panel favorable to his own point of view or to excuse for one reason or another some senator on whom the lot had fallen: the emperor is evidently refusing to allow something of this sort in a case before the prefect of the City at the time of the promulgation of the statute. (As we shall see presently, though, this statute may also have ratified a considerable expansion of the territorial jurisdiction of the tribunal, somewhat, but not wholly, along the lines suggested by Stein.)

As to the second point, *de praesentibus et administratorum honore functis,* it seems to me that Stein's interpretation should be accepted. We are agreed that the associate judges were to be selected from the enrolled members of the senate and that the senate of this period was composed, with every fewer exceptions as time went on, of persons *administratorum honore functis*. There are, perhaps, two differences. Under the translation proposed by me, such officials *in actu positi* as had already been inscribed on the roster of the senate would be eligible for the panel, and so would other enrolled senators who were not in Rome at the time. It might be unnecessarily inconvenient if the lot were to fall on some important member of the government who could not well spare time from his administrative duties to sit on the panel, or upon some other senator temporarily absent. It should be noted, though, that the translation of the Theodosian Code which, with other matter, forms the first volume of the *Corpus Juris Romani,* renders the passage: "from persons who are present and who have held the honor of office as administrators." [2] Further, in note 48 to the passage, the translation comments on *praesentes,* "present in the City, present at the imperial court, at present in office." It seems to me that the first of these, in accord with Stein's suggestion, is the best. Of *administratores,* the translation comments, in note 49 to this passage, "judges ordinary, governors of provinces." This interpretation seems to me mistaken, since the statute provides for the associate judges to be members of the senate, and that body, at the time of which we are speaking, was mainly composed of persons of higher rank than would ordinarily have been held by officials of these categories. It seems to me certain that we are dealing here with persons who have held positions of what we might call cabinet rank — former prefects, former

[2] Clyde Pharr, *The Theodosian Code and Novels and the Sirmondian Constitutions, a Translation* etc. (Princeton 1952) 226.

heads of the great departments of the central government, of the palace, or of the army.

Let us next turn to Stein's argument that the case of Arvandus must have come before the *iudicium quinque-virale* by special delegation from the emperor. He wrote: "Comme il est de la dernière évidence qu'une plainte du *concilium septem provinciarum* contre un préfet du prétoire des Gaules en activité de service, ne pouvait être addressée au préfet de la Ville ni au sénat, mais uniquement à l'empereur, il s'agit manifestement d'une procédure *ex delegatu.*" Neither in the preceding paper nor in *The Iudicium Quinquevirale* had I discussed the procedure through which this case, as Stein and I (both following Dalton) believe, came to be brought before our tribunal; I had not, quite frankly, understood how it had happened, but the letter of Sidonius,[3] which is our sole source of information concerning the matter, established (if one may suppose *decemviri* to be an error for *quinqueviri*) that it did. Stein's suggestion, then, seems at first sight both brilliant and sound, but yet there is a double possibility that it may not be in all respects the right one. There are passages in the letter of Sidonius that suggest another explanation. The letter does not seem to tell us that a charge of treason was brought against Arvandus while he was still in Gaul. It tells us that he was unpopular, crushed by debts, and in fear of his creditors. He was divested of

---

[3] Sidonius, *Epist.* 1.7. In addition to the translation by Dalton (O. M. Dalton, *The Letters of Sidonius,* translated with Introduction and Notes, 2 vols. [Oxford 1915]), these letters are now available in the Loeb Classics: Sidonius, *Poems and Letters,* with introduction, translation and notes, by W. B. Anderson, 2 vols. (vol. I, Cambridge, Mass., and London 1936; vol. II, completed after the death of Professor Anderson, Cambridge, Mass., and London 1965).

his authority, and sent to Rome under guard. There, he was lodged in the Capitol in custody of his friend, Flavius Asellus, the *comes sacrarum largitionum,* who treated him with conspicuous respect. He seems not to have considered himself in serious danger, and when his friend, Sidonius Apollinaris, then[4] prefect of the City, came, with another friend, Auxanius, to warn him that the provincial delegates had arrived and that they apparently intended to charge him not only with accepting bribes but also to accuse him of treason, Arvandus replied that the only concession he would make would be to employ advocates to defend him on the charge of bribery. Hereupon, Sidonius left Rome, and a few days later Arvandus was tried in the senate hall and condemned by the *decemviri* (*sic*) on a charge of treason. All this strongly implies that at first Arvandus was accused only of having accepted bribes, that although he was put under arrest, he retained his rank (*prius cinctus custodia quam potestate discinctus*), that he was sent to Rome under guard and put in custody of the *comes sacrarum*

---

[4] Ensslin, following Stevens, accounts for Sidonius' absence from Rome by assuming that his term of office as prefect of the City had expired before this time. See his review of *Iud. Quinq.* (above, chap. 1, n. 14) 440, citing C. E. Stevens, *Sidonius Apollinaris and His Age* (1933) 103. It is true that if the term of office of Sidonius had been over, he would have encountered no legal difficulty in absenting himself from Rome during the trial. It would, though, have been a little less than human for him to have done so considering how interested he was in the issue. Further, Sidonius tells us that he had incurred considerable odium because of his help to the accused: "amicus homini [Arvandus] fui . . . testatur hoc propter ipsum nuper mihi invidia conflata, cuius me paulo incautiorem flamma detorruit." This is more than one might expect if Sidonius, as a private citizen, had given advice to an old friend who, though accused of bribery, was at the time almost more the honored guest than the prisoner of Asellus, minister of finance. A visit and advice, though, from Sidonius, prefect of the City, would be a far more serious matter. The question is of no great importance, and we shall probably never secure definite proof either way; so, though I cannot claim that my interpretation is correct, I may, I hope, be pardoned for putting it forward.

largitionum pending the arrival of the evidence. It seems
not at all improbable that the normal procedure in such
cases would be for the *comes* himself to investigate charges
of this kind on behalf of the government, especially if the
bribes which Arvandus was accused of having accepted had
to do with matters of taxation. It is of course possible, too,
that the emperor had especially delegated the *comes
sacrarum largitionum* to hear these charges. The delegates
appeared, however, with evidence not merely of bribery but
of treason. Information of this would, even if the delegates
tried to keep the evidence dark until the trial, as we are
told they did, be certain to come to the ears of Sidonius:
he was the prefect of the City; he was the son-in-law of a
former emperor, Avitus, himself a Gaul; he was by birth
one of the foremost members of the Gallo-Roman aristocracy; he was the personal friend of all three of the provincial
delegates, a blood relation of one of them, and a connection
of their leader through his wife's family.[5] Hence his warning to Arvandus, and hence his departure from Rome:
whatever official or tribunal might hear the charges of
bribery (Sidonius tells us nothing of their disposal), the
charge of treason made in Rome against a senator actually
in Rome at the time the charge was made — this charge
would come before the prefect of the City and the *iudicium
quinquevirale* under our statutes and without any special

[5] See Dalton (above, n. 3) I, clxxv, clxxxi, for the connections of these delegates with Sidonius; also Anderson (above, n. 3) I 321 n. 7, 325 n. 7, and 370
n. 2. Anderson has suggested (I 374 n. 1) that the associate judges were perhaps
expanded from five to ten in cases of treason. This is of course possible. Still
though it is dangerous to tamper with the texts in the manuscripts in order to
make them conform to our theories, the emendation would in this instance be
such a plausible one that it seemed to me proper to follow Dalton. Cf. p. 4 above
also G. W. Ensslin, *Theoderich der Grosse* (Munich 1947) 219–20, 318.

delegation by the emperor. Sidonius would certainly not wish to preside over the trial of his friend. If there existed, as one must suppose there did, some normal procedure by which a judge could disqualify himself in cases in which he had a personal interest, Sidonius no doubt availed himself of it. If not — if the statute was considered so precise that the prefect of the City had to preside — then he no doubt made what excuse he could to leave the City and at the same time to leave the duty of acting as presiding judge to whatever official, by normal practice or special appointment, assumed the position of acting prefect during the "unavoidable" absence of Sidonius.

It seems, then, at least possible that Stein was mistaken in believing that the case of Arvandus was proof that "Aux derniers temps de l'Empire d'Occident et dans le royaume d'Italie d'importants procès criminels concernant des territoires extérieures à celui de la préfecture urbaine . . . ont néamoins été jugés par ce tribunal [the *iudicium quinquevirale*] en vertu de délégations spéciales du prince qui témoignait ainsi de sa déférance à l'égard du sénat." Nevertheless, it is certain that we know only too little about matters of this kind, and, as we shall see below, it is quite probable that the *iudicium,* as early as the time of Honorius, became the normal tribunal to hear criminal cases against senators arising anywhere within the Empire in the West, but this by virtue of statute without any special delegation by the emperor.

The other case cited by Stein as an example of a territorial extension of the jurisdiction of our tribunal by special delegation of the prince, is that of Boethius. It is flattering to find that, in stating positively (p. 258 and note) that Boethius was tried before the prefect of the City and the *iudicium quinquevirale,* sitting in Pavia, Stein, though disapproving of my study of the case in *The Iudicium Quinquevirale,* appears nevertheless to accept the hypothesis advanced by me in that work. (See the passages cited by Stein in his note, more particularly pp. 59–62.) As for the special delegation of the case to the prefect by the king, Stein argues that since Boethius was *magister officiorum* at the time the charges were brought, he was officially resident outside the suburbicarian diocese and therefore would not have come within the normal jurisdiction of the prefect of the City. As we shall see below, there is some reason to suppose that the jurisdiction of the prefect had been extended by statute in such cases long before this time, so that special delegation by the prince may not have been necessary even in cases arising outside of the suburbicarian diocese; but apart from that, it seems probable that Rome remained the official seat of government even though the prince might actually reside in Ravenna or Ticinum or Verona (much as Versailles is the official seat of the French government today), so that Boethius might not necessarily lose his rights as a resident of Rome merely because he held an office in the administration of the king. There remains, however, a fact that seems to make the case exceptional the prefect of the City (if indeed I am right in my hypothesis that Eusebius was prefect of the City) was summoned to Ticinum to try Boethius.[6] It is true that there

---

[6] *Anonymus Valesianus* 14.87. Cf. *Iud. Quinq.* 59–62 and Ensslin, *Theoderich* 318–19 and note.

is nothing in the statutes that expressly provides that the *iudicium quinquevirale* should sit only in Rome, but considering the composition of the court and the reason for which it was set up — it was created to protect the senators from oppression by the ruler, and the selection of the associate judges by lot gave especial assurance that it would not be packed — it was certainly very exceptional that it should meet elsewhere. Ensslin believes very plausibly that Theodoric did not wish the tribunal to sit in Rome for fear of possible disturbances there and that he selected Ticinum rather than Ravenna in order to remove, as far as possible, suspicion of undue influence by the king.[7] This seems very probable, but the fact remains that Eusebius, in trying Boethius, appears not to have been left entirely to the guidance of normal procedure.

Perhaps more persuasive is Stein's argument that the trial of Basilius and Praetextatus came before it *ex delegatu*. All we know of the case is derived from two letters of Cassiodorus and from a passage in the *Dialogues* of Gregory the Great.[8] Stein wrote: ". . . la délégation est attestée explicitement par Cassiod. *var.* IV 23, 2; les accusés ne semblent pas avoir été sénateurs, puisqu'ils ne sont désignés que par leurs noms tout court." The last point is reinforced by the fact that Cassiodorus does mention the rank of everyone else he names in the two letters: Argolicus, the prefect of the City, the *comes* Arigernus, and the five associate judges of the *iudicium quinquevirale*.

There are, however, parallel cases. In a letter to Agapetus,

[7] *Ibid.*
[8] Cass. *Var.* 4.22, 23; Greg. *Dial.* 1.4, pp. 28–31 (Moricca).

a prefect of the City, concerning the admission of a certain Faustus to the senate, Cassiodorus wrote: "atque ideo illustris magnificentia tua Fausto adulto, filio illustris Fausti . . ." [9] The son of a *vir illustris* must have been at least a *vir clarissimus*,[10] but Cassiodorus did not mention his rank, although he did mention the rank of his father. In a message to the senate concerning the appointment of Cyprianus, son of Opilio, to the office of *comes sacrarum largitionum,* both are named, but the rank of neither is mentioned, though neither was a newcomer to the service of the state.[11] No rank is attributed to the Castorius of *Var.* 3.20, although his alleged oppressor is called *praefectus vir magnificus Faustus.* Yet, as Mommsen suggested, this is probably the Castorius mentioned, with Florus, by Ennodius as *nobilibus adulescentibus a Fausto institutis.*[12] There are many other instances in which Cassiodorus names people without mentioning their rank.[13] This may of course mean that they had none, though surely most of those about whom the king would have to write as named individuals would be people of considerable importance.

More cogent in support of Stein's argument is the fact that in *Var.* 4.23, Theodoric writes to *comes* Arigernus:

[9] Cass. *Var.* 1.41.

[10] Cf. A. H. M. Jones, *The Later Roman Empire* (Oxford 1964, hereafter referred to as Jones *LRE*) II 529.

[11] Cass. *Var.* 5.41. Cf. Jones *LRE* III 152 n. 16, concerning the admission of Opilio, the son of our Cyprianus, to the senate.

[12] *MGHAA* XII 490, citing Ennodius XVI (*Epist.* 1.11).

[13] Cf. Ablabius of Cass. *Var.* 10.22; Petrus, the envoy of Justinian to Theodahad, mentioned in Cass. *Var.* 10.22 and 24; Campanianus, whose wife and sons had been enrolled in the *curia,* 9.4; the Constantius, Venerius, and Tanca of 8.28; the Crispianus, Agnellus, and Candac of 1.37; Wiliarit, the young grandson of the *vir spectabilis* Boio (apparently both Goths) of 1.38; Firminus of 3.36; Frontosus of 5.34, the Germanus and his father Thomas of 3.37; Renatus and Inquilina in 4.37, and no doubt many others.

"Praefectus igitur urbis sua nobis relatione declaravit Basilium et Praetextatum magicis artibus involutos impeti accusatione multorum: quos elapsos intimat mentis alienatione custodum. eos te praecipimus ubicumque repertos *ad iudicium quinquevirale* ducere, *quod in praesenti negotio nostra delegavit auctoritas,* ubi te residere censemus, ut violenta omnium defensione summota hanc causam discuti facias legibus et finiri" (italics ours).

As we learn from this letter and the one preceding it, the case had already been brought before the prefect of the City, and he had (let us assume for the moment) already selected five associate judges by lot. He has reported these proceedings to the king and added that the prisoners have escaped. (Is there a hint in the words of Cassiodorus that the prefect has implied that they have escaped by bewitching their gaolers?) The *omnium violenta defensione summota* of the letter to the prefect and the *violenta omnium defensione summota* of the letter to the *comes* strongly indicate that the prefect in his report has intimated that he fears the accused will resist by violence any attempt to bring them once more before the court. He has probably added that popular feeling against the accused is running very high; that it was strong we shall see when we consider the passage from Gregory. He has written that, given all the circumstances, he does not feel he can easily go on with the case, and has asked the king for instructions. Perhaps he has referred to *Cod. Theod.* 9.16.10 of Dec. 6, 371, a statute one might at first sight think particularly applicable to the case before us. This law provided that when members of the senatorial order (*ex ordine senatorio*) were charged with magic, they

were to be tried before the prefect of the City, but that if
the prefect felt that he was unable to analyze and determine
the limits of such cases ("quae iudicio memoratae sedis
dirimi vel terminare non creditur . . ." which I take to
mean if the network should prove so extensive and complex
that the prefect could not unravel it), he was to transfer the
case to the consistory. (We should remember that magic
often had to do with treason, so that the ruler would be particularly anxious to get to the bottom of such matters.) The
king, though, whether or not this statute has been brought
to his attention, evidently sees no such difficulties in the
case of Basilius and Praetextatus, or else feels that it has
been superseded by the statute of 376 (*Cod. Theod.* 9.1.13)
creating the *iudicium quinquevirale.* He feels that there is
no reason why the trial should not take place before the
normal tribunal: "nos, qui nescimus a legibus discrepare,
quorum cordi est in omnium moderatam tenere iustitiam,
praesenti auctoritate decernimus, ut quinque senatoribus, id
est magnificis et patriciis viris Symmacho Decio Volusiano
atque Caeliano nec non illustri viro Maximiano hanc causam
legitima examinatione pensetis." The defendants, he continued, should be produced before the court by the *comes*
Arigernus, and the *comes* should see to it that no disorders
should be allowed to interrupt the judicial process.

That the trial did take its normal course seems very doubtful. St. Gregory tells us that Basilius, "qui in magicis operi-
bus primus fuit," had secured refuge in a monastery in the
country.[14] Expelled because of a scandal he "non post
longum tempus in hac Romana orbe [*sic*], exardiscente zelo

---

[14] Above, n. 8.

christiani populi igni crematus est." This hideous and too
familiar zeal sounds more like a lynching than an execution
after trial and condemnation; it might, of course, have been
a lynching after trial and acquittal. At any rate, it leaves us
quite certain that Stein was right when he pointed out that
this Basilius was not the Basilius who later figured as an
accuser of Boethius.

However that may be, what was the meaning of the extreme emphasis put by Cassiodorus on following the strict
letter of the law? (This emphasis is the more striking because, as we have seen, there existed another statute, *Cod.
Theod.* 9.16.10, permitting the transfer of cases not so unlike
that of Basilius and Praetextatus as to make too implausible
a transfer of this case also.) It would have been nonsensical
for the king to have claimed that he was strictly following
the law if in fact he was appointing the associate judges
instead of merely confirming those that had already been
chosen by lot. It would have been absurd, too, if the accused
were not senators, for the king to have insisted that he was
bound by law to assign the case to the *iudicium quinquevirale*. He might, one supposes, have such a tribunal set up,
if he chose to, to hear cases that would not normally be
brought before it under the statutes defining its jurisdiction,
but he could hardly insist that he was bound by law to do
so. The most, then, that the *delegavit* of the letter of Cassiodorus can have meant is, it seems to me, that the case has
come before the prefect of the City and five associate judges
chosen by lot, that the tribunal has not been able to proceed
with the trial, that the prefect has reported the situation to
the king and requested instructions, that the king has re-

committed the case to the prefect and the associate judges, saying that he has no choice in the matter since under the law the case must be tried before the *iudicium quinquevirale*. He will, however, take steps to see that the difficulties which stand in the way of such a trial are removed. If this view may be accepted, the case of Basilius and Praetextatus, far from being evidence of delegation to the *iudicium quinquevirale* of a case which would not have come before it under the statute, is striking proof that the ruler felt himself bound not to impinge upon the strict terms of the statute concerning the jurisdiction of our tribunal.

Turning to the trial of Isocasius during the reign of Leo I, Stein and I seem agreed that the defendant, a *vir quaestorius,* was not tried before Pusaeus, prefect of Constantinople, and the *iudicium quinquevirale,* but before the praetorian prefect Pusaeus. Stein is certain that the whole senate participated with Pusaeus in the trial as associate judges. I am not certain of this, but think that the prefect may have been assisted by only a small commission of magnates. The issue depends on whether Malalas used the words παρὰ τῆς συγκλήτου in their strict meaning in the pertinent passage[15] or, as he sometimes did, to mean a group of high dignitaries, an informal consistory. In several other passages of Malalas, noticed by Ensslin and cited by me in the preceding chapter, σύγκλητος appears to be used in this more general sense. Stein seems to offer no explanation of the use of the word to refer to a council of war held by the emperor Julian before Babylon (Malalas II 22 Oxford), and it is hard to follow his argument that because Malalas, writing of the trial of

[15] Bonn ed. XIV 370 or Oxford ed. II 76.

the patrician Probus (Malalas II 171 Oxford), used both συγκλήτου and σιλεντίου κομβέντου in the same passage, he meant the same thing by both terms and was merely indulging in a literary flourish not characteristic of this chronicler. Rather, Malalas used the words with intention: Probus was tried and condemned before the praetorian prefect and a commission of dignitaries; he was pardoned by Justinian; the consistory and the senate met jointly to thank the emperor for his grace. Stein further pointed out that the instances cited by Ensslin and me of the loose use of συγκλητική Ῥώμης and of δύο συγκλητικούς of the king of Persia did not constitute a strong argument in support of our position. This must certainly be conceded, but one may perhaps feel that they were worth mentioning in corroboration of the more cogent passages, one of which, it seems to me, remains without a satisfactory explanation and the other without any explanation whatever. For the present, then, the case of Isocasius remains uncertain: he was tried before the praetorian prefect Pusaeus, but we cannot know whether, as seems probable enough, Pusaeus was assisted by the senate as a whole or, as is possible, by a commission of magnates.

It is perhaps pertinent to point out that if Stein's view should prove to be the correct one, it would become more certain than ever that Isocasius was not tried before the *iudicium quinquevirale:* not only would the presiding judge have been the praetorian prefect instead of the prefect of Constantinople, but he would have been assisted by the whole senate, not by a small committee — a committee consisting, for all we could prove to the contrary, of five senators chosen by lot. (On the other hand, the procedure would have been less in accord with what I believe to have been the usual practice in the East.)[16]

If, then, the *iudicium quinquevirale* never existed in the eastern portion of the Empire, we cannot be surprised at finding no mention of it in the great histories of Ostrogorsky and Vasiliev.[17] Unfortunately, since neither writer mentions the trial of Isocasius — not, after all, an event of such importance that we should expect it to be mentioned in works covering more than a thousand years — we cannot know what they felt about that trial. In view, though, of my insistence that any influence that the *iudicium quinquevirale* had in the development of later western law came, not from the East, but from the West through the inclusion of the second of the statutes concerning it (*Cod. Theod.* 2.1.12) in the Breviary of Alaric, and its repetition in various forms in the epitomes[18] — in view of this, it is comforting to read in Vasiliev[19] of the "direct influence exerted by the code of Theodosius upon barbarian legislation. But still more frequent was its indirect influence through the Visigothic code. During the early Middle Ages, including the epoch of Charlemagne, western European legislation was influenced by the *Breviarium* . . . not through the code of Justinian, which spread to the West much later, sometime during the twelfth century."

A. H. M. Jones, in his most impressive work on the later

[16] See above, chap. I, pp. 16–18.
[17] George Ostrogorsky, *History of the Byzantine State,* translated by Joan Hussey (Oxford 1956); A. A. Vasiliev, *History of the Byzantine Empire* (Madison 1958).
[18] See chap. I, pp. 1–2, 21.
[19] I 102 (above, n. 17).

Roman Empire, does mention Isocasius, but not in connection with his trial.[20] He also refers to the *iudicium quinquevirale:* "Gratian modified this rule, ordering provincial governors after passing sentence to refer the penalty to himself or to the urban prefect (from the Suburbicarian provinces) or to the praetorian prefect (from other provinces). In judging such cases the urban prefect was assisted by five senators chosen by lot." He mentions the trials of Arvandus and of Basilius and Praetextatus as having taken place before it (pointing out, however, that if we are to accept the trial of Arvandus as having been before that tribunal, we must read "Vviris" for "Xviris"). He does not appear to consider either case an enlargement of the jurisdiction of the tribunal as established by Gratian's statute.[21]

In writing that the provincial governors are to refer appropriate cases, after the preliminary stages, to the emperor *or* (italics mine) to the urban prefect, Jones is, as I also did in *The Iudicium Quinquevirale,*[22] translating *vel* by "or." In later Latin, though, *vel* came increasingly to have a conjunctive meaning, not a disjunctive one. Indeed, it is clearly used in a conjunctive sense in the opening words of our statute, "Provincialis iudex vel intra Italiam," which I should incline to render by "a provincial governor, including the governors of the Italian provinces." Similarly, it now seems to me, these governors are directed to refer the case, not "to Our Wisdom or to the glorious authorities," but "to Our

[20] Jones *LRE* II 863.
[21] *Ibid.,* I 491 and III 139 (note 47).
[22] *Iud. Quinq.* 3.

Wisdom and the glorious authorities." It would surely have been very odd if provincial governors, even of such high categories as vicars and proconsuls, were to have been left to choose whether the final stages of these important cases were to be heard by the emperor or by the prefect. Rather, they were to refer the cases to both.

If so, though, what did the emperor do, and what the prefect? Was the emperor merely to be kept informed, and was the prefect under all circumstances to determine the sentence? Or was it, as one might more plausibly suppose, the emperor who determined whether the case was to be concluded before him or else remitted to the prefect? But if the latter, then why did Cassiodorus insist with such extreme emphasis that the *iudicium quinquevirale* was the only tribunal before which Basilius and Praetextatus could legally be heard? Perhaps *Cod. Theod.* 2.1.12, the second of the statutes concerning the *iudicium,* is the answer: "In criminalibus causis senatus statuta iamdudum quinqueviralis iudicii forma servabitur. In quo cum perfacile esse credamus optimos legere de summis, sortito tamen ad iudicium vocabantur, ne de capite atque innocentia alterius iudicio electi iudicent." It will be noticed that all reference to the emperor and to the prefects has disappeared — though the trial of Basilius and Praetextatus, which was long posterior to this law, makes it certain that the prefect of the City remained the presiding judge of the *iudicium* — that the *iudicium* is the only tribunal we hear of, that there is nothing about preliminary determination of the facts of the case and of the questions at issue before the provincial governors. I have hitherto taken this law, promulgated by Honorius in 423, to have been a mere confirmation of Gratian's law of 376, insisting on the importance of the selection of the associate judges by lot, and making it clear, by the use of *senatus* instead of the *senatorum* of the earlier statute, that not all *viri clarissimi,* but only those — by this time entirely or almost entirely of the higher ranks of the senatorial order — who had actually been received as active and voting members of the senate, were entitled to trial before the *iudicium.*[23]

If, though, this law of Honorius was a mere confirmation of the law of Gratian, it seems surprisingly loosely worded. Can it be, rather, that it summarizes changes in practice that have taken place during the interval of nearly half a century between the two statutes? The Theodosian Code, as we have only recently been reminded, deliberately included obsolete as well as current statutes,[24] so that there would be no reason for surprise at finding Gratian's law in it as well as that of Honorius, even if the latter should be construed as replacing the former. If this should be the case — if the law of Honorius, that is, constitutes a substantial modification of the earlier statute — then it completely explains the attitude of Theodoric and Cassiodorus in the case of Basilius and Praetextatus: under the law of Gratian it might be argued, as we have seen, that the emperor could reserve jurisdiction in such a case; the law of Honorius, unless it is to be construed as a mere loosely worded confirmation of the law of Gratian, allows of no alternate jurisdiction to the *iudicium quin-*

[23] *Ibid.,* 4–7.
[24] Jones *LRE* I 475.

quevirale. This hypothesis, too, would offer a simpler explanation than I have given above to the trial of Arvandus before our tribunal (always assuming that we may read "Vviris" for "Xviris"): criminal charges against a senator would be heard before the *iudicium* no matter what part of the Empire in the West they arose in.

There are two weighty arguments against this hypothesis: the use of the word *iamdudum* with no suggestion that there have been any changes in the jurisdiction of the court since the promulgation of the only other extant statute we have concerning it, and the fact that the composition of the court is not more clearly defined. There is, though, an extremely strong argument in its favor, an argument that surprisingly enough seems not to have struck any of those, including myself until recently, who have written about the *iudicium:* the law of Honorius was incorporated into the Breviary of Alaric. Why would Alaric have incorporated into a code that was promulgated for the use of his Gallo-Roman subjects a law setting up a tribunal that dealt only with cases arising within the suburbicarian provinces of the Empire in the West? In 506, the date of the promulgation of the Breviary, how many among the Gallo-Roman magnates would have been in a position to benefit by the provisions of Gratian's law? Yet the *iudicium quinquevirale* of the law of Honorius must have been a living and valuable institution in their actual experience, one which they would wish to have securely established, with such changes as altered conditions should make necessary, in the Visigothic kingdom. The law of Honorius, then, must have reflected real changes in the

jurisdiction of the original tribunal, changes which had made
it and left it an institution of genuine importance to the
Gallo-Roman magnates of the time of Alaric.

This brings us to the last point which remains to be discussed in this chapter. If our tribunal was to be really important to these Gallo-Roman magnates, it was necessary not
only that its jurisdiction should have been extended to cases
arising outside the suburbicarian provinces but also that it
should have included criminal charges against all *viri clarissimi,* not merely criminal charges against members of those
higher ranks of the order which by this period constituted
the whole, or practically the whole, of the formally received
and voting membership of the senate. In the Gaul of 506,
some thirty years after Eurich had conquered the region
between the Rhone and the Alps, there can have been very
few men, and those old, who had ever been formally received into the Roman senate. On the other hand, the clarissimate, the great senatorial families of whom we hear constantly in Gregory of Tours — to one of which, indeed,
Gregory himself belonged — preserved great importance in
the Visigothic kingdom, it was mainly for their benefit that
Alaric promulgated his code, it was to them that it must
have mattered whether the essence of the *iudicium quinquevirale* should be preserved.

I have already mentioned that I have hitherto taken the
law of Gratian, and even more clearly, the law of Honorius,
to apply, not to the whole clarissimate, but only to those —
by this time most of them *viri illustres* — who had actually
been received into the active membership of the senate. The

44 *Late Roman Studies*

citations from the Theodosian Code which I had advanced to sustain my former view still seem to me far from negligible, especially *Cod. Theod.* 16.5.52 of 412. This law imposes a fine of fifty pounds of gold on *inlustres* who refuse to abjure the heresy of Donatism, a fine of forty pounds of gold on *spectabiles* for the same offense, of thirty pounds on *senatores,* of twenty pounds on *clarissimi,* etc., etc. It is evident that our statute distinguishes clearly between the various grades of the clarissimate, and specifically between *senatores* and those *clarissimi* who had not been formally accepted into the membership of the senate. It may be, though — indeed, I now incline to say that it must be — that when there was no reason for making these distinctions, the Code contented itself with using *senator* to signify any member of the clarissimate, *senatus* to cover the whole senatorial order. How else can we account for the inclusion of the law of Honorius in the Breviary of Alaric? [25]

In conclusion, it may not be superfluous to quote the *interpretatio* of the statute that follows it in the Breviary: "Cum

[25] In favor of the opinion that the *iudicium quinquevirale* heard charges against all members of the senatorial order and not merely against enrolled members of the senate, see Charles Lécrivain (above, chap. 1, n. 10) 11f; A. Hoepffner (reviewing *Iud. Quinq.*), *Revue des Etudes latines* 14 (1936) 214; cf. also H. F. Jolowicz (reviewing *Iud. Quinq.*), *History* 21 (1936) 158. See also Jones *LRE* I 491. In this passage he writes that the *iudicium quinquevirale* heard charges against "senators"; if I understand him correctly, he is using the word in the broad sense of all members of the senatorial order. On p. 529 of vol. II of the same work, he points out that by the time of Justinian only *viri illustres* were members of the senate and that even the title of *senator* was reserved for them. He adds that the same change took place in Rome under Theodoric, or perhaps even so early as the reign of Anthemius. It does not seem entirely clear from his text, notes, and citations that in the West also the *clarissimi* lost the title of *senator* as well as eligibility to the senate; but if they did, and if the loss took place as early as the reign of Anthemius, who was still a power in Gaul, it becomes difficult to account for the survival of our *iudicium,* even in modified form, in Visigothic Gaul in the time of Alaric.

pro obiecto crimine aliquis audiendus est, quinque nobilissimi viri iudices de reliquis sibi similibus missis sortibus eligantur, ne studio videantur electi et de capitali re aut innocentia alterius videatur facile iudicari." [26]

[26] Th. Mommsen and Paulus M. Meyer (edd.), *Theodosiani Libri XVI*, etc., I (Berlin 1905) 77. The *aliquis* of this text reminds one pleasantly of the song from *The Pirates of Penzance*,

> When everyone is somebody,
> Then no one's anybody.

We may, I think, feel certain that our *aliquis* was very much a "somebody." The *aliquis* is repeated in the *Epit. Suppl. Lat.*, which follows the text of the *interpretatio* fairly closely and is believed to have been composed in France before 838, perhaps as early as the 8th century. But the even earlier *Epitome Codicis Guelpherbytani*, also written in Gaul, after 754 but before 769, has: "Senatoris accusati a quibus iudicibus audiatur. Id est quinque nubilissimis [*sic*] viris et de reliquis militibus sortibus electis." See Gustavus Haenel (above, chap. 1, n. 5) 35f, and (for dates) pp. xxvi ff.

In an article of exceptional interest (A. H. M. Jones, "The Constitutional Position of Odoacer and Theoderic," *Journal of Roman Studies* 52 [1962] 126–30), Jones concludes with a discussion of the inclusion of an analogous law, *Cod. Theod.* 9.40.10, in the *Breviary*. In this instance, the "senatorii ordinis viri" of the *Code* becomes "aliquae maiores personae aut alicuius dignitatis viri" in the *interpretatio*.

CHAPTER III

PROCOPIUS AND BOETHIUS, I

Ɪɴ *Speculum* 22 (1947) 443–45, Mr. Howard R. Patch investigates "The Beginnings of the Legend of Boethius." He points out that "in the preface of King Alfred's Old English rendering of the *Consolatio Philosophiae* there is a fairly clear implication that Boethius died as a martyr who had perceived the 'wrongs wrought by Theodoric upon the Christian faith,' and who had 'cast about within himself how he might wrest the sovereignty from the unrighteous king . . .'" He adds that "a considerable time must have elapsed" for the story to have formed and spread across Europe, and perhaps even more "since the idea of Boethius as a martyr first began." In his article, he seeks to establish when the story first arose. He writes that "At least as early as the manuscripts containing the *Vitae,* and presumably then much earlier, the stand taken by Boethius was interpreted as that of opposition to a tyrant. Nor can it be fairly supposed that in the sixth century the conduct of Theodoric had only a political significance for the people, especially when in later allusions the religious implication is steadily borne in mind."

This article and the reply by Howard R. Patch are reprinted from *Speculum* 23 (1948) 284–87.

In *The Iudicium Quinquevirale,* I took a similar, and indeed, more extreme, position.[1] I argued that the position of Boethius as a leader of the senate and a Catholic, made it inevitable that, after the reconciliation between the emperor and the papacy, Boethius should choose the side of the emperor if a breach were to develop between the emperor and Theodoric, especially if that breach were to develop, as most political questions did at that time, on a religious issue. After an analysis of the texts, I propounded the following hypothetical reconstruction of the course of events: Justin's persecution of Arians in the East was very probably designed to create trouble between Theodoric and his Catholic subjects, and at any rate, it did create trouble; Theodoric sent the pope and other ecclesiastics on a mission to the emperor, either to seek tolerance in the East, or to threaten reprisals in Italy, or both; the senatorial leaders were probably anxious that an accord should be reached and certainly anxious that if no accord were to be reached, the emperor should at least take steps to protect the Catholic Italians from reprisals; Albinus, a senator, wrote to the emperor about the matter; the correspondence (of course treasonable from the point of view of Theodoric) came to light; Boethius, both because he thought the charge primarily a partisan conspiracy to ruin Albinus, and because he feared that the senate as whole would be endangered if Theodoric, irritated and suspicious as he already was, were to learn of it, tried unsuccessfully to prevent the case from being brought before the consistory; when the charges were discussed in the consistory, Boethius exclaimed that they were false, but that if the correspondence

---

[1] *Iud. Quinq.* 40–63 and notes.

were genuine, then it would implicate not only Albinus but the senate as a whole, Boethius himself included; the prosecutor, probably in order to save the senate by putting the whole blame on Albinus and Boethius, now *haesitans* brought false evidence against Boethius; his condemnation and death and that of Symmachus followed.[2]

It will be seen, then, that I go fully as far as Patch in this matter, that I entirely agree that Boethius may have been considered a martyr by "his Catholic friends." Indeed, it seems to me that, if we can accept my hypothesis, he has a valid claim to martyrdom. He probably was not primarily interested in the religious issue (he does not mention it in the *Consolatio*); he certainly was not put to death because he was a Catholic, but because he had been found guilty of treason. But his treason, if my hypothesis is tenable, consisted in an attempt to cover the senate, which seemed implicated in an attempt to protect the Italian Catholics, menaced with persecution, by imperial intervention in the affairs of Theodoric's kingdom. From the point of view of the Church, then, Boethius was put to death for trying to protect the Roman Church from persecution by heretics.

It is more difficult to follow Patch, though, when he writes that the passage in Procopius which refers to the matter[3] makes it "clear that even to a skeptic like Procopius the author of the *Consolatio* was a martyr." Procopius says that because Symmachus and Boethius practiced philosophy and were mindful of justice and were generous, they attained

---

[2] I further maintained that there was evidence tending to establish that Boethius was tried before the *iudicium quinquevirale;* this still seems to me true, but it is not material to the point at issue.

[3] *Hist.* 5.1.33–34, trans. H. B. Dewing, Loeb Classical Library.

great reputation, and attracted the envy of "men of the basest
sort," that "such persons slandered them to Theodoric, and
he, believing their slanders, put these two men to death, on
the ground that they were setting about a revolution, and
made their property confiscate to the public treasury." Patch,
in analyzing this passage, writes: "These two then, Symmachus and Boethius, 'because they practised philosophy'
(φιλοσοφίαν δὲ ἀσκήσαντε) and were known to be just and
charitable, were put to death; this is the way the story was
circulated. Once and for all it is made clear that even to a
skeptic like Procopius the author of the *Consolatio* was a
martyr." He adds in a footnote, "At the very least in the
sense used in the twelfth century regarding Symmachus:
'Teotricus rex Simmachus martyrizauit' (E. T. Silk, *Saeculi
Noni Auctoris in Boetii Cons. Philos. Commentarius,* in
Papers and Monographs of the American Academy in Rome,
IX (1935), p. liii, note 1)."

With this one cannot agree. Procopius does not say that
Symmachus and Boethius were *put to death* because they
"practised philosophy and were known to be just and charitable." He does say that they acquired a great reputation
because of these practices, and that certain people envied
them because of their reputation. Envying them, Procopius
continues, these people slandered them to Theodoric, and
he, believing the slanderers, put the two to death *on the
ground that they were setting about a revolution.* Procopius
gives a purely political aspect to the executions; he regards
Symmachus and Boethius as innocent, but not, in any sense
whatever, as martyrs.

It is the more necessary that this should be clear because

the account of Procopius is perhaps the strongest argument against the position taken by Patch ("Nor can it be fairly supposed that in the sixth century the conduct of Theodoric had only a political significance for the people") and, even more emphatically, by me, that religious and political issues were inextricably mixed in this case. The weight of the passage from Procopius cannot be disputed; indeed, I have elsewhere[4] given my reasons for attaching the highest importance to it. If, then, I am right in insisting that this passage is not to be construed as evidence that Procopius considered Boethius to be a martyr, but as giving a purely political explanation for his death, then it becomes necessary either for Patch and for me to give up our point of view, or else for some satisfactory explanation of the negative testimony of Procopius to be found.

Such an explanation exists. Patch is right in referring to Procopius as a "skeptic," or, at the very least, as far removed from the fanaticism which generally prevailed in religious matters in the sixth century. Bury says of him: "As to religion, the historian generally uses the language of a skeptic and a fatalist, regarding Christianity as an outsider with tolerant indifference, but never committing himself to any utterance against it."[5] Gibbon quotes a famous passage from Procopius as follows: "*that* religious controversy is the offspring of arrogance and folly; *that* true piety is most laudably expressed by silence and submission; *that* man, ignorant of his own nature, should not presume to scrutinize the nature of his God; and *that* it is sufficient for us to know that

---

[4] *Iud. Quinq.* 51.
[5] Bury's Gibbon (4th ed., 1911) IV 516.

power and benevolence are the perfect attributes of the Deity." [6] In another passage Gibbon, referring to Procopius and Agathias, writes: "Their religion, an honourable problem, betrays occasional conformity, with a secret attachment to Paganism and Philosophy." [7]

These judgments are well borne out by the passage from Procopius concerning Boethius, Symmachus, and Theodoric. He admires the moderation and justice of Theodoric, describes his repentance for having executed the two men, and says of the execution: "This was the first and last act of injustice which he committed towards his subjects, and the cause of it was that he had not made a thorough investigation, as he was accustomed to do, before passing judgment on the two men." We have already seen his praise of Symmachus and Boethius as philosophers and just and generous men. To him, the Theodoric of the "goldenes Wort," [8] the noble Symmachus, the Boethius of the *Consolatio,* were ideal figures, the crossing of their fates a true tragedy, high above the level of sectarian squabbling. He must, if Patch and I are right, have heard of the religious controversies of the time; he must have met many Italians who regarded Boethius as a martyr. But with these issues he had no sympathy, and to have presented his characters as moved by them would have been, in his opinion, to have slandered them. In his opinion, and in fact. For, though they became involved in questions arising from religious issues and though

[6] *Ibid.,* V 133; the passage from Procopius is *Bell. Goth.* 1.1.3.

[7] IV 210 n. 12.

[8] Felix Dahn, *Die Könige der Germanen* (Leipzig 1910ff) II 157 n. 5, quoting Cass. *Var.* II 27: "religionem imperare non possumus, quia nemo cogitur ut credat invitus."

they may have been sincerely religious men, Theodoric and Boethius and (we may presume) Symmachus were, as regards bigotry, far above the level of a Gregory the Great or a Justinian.

In conclusion, then, we may feel secure that Patch is right in believing that Boethius was regarded as a martyr "by his Catholic friends" from the time of his death; we cannot cite Procopius as evidence in favor of this point of view; on the other hand, we should not expect to find support for it in such a writer as Procopius.

PROCOPIUS AND BOETHIUS, II
by Howard R. Patch

Mr. Charles Henry Coster has raised some question regarding my article on the "Beginnings of the legend of Boethius" (*Speculum* 22 [1947] 443ff). He disagrees with my interpretation of the passage in Procopius because "Procopius does not say that Symmachus and Boethius were *put to death* because they 'practiced philosophy and were known to be just and charitable.'" It was not my contention that he did; but, even so, such is precisely the course of the argument in the Greek passage. The chain of cause and effect is clear: the idealism and goodness of Symmachus and Boethius brought these men a great fame; this reputation was presumably that of their nobility of thought and action; it attracted the envy of "men of the basest sort"; such persons slandered them to Theodoric; and he, "believing their slanders," put Symmachus and Boethius to death "on the ground that they were setting about a revolution." What bothers Mr.

Coster, I believe, is that of course Procopius does not tell us that Theodoric himself had the idealism and goodness of these men in mind when he put them to death. But that is no essential to the idea of martyrdom, which may as often spring from circumstance as from intention. It is clear that Procopius recorded the general view of Boethius as the innocent victim of Theodoric; for people closer to the scene the idealism that led to his death could only be the Catholic religion; and the passage in question does say that it was the good life of the two men (practicing philosophy and spreading abroad their generosity) that through the malice of others led to their death.

CHAPTER IV

THE FALL OF BOETHIUS:
HIS CHARACTER

I T IS at most a pardonable exaggeration to say that the fall
of Boethius has been almost as much discussed as the fall
of Adam. Not that there has been any doubt that the fall of
Boethius did in fact take place, but that exactly when it took
place, and exactly why, have been less clear. Some have
thought Boethius was a martyr,[1] some have doubted that he
was a Christian,[2] most have thought that he was the innocent victim of enemies who accused him falsely,[3] William

This article is reprinted from the *Annuaire de l'Institut de Philologie et d'Histoire Orientales et Slaves* (1952, Vol. IV in the *Mélanges Henri Grégoire*) 45–81.
    [1] For the authorities on this question, see William Bark, "The Legend of
Boethius' Martyrdom," in *Speculum* 21 (1946) 312 n. 1. Cf. "The Beginnings of
the Legend of Boethius," by Howard R. Patch, in *Speculum* 22 (1947) 443–45;
also, Charles Henry Coster and Howard R. Patch, "Procopius and Boethius," in
Speculum 23 (1948) 284–87, reprinted in chap. 3 above. The essence of the
difference of opinion between Patch and me seems to be that the former accepts
a broader definition of martyrdom than I do.
    [2] For the authorities maintaining this point of view, see Giovanni Semeria, "Il
cristianesimo di Severino Boezio rivendicato," in *Studi e Documenti di Storia e
Diritto* 21 (Rome 1900) 68–178, cited by Bark in note 4 of the article just referred to, and other authorities cited by Bark in the same note.
    [3] See, among many, Procopius, *History of the Wars* 5.1.33–34; Viktor Schurr,
Die Trinitätslehre des Boethius im Lichte der "skytischen Kontroversen" (Pader-
born 1935) 201 n. 316; E. K. Rand, *Founders of the Middle Ages* (Cambridge,
Mass. 1929) 159. Stein believes that Theodoric sincerely thought Boethius guilty
but that Boethius sincerely thought himself innocent (Stein II 257). I still hold
to my view that Boethius was guilty of acts (trying to prevent the charges against
Albinus from coming to the notice of Theodoric and trying to minimize the
matter when it was brought before the King) that he knew would amount to

Bark has maintained that he did actually attempt to overthrow Theodoric.[4] The character of Boethius has generally been thought one of the noblest of that antique world which was about to expire;[5] Bark, on the other hand, feels unable to "avoid the conclusion that Boethius could be harsh, selfish and arrogant, and that he well knew how to consult his own interests . . ." that he "lacked the steadfastness of Cassiodorus, being apparently unaware of the inconsistency of accepting gifts of power and prestige from Theodoric while working for the King's overthrow."[6]

Much of the severity of Bark's estimate of the character of Boethius is of course due to his belief that Boethius was guilty of treachery. Let us see, then, how he supports his contention that Boethius conspired to overthrow Theodoric. In the first place, he accepts with justified enthusiasm the brilliant and scholarly analysis of the theological tractates of Boethius by Father Schurr.[7] Schurr demonstrates beyond pos-

treason in the eyes of Theodoric, acts which Boethius himself thought justified because his first loyalty was to Romanism and Catholicism. Cf. *Iud. Quinq.* 62f.

[4] William Bark, "Theodoric vs. Boethius: Vindication and Apology," in *American Historical Review* 49 (1944) 410–26. M. L. W. Laistner seems to support this position. See his review of Pierre Courcelle, *Histoire littéraire des grandes invasions germaniques* in *Speculum* 24 (1949) 257f. Bark's article is also cited by Vasiliev. See A. A. Vasiliev, *Justin the First* (Harvard University Press, 1950) 328 n. 19.

[5] Among many, see Procopius (above, n. 3); Rand (above, n. 3) 135f, 157f, 180.

[6] Bark (above, n. 4) 425 n. 66 and 426. See also his "The Legend of Boethius' Martyrdom" (above, n. 1) 317 n. 18. One should add that Bark, elsewhere in the interesting and stimulating articles cited, fully recognizes that in spite of the defects which he finds in the character of Boethius, the latter was "one of the greatest men of the sixth century; his brilliant reputation has no need of spurious honors" ("The Legend" 312). He also says ("Theodoric vs. Boethius" 426), "At the end at least he was loyal to what he believed in and risked everything for it." For another very severe criticism of the character of Boethius, see Thomas Hodgkin, *Italy and Her Invaders,* III (2nd ed., Oxford 1896) 479, 493, 498. For a milder criticism, see *Iud. Quinq.* 50f.

[7] See above, n. 3.

sibility of denial the support given by Tractates 5, 2, and 1 to the formulae advocated by the Scythian monks ("ex duabus et in duabus naturis" and "unus ex trinitate carne passus") in the Theopaschite controversy, a dispute which had direct bearing on the healing of the Acacian schism, since the eventual acceptance of these formulae freed the papacy from all suspicion of Nestorianism in the eyes of the East.[8]

Schurr, however, perhaps influenced by the fact that Boethius' support was indirect,[9] seems to feel that the latter's interest was primarily dialectical rather than controversial. But the one does not exclude the other; and, since the manner in which Boethius handled these questions, if indirect, was still most pertinent to the current controversy, one is inclined to believe with Bark[10] that Boethius hoped to secure the acceptance — it was in fact secured — of the Scythian formulae not only for their own sake but also in order to provide a sound basis for ecclesiastical unity. In this connection, Bark is slightly troubled by the fact that Boethius said he was writing only for a friend or two, and wonders whether to attribute this to "rhetorical exaggeration or perhaps to caution." But one may take Boethius' statement quite

---

[8] Bark correctly points out ("Theod. vs. Boethius" 412 n. 7) that I was not justified in doubting (*Iud. Quinq.* 81 n. 214) the authenticity of "many of the theological works attributed to Boethius." Tractate 3 is not cited above because, though Schurr sufficiently demonstrates (above, n. 3; 225ff) its relationship with Tractates 2 and 1, it seems not to bear on the Theopaschite controversy.

[9] Schurr (above, n. 3) 221.

[10] "Theod. vs. Boethius" 416, 418f. It should be noted, however, that Vasiliev in his most interesting discussion of the healing of the Acacian schism makes no mention of the theological tractates of Boethius. He does however write that the Scythian monks, during their stay in Rome, "spread a good deal of propaganda for their formula among the population in general, and even in the Roman Senate." Cf. *Justin the First* 190ff.

literally without impairing the validity of Bark's thesis. It is obvious that even in the sixth century, works such as the theological tractates of Boethius could not be widely understood, though they might have great influence on those who did understand them. Boethius, we may suppose, was writing for a few friends, just as he said he was, but it was precisely those friends who could be helpful in bringing about the healing of the schism.[11]

The situation reminds us of one with which we are familiar. They say that Professor Einstein once remarked that there were perhaps only half a dozen people in the world capable of understanding his theory of relativity. Obviously, he wrote for that half dozen — and changed the course of science.

So far, so good. It is in the next steps of his argument that we find ourselves unable to follow Bark. He writes:

> His [Justinian's] chief purpose was to put an end to the dangerous theological dissension which rent the empire, *since there could be no thought of political unification until the Eastern church had made its peace with Rome* . . . *Justinian's plan for, first, theological and then political unification* had many ramifications and there is evidence that Boethius had something to do with certain aspects of this plan . . . It must be admitted, however, that Boethius' profound interest in theological matters and the probable use of his writings by the Scythians do not prove that the Roman Patrician was a partner in *Justinian's policy of ecclesiastical and political unification.* At the same time it is only fair to say that if Boethius' purpose in supporting the Scythian theology was the same as Justinian's, both men would have made every effort to conceal the fact . . . There is reason to believe that there was strong indication of treason [against

[11] Cf. Schurr (above, n. 3) 198ff; Bark "Theod. vs. Boethius" 420.

Theodoric on the part of Boethius]. What could it have been but *Boethius' unmistakable sympathy with Justinian's imperial policy,* a sympathy made plain both by his support of the Scythian theology and by his close contact with *those who strove for an ecclesiastical harmony which they hoped would be followed by political unification based on the destruction of Theodoric's power.*[12]

We should be the last to deny the intermixture of political and religious issues at that time, or that Justinian may from the outset have had in mind the restoration of imperial power in the West, or that he fully realized the necessity of reconciliation in the religious field if political unity was to be attained.[13] But it does not follow that he, or the Roman ecclesiastics and senators who also sought to heal the schism, thought of religious reconciliation merely as a step towards political unity or even that they considered political unity the more impotrant of the two. On the contrary, it seems likely that not only the ecclesiastics and senators but also Justinian would have preferred an empire loosely knit from the political point of view but united in orthodoxy, to an empire centralized politically but split by religious schisms.[14]

There is more here, though, than a mere error in emphasis. Bark has asserted that, probably as early as 519,[15] certainly in 523,[16] Justinian was actually conspiring with some Roman senators, Boethius among them, to bring about the forcible

[12] Bark, "Theod. vs. Boethius" 413, 416, 419, 425. Italics are ours.

[13] Cf. *Iud. Quinq.* 40–42. Also, Stein II 254.

[14] Cf. Charles Diehl, in *CMH* II (Cambridge 1913) 1ff, esp. 4 and 5. Such errors in emphasis are very difficult to avoid. Indeed, the present writer feels that he committed the same fault in an article written as recently as 1948 (see above, chap. 3, p. 47: "Justin's persecution of Arians in the East *was very probably designed* to create trouble between Theodoric and his Catholic subjects . . .")

[15] "Theod. vs. Boethius" 414.

[16] *Ibid.,* 410, 415, 424.

overthrow of Theodoric. The character of Justinian, the circumstances in which he was placed, and the art of politics all combine to make this most improbable. Politics, even the most Machiavellian, the most Byzantine politics, are highly empirical, based on the actualities of the moment. Long-term plans and fixed policies may indeed exist, but they are put into execution only as expedience and opportunity offer. In the meantime, opinion may be molded to favor them, steps inconsistent with them may be avoided so far as possible, but the fewer who actually have knowledge of them, the better.

"Time and myself against any three," said Charles Fifth — and he, if anyone ever did, knew what it meant to have many problems and many people to deal with simultaneously, knew when to act, and when to let things ripen. Justinian, too, had many people and many problems to deal with. He was sometimes too hasty in believing that he had disposed of one or another, but, cautious by nature, always short of money, always short of troops, he at least sought to take his problems one at a time and to a very considerable extent was successful in doing so. Whatever his ultimate intentions may have been, he attacked neither Africa nor Italy nor Spain until he had, as he supposed, secured himself from difficulties in other quarters. The very year after the apparent conclusion of the Persian war, he gained the support of the Ostrogoths and overthrew the Vandal kingdom. The very year after he had concluded the Vandalic war — one may presume that he did not realize that his troubles with the Berber tribes would be so long or so serious — he undertook the Gothic war. When he intervened in Spain, the Italian war was, to be sure, not yet over, but he seized a moment when the Visigoths were divided among themselves, and the Ostrogoths unable to help them.

Can we believe that this methodical man would have wished a revolt against Theodoric to break out before his own domestic position was secure, before he had fortified his frontiers, while he was still in very serious danger from the Persians, while the Vandal fleet still existed on his flank? [17]

Under such conditions, an Italian revolt could not possibly have been successful; it would have meant the premature ruin of his potential supporters, and the creation of resentment against the East among the Italians, who would have felt that he had roused them to revolt and then left them without adequate support. In the absence, then, of very definite proof, we cannot assume that at the time of the healing of the schism, or even in 523, Justinian either wished or expected the overthrow of the Gothic kingdom in the near future.

Under such circumstances, it seems extremely improbable that he would have gone so far as to discuss with a group of Roman senators — to say nothing of discussing by letter — any hopes he might have had for the restoration of the Empire in the West at some indefinite time in the future. He might work with them for Catholic unity, he might, somewhat later, in adopting an anti-Arian policy in the East, be not unconscious that he was driving a wedge between Theo-

---

[17] To be sure, the Vandal fleet was not what it had been, and with the accession of Hilderich in 523, Vandal policy became friendly to the Empire. But that friendship was, as events proved, not stable, and that the Vandal fleet was still to be reckoned with, we see from Theodoric's own effort to create a fleet capable of opposing it. Cf. Wilhelm Ensslin (above, chap. 2, n. 5) 320f.

doric and the Italians; but he would not be likely to discuss his further plans, even if they were already developed, sooner than necessary. Political friendships are notoriously impermanent; secrets broadly shared are notoriously hard to keep; Justinian would have no reason to risk failure by premature disclosures.

To pass to our next point, Bark has assumed not only that Justinian was conspiring with a group of senators in 523 and even earlier for the overthrow of Theodoric's kingdom but that Boethius was one of the senators involved in the conspiracy. Against this assumption we have the definite testimony of Boethius himself. He wrote:

> Nam de compositis falso litteris, quibus libertatem arguor sperasse Romanam, quid attinet dicere? . . . Nam quae sperari reliqua libertas potest? Atque utinam posset ulla! Respondissem Canii verbo, qui cum a C. Caesare Germanici filio conscius contra se factae coniurationis fuisse diceretur: Si ego, inquit, scissem, tu nescisses . . .[18]

Bark discounts this statement of Boethius because there seems some reason to believe that Cassiodorus thought Boethius guilty.[19] He writes: "I think the latter [Cassiodorus] was in a better position to speak the truth and also . . . we cannot be sure that Boethius had given up hope of pardon." Noting that Cassiodorus in the writings that have come down to us spoke never a word, true or otherwise, on this subject, we must concede that he did praise the accusers of Boethius, so that, though praise is not rare in the letters of Cassiodorus, it does seem possible that he thought Boethius guilty or at

[18] *Cons. Phil.* 1.4.
[19] "Theod. vs. Boethius" 423. Cf. Hodgkin (above, n. 6) 488ff, and *Iud. Quinq.* 51, 63.

least was not unwilling to give the impression that he thought so.

But there can be no question that, whether Boethius was in a better position to speak the truth than Cassiodorus or not, or whether Cassiodorus spoke at all or not, Boethius was in a better position to know the truth than Cassiodorus could possibly be. Cassiodorus might feel — and still be mistaken — that the evidence was damning; Boethius would know whether he had or had not written the letters that he called false.

The question, then, is whether Boethius in writing this passage in the *De Consolatione Philosophiae* was telling the truth or whether he was trying to better his position in the eyes of Theodoric or in the eyes of posterity. In the passage he says in substance that he knew of no conspiracy but that, if he had known of one, he would have seen to it that it succeeded. One can only say that if Boethius was trying to excuse himself to Theodoric, he chose a very singular way of doing so. Nor was Boethius trying to save his reputation: he wrote that if he had known of a conspiracy, he would have gloried in bringing it to a successful conclusion. He did not, therefore, feel that his reputation would have suffered by an admission that he had been involved in it. He had, then, no motive, whether of safety or reputation, for distorting the truth when he wrote. And, as we have just seen, Cassiodorus might have been mistaken, but Boethius necessarily knew whether he had or had not written the letters that he called false. Further, Cassiodorus, perhaps for the most disinterested motives, continued to serve the Gothic rulers through every change; he must have shown considerable ability in not speaking out when to have done so might have meant, at the least, dismissal from office. One is driven to conclude both that Boethius was speaking the truth and that he was in a better position than Cassiodorus both to know it and to speak it. We may feel certain, therefore, that Boethius did not in fact know of any conspiracy against Theodoric until the evidence, whether true or false or distorted, against Albinus came to his attention in Verona.

We must, then, reject Bark's hypothesis. But the mention of Albinus and of the meeting of the consistory at Verona reminds us that certain obstinate facts remain. Evidence implicating Albinus in treason did come to light; Boethius by his own admission did try to suppress it; he was himself accused of treason, was tried and executed; his father-in-law, Symmachus, was tried and executed. And there is some reason to believe that Cassiodorus felt that Boethius was guilty, or at least that he was willing to have it supposed that he thought him to be so. It is not enough, then, to argue that Bark's hypothesis is anachronistic so far as concerns Justinian and untenable as regards Boethius; one must at least claim to have something more plausible to offer.

The present writer's hypothesis was published many years ago in his monograph, *The Iudicium Quinquevirale*.[20] It was not accepted for reasons of chronology, but for all that, it did have a certain influence.[21] It now seems possible to

---

[20] Pp. 40–63 and notes concern the case of Boethius.

[21] It is a pleasure to find that such a distinguished authority as Ensslin, though he accepts the usual chronology, does agree that Boethius was probably tried before the *iudicium quinquevirale*. He points out that if that was indeed the case, the tribunal was, exceptionally, meeting at Pavia instead of Rome (*Theod. der Grosse* 318). Cf. also Stein II 258. For chronology, see Laistner's review of *Iud. Quinq.* (above, chap. 1, n. 6); Bark, "Theod. vs. Boethius" 410 n. 2; A. E. F.

defend my chronology, but before taking up that question,
I wish to restate my position and then to add such modifications as further study has caused:[22] Justinian, having healed
the schism that divided the Catholic church, proceeded to
persecute the Monophysites with vigor and, outside of Egypt,
with considerable success. But the Monophysites were by no
means the only heretics in the Empire. Among others were
the Arians, no longer very important in the East, but most
important in the West, as they still included the great major-
ity of the Germans (the Burgundians and the hitherto heathen Franks had recently been brought into the Catholic
church by the conversion of their rulers), among them definitely Theodoric and his Ostrogoths. Presently (the question
of chronology will be taken up later), the emperor Justin
took measures[23] in accordance with which Arian churches
in the East were seized by the Catholics and many Arians
were induced to profess Catholicism. There is no reason to
suppose that Justinian, who was the power behind the throne
of his uncle, did not fully realize that measures taken against
the Arians in the East would be distasteful to Theodoric but
viewed with at least inward approval by the great senatorial
families of Italy, with their strongly Catholic sympathies.
Inward approval, perhaps, but also great uneasiness: if Theodoric were to retaliate, they would be the obvious victims.
Theodoric in fact did send a very impressive embassy to the

Boak's review of *Iud. Quinq.* in *Classical Philol.* 33 (1938) 120, and Ensslin's
review of the same work (cited above, chap. 1, n. 14); also Stein II 258.

[22] Originality is not claimed for this position. The main thesis was clearly
stated by Maurice Dumoulin in *CMH* I (1911) 452ff.

[23] Caspar doubts that these measures are reflected in any of the laws known to
us; he believes they were taken under powers of administrative discretion. Erich
Caspar, *Gesch. des Papstums*, II (Tübingen 1933) 184 n. 3. Cf. Louis Bréhier,
in *Histoire de l'Eglise depuis les origines jusqu'à nos jours*, IV (1937) 434 n. 4.

Emperor to threaten reprisals. It was headed by the Pope himself; of the other nine members, one was a patrician, three others were ex-consuls, and the remaining five were bishops, among them the bishop of Ravenna. Justin agreed to return the seized churches to the Arians, but did not agree (and in all probability the Pope did not ask him to agree) to allow the converts to apostatize. *During the absence of the embassy,* there came to light in Italy documents that either were or purported to be letters written to the Emperor by the patrician Albinus. "In all probability, the letters, whether genuine or forged, either requested the Emperor, in the event that the anti-Arian decrees were not to be rescinded, to devise some means of protecting the Italian Catholics, or else they went even further and encouraged Justin to maintain his attitude and to extend it to Italy by overthrowing Theodoric. Given the rather cautious policy which the senate appears to have pursued throughout the period we are studying, the former of these suppositions is the more probable." [24] Boethius, fearing that the documents would be used merely to exacerbate the situation to the prejudice of the senate, tried to keep the *referendarius* Cyprian from bringing them to the attention of the consistory. Cyprian, though, did bring them to the attention of the consistory and, when Boethius took the defense of Albinus, brought charges of treason and divination against Boethius himself. Boethius and Albinus were imprisoned. *On the return of the embassy,* Boethius was executed, and his father-in-law Symmachus was arrested and executed. Pope John was imprisoned and died in prison. Theodoric himself died shortly afterwards.

[24] *Iud. Quinq.* 57.

Since 1935, I have changed my views in four particulars.
I then thought it unlikely that the letters attributed to
Albinus went so far as to urge the overthrow of Theodoric;
I now think it even less probable than I did then. Next, I
believe that Albinus and Boethius were accused in connection, indeed, with the anti-Arian measures of Justin, but
possibly in the late autumn of 524, before, not after, the
departure of the embassy of Pope John. More probably,
however, *after* the departure of the embassy. Third, I doubt
that there was any considerable interval between the arrests
of Boethius and Symmachus, or between the executions of
the two. The interval probably came after the two arrests
and before the two executions. Fourth, in spite of a very
clear statement in the *Anonymus Valesianus,*[25] I am not
at all certain that the Cyprian was *referendarius* at the time
Boethius was arrested.

However plausible this hypothesis, amended or not, may
be in other respects, it cannot be sound if Boethius was
arrested in 523.[26] For the anti-Arian measures were probably
not put into force until toward the end of 524; the Pope
and his embassy left Italy not before October or November
of 525; it is certain that the Pope was in Constantinople
on Easter Day, 526; there seems no reason to doubt that he
died in Italy on May 18, 526 or that Theodoric died on
August 30th of that year.[27] In short, the Arian crisis would

---

[25] *Anon. Vales.* 14.85.

[26] Cf. above, n. 21.

[27] Bréhier (above, n. 23) IV 434–36. But Bréhier well observes that we date
the anti-Arian measures solely by a single passage in Theophanes. Caspar does
not date the anti-Arian measures or the departure of the embassy; he agrees that
the Pope was in Constantinople on Easter Day, 526, that he returned directly
afterwards and shortly died, and that Theodoric in turn died on August 30, 526

have arisen after the arrest of Boethius and so could not have been the cause of it.

We must therefore once more review the sources. There are four major contemporary, or almost contemporary, sources: Boethius himself, Procopius, the *Liber Pontificalis,* and the *Anonymous Valesianus.* Boethius[28] makes it clear that he had political enemies; that he did attempt to suppress consideration by the consistory of documents that, he considered, were false but purported to incriminate Albinus and the senate as a whole; that he did this (we have already given our reasons for believing his statements) because he did not believe there would be a fair trial (*praeiudicatae accusationis poena*); that he himself was accused of plotting to overthrow Theodoric, but that of this he was innocent (*Nam de compositis falso litteris, quibus libertatem arguor sperasse Romanam*). Unfortunately, he tells us nothing bearing on the date of the accusation; the only fact of chronological importance that we learn from the *Consolation* is that he lived long enough after his arrest to compose it.

Procopius is a witness not lower in standing than Boethius himself. He was the major historian of his period and a considerable historian for any period. "He is industrious in collecting facts, careful and impartial in stating them; his judgment is sound, his reflections generally acute, his con-

---

(above, n. 23; II 184–91). Stein also believes the anti-Arian measures to have been put into effect in 524–525, and the Pope to have left Italy in the fall of 525 (Stein II 259f). Ensslin states that the Pope and his embassy left Italy at the very beginning of 526 (above, chap. 2, n. 5; 323). Bark accepts the chronology of Bréhier and Stein. See "The Legend of Boethius' Martyrdom" (above, n. 1) 315 n. 13. For a recent and most interesting discussion of Pope John's embassy and its date, see W. Ensslin, "Papst Johannes I. als Gesandter Theoderichs des Grossen bei Kaiser Justinos I," *BZ* 44 (1951) 126–34.

[28] *Cons. Phil.* 1.4.48ff.

ceptions of the general march and movement of things not unworthy of the great events he has recorded." [29] He was already of age when the events with which we are dealing occurred; he was familar with the fortunes of the widow[30] and the children[31] of Boethius. He obviously had every opportunity of obtaining first-hand information concerning the deaths of Boethius, Symmachus, and Theodoric, and we may be certain that he was careful to obtain it. He wrote:

> Symmachus and his son-in-law Boetius were men of noble and ancient lineage, and both had been leading men in the Roman senate and had been consuls. But because they practised philosophy and were mindful of justice in a manner surpassed by no other men, relieving the destitution of both citizens and strangers by generous gifts of money, they attained great fame and thus led men of the basest sort to envy them. Now such persons slandered them to Theoderic, and he, believing their slanders, put these two men to death, on the ground that they were setting about a revolution, and made their property confiscate to the public treasury. And a few days later [ἡμέραις ὀλίγαις ὕστερον], while he was dining, the servants set before him the head of a great fish. This seemed to Theoderic to be the head of Symmachus newly slain. Indeed, with its teeth set in its lower lip and its eyes looking at him with a grim and insane stare, it did resemble exceedingly a person threatening him. And becoming greatly frightened at the extraordinary prodigy and shivering excessively, he retired running to his own chamber, and bidding them place many covers upon him, remained quiet. But afterwards he disclosed to his physician Elpidius all that had hap-

---

[29] This quotation from the eleventh ed. (1911) of the *Encycl. Britannica,* art. "Procopius," seems fully justified, at least so far as the *Histories of the Wars* are concerned. See also G. Soyter, "Die Glaubwürdigkeit des Geschichtschreibers Prokopios von Kaisareia," *BZ* 44 (1951) 541–45.

[30] *Hist.* 7.20.27–30.

[31] *Ibid.,* 5.2.5.

pened and wept for the wrong he had done Symmachus and
Boetius. Then, having lamented and grieved exceedingly over
the unfortunate occurrence, he died not long afterwards
[οὐ πολλῷ ὕστερον]. This was the first and last act of injustice
which he committed toward his subjects, and the cause of it
was that he had not made a thorough investigation, as he was
accustomed to do, before passing judgment on the two men.[32]

There is a picturesqueness in the account of Procopius that
tends to discredit it to modern ears. But there is nothing
intrinsically improbable in it. Theodoric, upset by the recent
executions and by the all too evident collapse of his life's
work, sits down to his dinner as a bout of chills and fever
comes on. The feverish imagination of the old barbarian sees
the fish's head as that of Symmachus. Overcome by horror,
remorse, and sickness, he takes to his bed, and, the chills
increasing, asks for covers.

Procopius does not say that he had the story directly from
Elpidius, but he does cite him as the source, and the details
of the sudden attack of chills and the request for covers in
August in Ravenna are just what a doctor would notice in
diagnosing an illness. In any case, we may be sure that
Procopius made every effort to secure the most accurate
information concerning an event so important as the death
of Theodoric.

Next, the account of Procopius confirms the statements
of Boethius in many particulars and contradicts them in
none. His confirmation is the more valuable because he
speaks with admiration of Theodoric, particularly of his
administration of justice, although admitting that in this

[33] *Ibid.*, 5.1.32–39. The translation given is that of Dewing, in the Loeb Classical Library.

particular case the King was unjust; he has not been biased
by resentment such as crept into the writings of Boethius
himself, such too as we find in the two sources with which
we shall have next to deal.

From the chronological point of view, Procopius brings
out one fact which is of extreme importance to our argument. Boethius and Symmachus were executed only *a few
days* before the final illness of Theodoric, and that final
illness ended in death *not long afterwards*. As we have
seen,[33] Theodoric died on August 30, 526, and Pope John
had returned from Constantinople after Easter of that year.
This is consistent with our hypothesis that Boethius and
Symmachus were executed shortly after the return of the
Pope from his embassy; it is wholly inconsistent with Bark's
belief that Boethius was executed in 524 or 525.[34]

Our next text is from the *Liber Pontificalis*.[35] There we
are told of the embassy of Pope John. The passage continues:

> Eodem tempore cum hii suprascripti, id est papa Iohannes
> cum senatores, Theodorum excons., Inportunum excons., Aga-
> pitum excons. et Agapitum patricium defuncto Thessalonica et
> suprascriptos positos Constantinopolim, Theodoricus rex hereticus
> tenuit duos senatores praeclaros et exconsules, Symmachum et
> Boetium, et occidit interficiens gladio. Eodem tempore rever-
> tentes Iohannes venerabilis papa et senatores . . .

The repetition is awkward but entirely clear: Theodoric
arrests Boethius and Symmachus *after the embassy has left*

---

[33] Above, p. 66 and n. 27.

[34] "Theod. vs. Boethius" 410.

[35] *Liber Pontificalis* 55, Iohannes (L. M. O. Duchesne ed., Paris 1886, I 275).
There are no significant differences in the relevant passages in Mommsen's edition
(MGH, *G st. Pont. Rom.,* I [Berlin 1898] 133ff).

Italy, and they are executed *on its return.* According to this text, then, Boethius was arrested not earlier than the fall of 525 and executed in the late spring or summer of 526.[36] This is consistent with Procopius; it is inconsistent with the hypothesis that Boethius was arrested in 523 and executed in 524 or 525.

In the *Abridgement of Felix,* an older version than the text as found in the present *Liber Pontificalis* — probably, indeed, based on a text composed about 535, or some ten years after the events with which we are concerned — [37] the wording of this passage is somewhat different, but if possible even clearer. The account of the fate of Symmachus and Boethius is introduced by the following words: "Et dum actum fuisset in partes Greciarum secondum voluntatem Theoderici regis heretici [ne] maxime sacerdotes vel christiani ad gladio mitterentur, illud vero beatissimo Iohanne episcopo et viros inlustres positos Constantinopolim . . ." [38]

Fourthly, we turn to the *Anonymus Valesianus.*[39] As this is the most detailed account which has come down to us, and as it is also the one which in its usually accepted form makes difficult the acceptance of the hypothesis advocated in this paper, the reader will excuse one more — the last — long quotation.[40]

XIV . . . 83. Ex eo [Theodoric had compelled the Catholics to pay for the restoration of synagogues they had burnt down

---

[36] See above, n. 27, for the dates of the embassy.
[37] See *RE* XIII 77f.
[38] Duchesne (above, n. 35) 227 n. 6; Mommsen (as above, n. 35).
[39] *Anonymi Valesiani Pars Posterior,* in *MGHAA* IX (Theodor Mommsen ed., Berlin 1892) 326ff, and, a more recent edition, L. A. Muratori, *Rerum Italicarum Scriptores,* ed. by G. Carducci and Vittorio Fiorini, vol. XXIV, part 4 (*Anonymus Valesianus,* ed. Roberto Cessi, Città di Castello 1913).
[40] *Ibid.,* 14.83–15.93.

in Ravenna] enim invenit diabolus locum, quem ad modum hominem bene rem publicam sine querella gubernantem subriperet. nam mox iussit ad fonticlos in proastio civitatis Veronensis oratorium santi Stephani id est altarium subverti. item ut nullus Romanus arma usque ad cultellum uteretur, vetuit.

84. item mulier pauper de gente Gothica, iacens sub porticu non longe a palatio Ravennati, quattuor generavit dracones: duo de occidente in orientem ferri in nubibus a populo visi sunt et in mari praecipitari, duo portati sunt unum caput habentes. stella cum facula apparuit, quae dicitur comes, pendens per dies quindecim. terrae mota frequenter fuerunt.

85. post haec coepit adversus Romanos rex subinde fremere inventa occasione. Cyprianus, qui tunc referendarius erat, postea comes sacrarum et magister, actus cupiditate insinuans de Albino patricio, eo quod litteras adversus regnum eius imperatori Iustino misisset: quod factum dum revocitus negaret, tunc Boethius patricius, qui magister officiorum erat, in conspectu regis dixit: 'falsa est insinuatio Cypriani: sed si Albinus fecit, et ego et cunctus senatus uno consilio fecimus: falsum est, domne rex.'

86. tunc Cyprianus haesitans non solum adversus Albinum sed et adversus Boethium eius defensorem deducit falsos testes. sed rex dolum Romanis tendebat et quaerebat quem ad modum eos interficeret: plus credidit falsis testibus quam senatoribus.

87. tunc Albinus et Boethius ducti in custodiam ad baptisterium ecclesiae. rex vero vocavit Eusebium praefectum urbis Ticini[41] et inaudito Boethio protulit in eum sententiam. quem mox in agro Calventiano, ubi in custodia habebatur, misere fecit occidi. qui accepta chorda in fronte diutissime tortus, ita ut oculi eius creparent, sic sub tormenta ad ultimum cum fuste occiditur.

XV. 88. rediens igitur rex Ravennam, tractans non ut dei amicus sed legi eius inimicus, inmemor factus omnis eius beneficii et gratiae, quam ei dederat, confidens in brachio suo, item

[41] The present writer believes the alternative reading "Ticinum" to be the correct one. Cf. Mommsen (above, n. 39) IX 328f, and *Iud. Quinq.* 59f. In the Cessi ed., p. 20, "Ticinum" is given as the main reading (above, n. 39). And cf. Ensslin, *Theod. der Grosse* 318.

credens quod eum pertimesceret Iustinus imperator, mittens et evocans Ravennam Iohannem sedis apostolicae praesulem et dicit ad eum: 'ambula Constantinopolim ad Iustinum imperatorem, et dic ei inter alia, ut reconciliatos in catholica restituat religione.'

89. cui papa Iohannes ita respondit: 'quod facturus es, rex, facito citius: ecce in conspectu tuo adsto. hoc tibi ego non promitto me facturum, nec illi dicturus sum. nam in aliis causis, quibus mihi iniunxeris, obtinere ab eodem, annuente deo, potero.'

90. iubet ergo rex iratus navem fabricari et superinpositum eum cum aliis episcopis, id est Ecclesium Ravennatem et Eusebium Fanestrem et Sabinum Campanum et alios duos, simul et senatores Theodorum Inportunum Agapitum et alium Agapitum. sed deus, qui fideles cultores suos non deserit, cum prosperitate perduxit.

91. cui Iustinus imperator venienti ita occurrit ac si beato Petro: cui data legatione omnia repromisit facturum praeter reconciliatos, qui se fidei catholicae dederunt, Arrianis restitui nullatenus posse.

92. sed dum haec aguntur, Symmachus caput senati, cuius Boethius filiam habuit uxorem, deducitur de Roma Ravennam. metuens vero rex ne dolore generi aliquid adversus regnum eius tractaret, obiecto crimine iussit interfici.

93. revertens Iohannes papa a Iustino, quem Theodoricus cum dolo suscepit et in offensa sua eum esse iubet. qui post paucos dies defunctus est . . .

The account goes on to tell us of the funeral of the Pope, and of the miraculous circumstances which attended it, of Theodoric's decree that the Catholic churches should be turned over to the Arians, and of his death on the very day that the decree was to be carried out.

This account, impressive because of its detail, adds substantially to what we know from other sources, but, at least in the form just given, it is inconsistent with them in one

particular. Boethius is arrested, tried, and executed before
the departure of the embassy. Not only is this inconsistent
with Procopius (since he makes the execution occur only
just before the death of Theodoric) and with the *Liber
Pontificalis,* it is also inherently improbable. "Boethius is
executed before the Pope goes on his embassy. But just after
such a drastic step, Theodoric would scarcely have been in
the mood to send an embassy, and Justin would certainly
have felt little inclination to make concessions. And once
things had gone to these extremes, Theodoric would have
been very foolish to have loosed his grip on such valuable
hostages as the Pope, the Bishop of Ravenna, four other
bishops, and four of the leading senators. Finally, one is at
a loss to understand why, if Symmachus was to be [arrested
and] executed at all, he was not [arrested and] executed
sooner." [42] According to this account in its present form,
Theodoric was not afraid of Symmachus when he arrested
Boethius; he was not afraid of Symmachus during the long
period Boethius was in prison writing the *Consolation*; then
Theodoric had Boethius most cruelly executed — but he was
still not afraid of Symmachus; then Theodoric summoned
the Pope to Ravenna; then he had a boat built for the Pope
and the other ambassadors. When the boat had been built
and when the embassy had reached Constantinople, then
suddenly Theodoric became afraid that Symmachus might
attempt to avenge Boethius. This simply does not make
sense.

The solution of the difficulty seems to have been found
by Roberto Cessi, the editor of the *Anonymus Valesianus*

[42] *Iud. Quinq.* 55.

in the Muratori Collection. Though he gives the text in the order in which it appears in the manuscripts, he believes that sections 88–91 should go between sections 84 and 85, thus bringing section 87 next to section 92.[43] If this order is followed, we hear first of growing religious excitement, of prodigies and portents. Then of the departure of the embassy. Then of the affair of Cyprian, Albinus, and Boethius. Then "dum haec aguntur" of the arrest and execution of Symmachus. And, immediately following, of the return of the embassy, the arrest of the Pope, his death, and that of Theodoric. We find the *Anonymus* in complete accord with Procopius and the *Liber Pontificalis*.

The difficulties disappear — but only to rise again. *Cyprianus, qui tunc referendarius erat, postea comes sacrarum et magister* . . . The *Anonymus* tells us, that is, that Cyprian did not become *comes sacrarum* until after the arrest of Boethius. But, as was first pointed out by Usener[44] and very properly brought up by Laistner and Bark in opposition to the present writer's hypothesis,[45] we possess the letter appointing Cyprian to the post of *comes sacrarum:* "Sume igitur per indictionem tertiam sacrarum largitionem deo propitio dignitatem . . ."[46] No one disputes that the third indiction started on September 1, 524. It is therefore argued that the arrest of Boethius, if it occurred while Cyprian was still *referendarius,* must have taken place before that date.

The argument, though, is not conclusive. Cessi points

---

[43] Cessi (above, n. 39) pp. cxxvi and following. His argument is based not merely on an hypothesis concerning chronology but on close and convincing analysis of the text itself.

[44] *Anecdoton Holderi,* ed. Herman Usener (Leipzig 1877) 77ff.

[45] See above, n. 21.

[46] *Cass. Var.* 5.40. Cf. also 5.41.

out[47] that in practice the magistracies changed on January 1st, so that Cyprian would not have assumed his duties as *comes sacrarum* until January 1, 525. He also well remarks that the letter appointing him to office for the third indiction was not necessarily written before September 1, 524, that the expression *per indictionem tertiam* merely indicated that Cyprian was to assume office on the January 1st following that date, and so the letter itself may perfectly well have been written only a short time before the new year.

As we have seen,[48] the consensus of authority is that the anti-Arian measures of Justin were put into force toward the end of 524. This would seem very easily to have given Albinus time to have heard of them and to have written to Justin about them while Cyprian still held the office of *referendarius*. We are, then, not compelled to assume anything so improbable as a conspiracy to overthrow the regime of Theodoric, much less compelled to suppose such a conspiracy in 523 or even 519.

But, since the embassy of the Pope did not take place until the following year,[49] this explanation does oblige us to place the arrest of Boethius before the departure of the Pope. It is for this reason that I have written that I now believe that this may possibly have been the order of events.[50]

This hypothesis, though, leaves us with one very awkward fact. Albinus' difficulties arose, we may suppose, not because he was plotting to overthrow Theodoric, but because he was

[47] As above, n. 39: p. cxxxix.
[48] See above, n. 27.
[49] *Ibid.*
[50] See above, p. 66.

corresponding with Justin about the anti-Arian measures. Still, the crisis, on this assumption, comes *before* the departure of Pope John for Constantinople. But both our sources, the *Liber Pontificalis* and the *Anonymus Valesianus* as restored by Cessi, are most clearly agreed that it arose *after* the departure of the Pope. This solution, therefore, is not wholly satisfactory.

There is another possible explanation. Is the *Anonymus* correct in telling us that Cyprian was *referendarius* at the time of the arrest of Boethius? It seems probable[51] that the second part of the *Anonymus*, with which we are concerned here, is itself divisible into two parts; that there were two chroniclers, each contemporary with the events described by him; that the first, writing before the healing of the Acacian schism, was favorable to Theodoric but that the second, writing after the healing of the schism, was opposed to him; that at a later date a third writer, possibly Bishop Maximian of Ravenna, joined the two fragments together and somewhat revised them. The opening sentence of 14.83 is the compiler's charming attempt to account for the change in tone of his sources: "Ex eo enim invenit diabolus locum, quem ad modum hominem bene rem publicam sine querella gubernantem subriperet." In another passage, as Mommsen has noticed,[52] the compiler speaks of the memory of Theodoric as still persisting into his own time (*usque nunc*). It is obvious, then, that the reviser of the chronicle was

---

[51] Cf. *RE* I 2334; Hodgkin (above, n. 6) III 26of; Cessi (above, n. 39; pp. clxvi and following); Bury's Gibbon, *The Decline and Fall of the Roman Empire* (4th ed., London 1911) IV, app. I, p. 522; J. B. Bury, *History of the Later Roman Empire* (London 1923) I 423 n. 1; Mommsen, in his introduction to the *Anon. Vales.* (above, n. 39; 258). The question is reviewed in *Iud. Quinq.* 49f.

[52] Mommsen (as in n. 51 above), writing of c. 61.

working a very considerable number of years after these events had taken place, so that his comments and explanations do not have the force of contemporary evidence.

Now, the passage that we have quoted above outlining the career of Cyprian[53] is clearly the compiler's attempt to identify for his readers the Cyprian referred to in the original sources which he was working into his chronicle: the contemporary chronicler would probably not have thought any identification necessary, and in any case, though he might have identified Cyprian through references to his family or his past career or present position, could not have identified him by mentioning the posts that he was to hold in the future. The compiler, then, perhaps Bishop Maximian, writing many years later, might remember his career too. But he would realize that this Cyprian, though he had been a considerable figure at the time, was more or less forgotten and might easily be confused with others — notable contemporaries were Cyprian, bishop of Toulon from approximately 520 to 550, and the Cyprian who was an officer of Belisarius in the Vandal and Gothic wars.[54] It would be natural, then, for our compiler to insert a few words about the Cyprian referred to in this passage. He would remember that this Cyprian had been *referendarius,* and later *comes sacrarum largitionum,* and later still *magister officiorum.* But, writing from memory many years later, he might very easily make a mistake about the precise office held by Cyprian at the time of the scene in the consistory at Verona.

It has been argued that Cyprian was promoted from

[53] *Anon. Vales.* 14.85.
[54] *RE* IV 1942.

referendarius to *comes sacrarum largitionum* in 524 precisely as a reward for the part played by him in the Boethius
affair.[55] But if we are to take 525 (after the departure of the
Pope for Constantinople) as the date of the arrest of Boethius,
and the spring or summer of 526 (at the time of the return
of the Pope) as the date of his execution, then, if we must
reward Cyprian with a promotion, his elevation to the rank
of *patricius* will do at least as well. That took place in 527,
shortly after the deaths of Boethius, Symmachus, Pope John,
and Theodoric.[56]

It is obvious that it would be unsound to assume an error,
even a plausible error, in one's source in order to support
an hypothesis based primarily on that source. But such an
assumption is not only permissible but mandatory if one is
dealing with three sources (Procopius, the *Liber Pontificalis,*
the *Anonymus Valesianus*) of approximately equal weight,
two of which are in agreement, but the third of which is
not, unless one is to make the plausible assumption in
question. And that is our case. If we may assume that
Cyprian was not *referendarius* but *comes sacrarum largitionum* at the time of the consistory in Verona and if we
may also accept Cessi's convincing arguments concerning
the order of the text of the *Anonymus,* then we find both
the *Liber Pontificalis* and the *Anonymus* telling us, un-
contradicted by the letter of Cassiodorus,[57] that the scene in
Verona took place after the departure of Pope John for
Constantinople, and we find all three authorities, Procopius,

---

[55] Laistner (above, n. 21); Stein II 257.
[56] Cass. *Var.* 8.21, dated by Mommsen *ca.* 527. See also 8.22. (*MGHAA* XII
252–54.)
[57] See above, n. 56.

the *Liber Pontificalis* and the *Anonymus Valesianus*, telling us that Boethius and Symmachus were executed only very shortly before the death of Theodoric.

Ernst Stein, however, in the second volume of his history, published in France after his death, was also of the opinion that Boethius was arrested in 523 and executed in 524.[58] Somewhat inconveniently, he cites not the authorities which we have been discussing but "Mommsen, M. G., Auctt. antt. XII, p. xi. xxix" and mentions, as further proof, that Boethius could not have been *magister officiorum* at the time that Honoratus succeeded his brother Decoratus as *quaestor*. As Stein was perhaps the leading authority of our time on the later Empire, we feel some diffidence in stating that his arguments in this instance do not add to the strength of the case against us. But in fact, they seem to us neither sound in substance nor clearly stated.

Mommsen, in the passages cited by Stein, establishes that the letters in the fifth, eighth, and part of the ninth books of the *Variae* were written between 523 and 527, and therefore *in Mommsen's opinion* ("existimamus") while Cassiodorus held the office of *magister*. Mommsen does not state in so many words why he held this opinion, but it is clear that he accepted Usener's chronology.[59] As it is extremely probable that Cassiodorus directly succeeded Boethius as *magister*,[60] it follows that anyone accepting Usener's chronology would think it probable that letters written by Cassiodorus between 523 (or at least the later part of 523, after

[58] Stein II 254ff, esp. 258 n. 1.
[59] Cf. *MGHAA* XII 489 (*index personarum* under *Boethius*), where he cites Usener's chronology on the point with approval.
[60] Cf. *Iud. Quinq.* 51. Stein II 257 states this as an established fact.

the disgrace of Boethius) and 527 were written by him while he was holding the office of *magister*. The establishment of the date, though, goes back to Usener's argument, which we have just been discussing. The reader may or may not agree with our hypothesis, but he will realize that Stein, in citing the passage from Mommsen's introduction to the *Variae* of Cassiodorus, has not brought forward any further evidence. We may add, incidentally, that if Boethius was disgraced in 523 and if Cassiodorus immediately succeeded him as *magister,* then Cassiodorus held that office for a most unusually long period. If, however, the disgrace of Boethius took place in 525, as we argue, then Cassiodorus' term of office as *magister* was of far less exceptional length.

But Stein advanced a further argument which he felt to be in favor of the generally accepted chronology. He pointed out that Boethius could scarcely have held the position of *magister* at the time that Honoratus succeeded his brother Decoratus as *quaestor*.[61] Though we cannot agree with Stein's chronological deduction, he is unquestionably right as to the fact. In the *Consolation,* Boethius makes Philosophy say to him: "Tu quoque num tandem tot periculis adduci potuisti ut cum Decorato gerere magistratum putares, cum in eo mentem nequissimi scurrae delatorisque respiceres?"[62] That is, Boethius thought of holding office as *magister* in the same cabinet as Decoratus but did not in fact do so. Now, we know that Decoratus held the office of *quaestor* in 524, died in that year, and was succeeded by his brother

[61] Stein II 258 n. 1.

[62] *Cons. Phil.* 3.4.10. To the best of my recollection, Stein is mistaken in implying that I was unaware of this passage in 1934. It is certain, though, that I did not then, and that I do not now, see it as a difficulty in the way of the chronology which I advocate.

Honoratus.[63] It has usually been supposed that Theodoric
had intended to appoint Decoratus *quaestor* in 523, but that
he did not do so because Boethius objected. Then, on
Boethius' disgrace, Decoratus was appointed.[64] It may of
course well be that Boethius enjoyed such prestige that he
could control Theodoric's choice of cabinet ministers. But
that certainly is not what Boethius said. He said not that he
had kept Decoratus out of office but, on the contrary, that
he had intended to sit in the same cabinet as Decoratus,
though, as things turned out, he did not do so.

If we may accept the chronology advocated in this paper,
the difficulty disappears at once. Decoratus was in office as
quaestor in 524. Theodoric planned to continue him in that
position for the following year. He also offered Boethius the
position of *magister officiorum* for 525. Boethius did not like
the idea of sitting in the same cabinet with Decoratus, but
nevertheless he did accept the appointment. However,
Decoratus died before Boethius took office. This accords
perfectly with the text in the *De Consolatione,* with the
letters in the *Variae,* and with the chronology we are defending. It is also in accord with the fact that, although
Boethius calls Decoratus a *delator,* he does not refer to him
as one of the group which accused Albinus and Boethius
himself. If Decoratus had been alive at that time, he would
no doubt have struck a blow against his enemy, and Boethius
would no doubt have remembered to hold it against him

Finally, Stein believed that the letters which got Albinus
into trouble were official communications sent by him as

---

[63] Cass. *Var.* 5.3 and 4 (*MGHAA* XII 144f).
[64] Ensslin, *Theod. der Grosse* 316, 319; Stein II 255, 257.

one of the leading senators and in the name of the senate to the emperor in connection with the ordination of the new pope, John.[65] This would of course mean that they were written in 523, since Pope John was elected in that year.[66] To accept this hypothesis, however, one would have to be so ingenuous as to believe that official letters of this sort were, for no reason whatever, so worded as to expose the writer to a charge of treason. Schurr calls our attention[67] to an instance in which the senate, in writing to the emperor upon a controversial point, took the natural precaution of obtaining the approval of Theodoric before sending the letter, and no doubt this would have been done in any official communication concerning which there was the least doubt. Nor, if we were concerned with public, official letters of this sort, could there be any question of informers or of attempting to suppress the matter, as Boethius said he did.

So much, then, concerning the arguments advanced by Bark and Stein in favor of the generally accepted chronology, and for the authorities cited by them. There remain, however, some minor sources which should be mentioned, the more so since one of them, at least, is not consistent with our position. First, the *Fasti Vindobonenses Posteriores* give 523 as the date of the executions of both Boethius and Symmachus, but they also place the death of Theodoric in the same year.[68] There is no doubt, so far as the death of Theodoric is concerned, that they are incorrect about the year; it is less probable that they would be wrong in placing

---

[65] Stein II 255 n. 4.
[66] *RE* IX 1808 (49).
[67] As above, n. 3; 138.
[68] *MGHAA* IX 332.

the three events in the same year. To the extent that the
may be relied upon, they support our position.

The *Agnelli Liber Pontificalis Ecclesiae Ravennatis,* a lat
source, tells us of these events in the following order: th
executions of Boethius and Symmachus; the return of Pop
John from his embassy (there is no mention of his havin
been sent); the imprisonment, death, and burial of the Pope
the location of the sarcophagi of Symmachus and Boethius
measures hostile to the Catholics taken by Theodoric; hi
death and burial; the subsequent history of his tomb.[69] Thi
seems to indicate that the deaths of Symmachus, Boethiu
and the Pope all occurred at about the same time and tha
that time was very shortly before the death of Theodori
himself. The passage, for what it is worth, is not consister
with the generally accepted chronology but is consister
with the chronology advocated in this chapter.

Finally, Marius, bishop of Avenches near Lausanne fror
574 to 594,[70] gives 524 as the date of the execution of Boethi
and 525 as that of the execution of Symmachus.[71] This (
course is inconsistent with both the hypotheses concernin
the arrest of Boethius that have been advanced here — fir
that the letters of Albinus came to light late in the autum
of 524; second that they came to light after the departu
of Pope John for Constantinople — and against our beli
that Boethius and Symmachus were not executed unt
shortly before the death of Theodoric. This source, in shor
fully supports the generally accepted chronology and cann

[69] *De Sancto Iohanne* 20.39 (MGH, *Script. Rer. Langobard. et Ital. Saec. VI–I*
Hannover 1878, pp. 303f).
[70] *RE* XIV 1822.
[71] *Chronicle, a.* 524, 525, ed. Mommsen (*MGHAA* XI 235).

so far as we can see, be explained in any other way. Further, Marius, though by no means free from errors, wrote on good authority; among other sources, he made use of consular *fasti* of Italian origin.[72] There is no way, though, of knowing how many times or how accurately these had been copied during their journey to Avenches and during the half century or more between the death of Boethius and the compiling of the chronicle. That records of this sort are not immune from error, we know from many instances; we have just seen that the *Fasti Vindobonenses Posteriores* give 523 as the date of the death of Theodoric. Taken alone, the text of Marius would be decisive, but he cannot outweigh or equal such witnesses as Procopius and the *Liber Pontificalis,* he cannot be held an insurmountable obstacle to an hypothesis, otherwise plausible, which brings the *Anonymus Valesianus* into full accord with these two.

It should seem, then, to judge from what we know of the general situation and from such chronological information as we can derive from the sources, that Boethius was not engaged in an attempt to overthrow Theodoric but that his fall was caused by the reaction in Italy to the anti-Arian measures of Justin; that he was not arrested in 523; that he may have been arrested toward the end of 524; that far more probably he was arrested in 525 after the departure of Pope John for the East; that the arrest of Symmachus followed hard upon the arrest of Boethius; that both were executed after the return of the Pope, and only shortly before the death of Theodoric.

So much for the causes which led to the fall of Boethius

[72] See *RE* XIV 1822.

and Symmachus and for the dates of these events. What, now, of the claims of Boethius to martyrdom? If we could agree with Bark that Boethius had been conspiring for years to overthrow Theodoric, we should entirely agree with him[73] that the case for his martyrdom was lost. For those of us who cannot accept Bark's explanation, the question becomes largely one of definition. If one is satisfied with the second definition of "martyr" in the *Oxford Dictionary* ("One who undergoes death . . . on behalf of any religious or other belief or cause, or as a consequence of his devotion to some object"), then, even if one restricts this to specifically Christian beliefs or causes and to devotion to specifically Christian objects, martyrdom could be claimed for Boethius on the basis of the hypothesis advanced in this paper. When he found that Albinus and the senate seemed implicated in correspondence with Justin — either approving Justin's anti-Arian measures or seeking protection against reprisals by Theodoric — he sought to suppress the evidence and, that failing, to defend Albinus. He sought, that is, to defend the Catholic position, and that was the real cause of his fall, although he was actually condemned for having written letters, which we believe to be false, advocating the overthrow of Theodoric's government, and for sacrilege. On this basis, indeed, we have claimed martyrdom for him in the preceding chapter.[74]

The second definition in the *Oxford Dictionary* is, however, insufficient for our purpose: the first definition given is the theological usage, and it is that of course with which

---

[73] See his "The Legend of Boethius' Martyrdom," cited above, n. 1.

[74] See "Procopius and Boethius" (above, chap. 3). This seems also to have been the position of Rand. See E. K. Rand (above, n. 3) 180.

we are here concerned. It reads: "1. *Eccl.* The specific designation of honour (connoting the highest degree of saintship) for: One who voluntarily undergoes the penalty of death for refusing to renounce the Christian faith or any article of it, for perseverance in any Christian virtue, or for obedience to any law or command of the Church." To bring Boethius within these terms, we should be obliged to hold either that Theodoric put Boethius to death because he was a Catholic or because he practiced the Christian virtues or else that the Church commanded Boethius to support the anti-Arian policy of Justin and Justinian — positions which seem to us frankly ridiculous.[75]

Finally, what of the character of Boethius? We have ourselves written[76] that in the *De Consolatione Philosophiae* he spoke bitterly of Theodoric, of his accusers, of some of the Roman officials and Gothic leaders. But we also pointed out his provocation, the generally low tone of political polemics, the special violence such controversies frequently take among southern peoples, and the probability that Boethius wished to draw the strongest possible contrast between his former prosperity and merits on the one hand and his present adversity on the other, in order to show that both prosperity and adversity were indifferent to the true philosopher. We might wish that he had not permitted himself to write these passages, but we cannot let them outweigh the evidence of his life as a whole.

Hodgkin has been more severe in his judgment of the political career of Boethius: ". . . utterly unfit for affairs;

---

[75] See, however, the very respectable authorities cited by Bark in his article on this subject, cited above, n. 1.

[76] *Iud. Quinq.* 50, 63.

passionate and ungenerous; incapable of recognizing the fact that there might be other points of view beside his own; persuaded that every one who wounded his vanity must be a scoundrel, or at best a buffoon; — in short, an impractical colleague, and, with all his honourable aspirations, an unscrupulous enemy." [77] But this harsh estimate, too, is based entirely on the passages in the *De Consolatione Philosophiae* and is, therefore, subject to the rebuttal we have just made. The rebuttal is not complete, but it does, we feel, plead strongly in mitigation.

We have seen[78] that Bark, too, is critical of some aspects of the character of Boethius, the more so because he believes him to have been conspiring against Theodoric at the very time of his *Panegyric* of the King, at the very time he was the King's *magister officiorum*. We doubt that his judgment would be so severe if it were not for that belief. Evidence of the harshness, selfishness, and arrogance of which he speaks is found only in the *De Consolatione Philosophiae*, and even there, as we have seen, it may be little more than a literary device. At the worst, although it is not admirable, it is certainly understandable. The charge that Boethius well knew how to consult his own interests seems, in part at least, refuted by his fate. Further, if one is not to accept Bark's hypothesis of the long-standing plot against Theodoric, there is left little more of this charge than the assertion that Boethius was for many years an able and successful public figure — a welcome antidote to the extreme view of Hodgkin.

[77] As above, n. 6; III 493.
[78] Above, p. 55.

But Boethius is not the only witness available. Let us turn to what his contemporaries said of him in the works that have come down to us. First, Cassiodorus. In two letters[79] he praises Boethius in superlative terms for his learning. Although Cassiodorus was accustomed to flatter, there seems no reason to doubt his sincerity in this instance: the accomplishments of Boethius in the field of scholarship were very considerable, even astounding when one considers the standards of the age in which he lived. These praises, though, do not touch on other aspects of his personality. In the *Anecdoton Holderi,* however, though the passage concerning Boethius treats mostly of his eloquence and learning, we do find the statement: "Boethius dignitatibus summis excelluit." [80] This probably means no more than that he was distinguished through having held the highest offices, rather than that he was distinguished by the manner in which he performed the functions of those offices or that he was distinguished because of his great merits. Yet both *dignitas* and *excello* have connotations such that one feels certain that Cassiodorus, who was surely choosing his words very carefully in this passage, would not have used them if he had a harsh view of the political capacity or of the character of Boethius. They are words that he might well have used of a contemporary whom he respected and admired, although

[79] Cass. *Var.* 1.45, 2.40 (*MGHAA* XII 39ff, 70ff).
[80] *Anecdoton Holderi* (above, n. 44) 4. Also printed in *MGHAA* XII, pp. v–vi, though, of course, without Usener's comments. Usener believes (p. 7) the *Anecdoton* to date from not later than 523, but Mommsen, in his introduction to the works of Cassiodorus in the *Monumenta* (*MGHAA* XII, p. xi) gives a conclusive reason for believing it to have been written after the *Variae:* it refers to the *Variae* in its text. It was therefore definitely written after the fall of Boethius, no matter what chronology we may accept.

he could not forget that he and that contemporary had taken opposite sides in the greatest crisis of their times.

If the silence of Cassiodorus concerning the trial and death of Boethius, if the praise bestowed by Cassiodorus on the accusers of Boethius — if these are susceptible of being stretched into evidence that Cassiodorus believed Boethius disloyal to Theodoric, even then, though they may be used as evidence on that point, they are no evidence whatever on any other point concerning Boethius. Neither by words nor by silence does Cassiodorus support the very severe strictures of Hodgkin, or even Bark's view that Boethius could be harsh, selfish, arrogant, and self-seeking.

Our next witness is Ennodius, writing at a time when he was already a well-known author and a prominent ecclesiastic, but not yet bishop of Pavia.[81] The last thing that could be said of Ennodius would be that he damned Boethius by faint praise; in general, he could not be more fulsome. The contrary, though, is true: when he attacks Boethius, he clears him of harshness, selfishness, arrogance, and self-seeking by not even hinting at such charges but attacking him on wholly other grounds.

Ennodius opens his letters to Boethius with *Epist.* 6.6, an

[81] The chronology of the writings of Ennodius has caused much discussion, but it is now generally conceded that the works as found in the manuscripts are, as a whole, in approximately chronological order. For a recent review of this problem, see Sister Genevieve Marie Cook, *The Life of Saint Epiphanius of Pavia by Ennodius, a Translation with an Introduction and Commentary* (Washington, D. C. 1942) 1–6. So far at least as concerns the particular letters, the *carmen,* and the *opusculum* with which we shall have to deal, the manuscript order, followed by Vogel in his edition (*MGHAA* VII, Berlin 1885), seems entirely satisfactory, and it is that text from which we quote. The principal letter and the *carmen* were, as appears from their text, written at the time of the consulship of Boethius. That was in 510, at a time when Ennodius was still in Milan. See *RE* V 2630.

amiable letter but of no particular significance. In *Epist.*
7.13, he praises Boethius for his learning and studious habits,
refers to the fact that he and Boethius are related, and requests that they correspond frequently. In *Epist.* 8.1, he
again praises Boethius most highly for his learning and his
scholarship, which, he writes, constitute his title to the
consulship. Further, he once more refers to their relationship
and asks Boethius to give him the use of ("mihi quo vultis
genere concedatis") a house in Milan that had belonged to
their family and was now owned by Boethius. As we have
just seen, Ennodius was still in Milan at the time, so that
it was probably of real importance to him to have the use
of this house.

We must pause to notice the words in which Ennodius
writes of the consulship in this letter:

> fuerit in more veteribus curulium celsitudinem campi sudore
> mercari et contemptu lucis honorem sole fulgere: sed aliud genus
> virtutis quaeritur, postquam praemium facta est Roma victorum.
> noster candidatus post manifestam decertationem debitum tri-
> umphum, dum numquam viderit bella, sortitur, iudicio exegit
> laureas et congredi non necessarium duxit armatis. inter Ciceronis
> gladios et Demosthenis enituit et utriusque propositi acumina
> quasi natus in ipsa artium pace collegit.

In *Epist.* 8.31, Ennodius reminds Boethius of his request
for the house. In *Epist.* 8.36, Ennodius mentions that
Boethius has reproached him for a certain coolness and asks
him not to be cool himself, but to write. *Epist.* 8.37 and
8.40 contain new requests for the house. We do not hear
that he ever received it.

Boethius may have had his reasons for distrusting the

flatteries of Ennodius: Vogel points out[82] that Ennodius was a friend of the praetorian prefect Faustus (Faustus Niger), whom Boethius opposed in the matter of levying grain in Campania. As Faustus was praetorian prefect from 507 to 511,[83] it is probable enough that his disagreement with Boethius took place at this time. If, indeed, Boethius did distrust Ennodius, his suspicion proved fully justified. Ennodius, in writing to Boethius, had turned the latter's lack of military experience into an excuse for making him a graceful compliment on his learning. Now, disappointed in his hope of getting the house, or annoyed for some other reason, he used the same topic as the basis for a savage jeer:

DE BOETIO SPATA CINCTO

Languescit rigidi tecum substantia ferri,
    Solvitur atque chalybs more fluentis aquae.
Emollit gladios inbellis dextra Boeti.
    Ensis erat dudum, credite, nunc colus est.
In thyrsum migrat quod gestas, inprobe, pilum.
    In Venerem constans linque Mavortis opem.[84]

We need not bother with the charge that Boethius was not a military figure: that distinction has never been claimed for him, and in any case, a Roman of his position would not have been allowed to follow a military career even if he had wished to.[85] Ennodius has merely chosen to introduce his charges of lechery and drunkenness by a somewhat heavy-handed joke, based on the martial traditions and pomp of the consular office and on the martial sound of the name of Boethius himself.

[82] As above, n. 81; p. xxiv.
[83] See *RE* VI 2095.
[84] CCCXXXIX (*Carm.* 2.132).
[85] See Stein II 120.

Nor need we be too shocked at the other charges. That a young Italian in his twenties,[86] very rich, of the highest position, should have sown a few wild oats is not surprising. Boethius himself has indeed given us a hint in the opening lines of the *Consolation:*

> Carmina qui quondam studio florente peregi,
> Gloria felicis olim viridisque iuventae . . .

But that hint alone would not have allowed us to clear him of the suspicion of priggishness that might otherwise have attached itself to him. At any rate, we may be quite certain that his dissipations did not go too far; no really dissolute man could have accomplished what we know Boethius did accomplish.

What interests us is that this is all that Ennodius in his moment of spite[87] could find to say against Boethius. We may be sure that he would have been quite ready to have called him harsh, selfish, arrogant, and self-seeking if he had thought for a moment that such charges would stick. Instead, he called him a "playboy."

We have already seen that the *Anonymus Valesianus* takes the part of Boethius.[88] It is so violently partial, however, that although it is a weighty authority for fact, we should scarcely cite it in this connection if it were not that we have also had to mention such doubtful evidence as the inferences that may be drawn from the silence of Cassiodorus.

---

[86] Boethius seems to have been born in 480 or not much later. See *RE* III 596.

[87] It is a pleasure to add that, if we may trust the order of the writings of Ennodius as given by Vogel (see above, n. 82), the hard feeling did not last. In CDLII (*Opusc.* 6) we find Ennodius writing: "est Boetius patricius. in quo vix discendi annos respicis et intellegis peritiam sufficere iam docendi, de quo emendatorum iudicavit electio."

[88] See XIV 86, quoted on p. 72 above.

Next, in favor of Boethius, we have what Procopius tells us of Rusticiana.[89] When Totila captured Rome, he protected her from his Goths. They wished to put her to death, charging that she had destroyed the statues of Theodoric. Her reason for doing this, they said, was that she wished to avenge the murders of her father, Symmachus, and of her husband, Boethius (τοὺς φόνους ἀμυνομένη Συμμάχου τε τοῦ πατρὸς καὶ βοετίου τοῦ ξυνοικήσαντος). Procopius also tells us that Rusticiana was a woman always lavishing her wealth upon the needy.[90] One gets the impression of a woman devoted to the memory of her husband and her father, seeking consolation in good works for the tragedy which had overtaken her. At the same time, no vapid character, but one who won the respect alike of her fellow Romans, of the Greek historian, and of the Gothic king. The loyalty of such a woman would not have been given to a harsh, selfish, calculating man.

Finally, we may repeat what Procopius has to tell us of Boethius himself:

> Symmachus and his son-in-law Boetius were men of noble and ancient lineage, and both had been leading men in the Roman senate and had been consuls. But because they practised philosophy and were mindful of justice in a manner surpassed by no other men, relieving the destitution of both citizens and strangers by generous gifts of money, they attained great fame and thus led men of the basest sort to envy them. Now such persons slandered them to Theodoric, and he, believing their slanders, put these two men to death . . . But afterwards he . . . wept for the wrong he had done Symmachus and Boetius. Then, having lamented and grieved exceedingly over the unfortunate

[89] *Hist.* 7.20.29f.
[90] *Ibid.*, 7.20.27.

occurrence, he died not long afterward. This was the first and last act of injustice which he committed towards his subjects, and the cause of it was that he had not made a thorough investigation, as he was accustomed to do, before passing judgment on the two men.[91]

This is high praise, and it comes, as we have seen, from an eminent historian who had every reason to try to ascertain the truth of the matter, who had every means of ascertaining it. More, the passage distinctly gives one the feeling that Procopius had heard of the controversies of which Boethius had written in the *De Consolatione Philosophiae* and that he gave his impartial and considered judgment in Boethius' favor.

To summarize. We cannot share the views of Bark that Boethius was involved in a conspiracy to overthrow Theodoric, or that such a conspiracy came to light in 523. We think that the cause of his fall was the reaction in Italy to the anti-Arian measures of Justin, that his arrest may possibly have taken place in the late autumn of 524, but far more probably after the departure of Pope John on his embassy, that Symmachus was arrested very shortly afterward, and that Theodoric waited until the Pope had returned before he executed them. We do not see how Boethius can be called a martyr in the strict, theological sense of the term. We think it unfortunate but very understandable that Boethius allowed himself to write of Theodoric and his other opponents in the terms that he did, but we do not think that sufficient evidence to justify the aspersions that have been

[91] See above, n. 32. In quoting this text there, we were emphasizing the chronological implications of the passage; we now repeat it to make sure that the reader gives full weight to its bearing on the character of Boethius.

cast upon his political ability, much less evidence of defects
so grave as to outweigh the strong evidence which we have,
both from his own work and from other contemporary
sources, of the nobility of his character as a whole.

On this last point, there is still a third source, which most
certainly ought not to be neglected. We should like, in end-
ing this paper, to make our own the sensitive passage with
which Patch concludes his delightful study, *The Tradition
of Boethius:*

> The total impression we get is that his work was good in
> effect; that it served to steady men, and taught them to use
> reason and wisdom. The greatness of Boethius in this and that
> realm or in the different centuries may seem to fluctuate; but
> the stature of his Lady Philosophy suffered change, and he is
> like her. Interestingly enough, after his death, he ceases to be
> the victim; he himself becomes the teacher and instructs the
> whole Middle Ages. Frequent complaints go up to Fortune for
> the same old causes, and he gives the answer of Philosophia.
> This may sometimes carry with it something of the music of
> Plato, but it is likely to be told in the words of Aristotle. Saint-
> liness and good sense mark the man's path through the cen-
> turies. In the absence of more details regarding the personal
> habits of his life and the various things he did, this, we may
> fairly assume, is what he was like.[92]

Postscript

L. BIELER, in his excellent edition of the *Consolatio*[93]
summarizes as follows (pp. vii–viii):

[92] Howard Rollin Patch, *The Tradition of Boethius* (New York 1935) 123. Cf.
also A. Pertusi, "La fortuna di Boezio a Bisanzio," *Annuaire de l'Institut de
Philologie et d'Histoire Orientales et Slaves* 11 (1951, vol. III in the *Mélanges
Henri Grégoire*) 301–22.

[93] Anicii Manlii Severini Boethii *Philosophiae Consolatio,* ed. Ludovicus Bieler
(Turnhout 1957), being part 1 of vol. XCIV of the *Corpus Christianorum, Series
Latina.*

Annis uero qui sequebantur [after 510/11] Boethius, cum defensorem strenuum et dignitatis senatoriae et fidei catholicae se praeberet, non solum aulicis sed regi ipsi magis magisque suspectus est. Denique cum anno 523 pro Albino consulari maiestatis reo minus prudenter quam liberaliter intercederet non solum non auditus sed mox ipse maiestatis accusatus est. Qui primum una cum Albino in agrum Caluentianum [Ager Caluentianus secundum probabilissimam, ut mihi uidetur, opinionem extra Pauiam situs erat.— Bieler's note] relegatus, deinde absens exsul a senatoribus pauore prostratis reus pronuntiatus morte et proscriptione damnatus est. Postremum anno 524 (si Fastis Rauennatibus credere debemus) capitis poenam soluit. De innocentia uel crimine Boethii cum aliis aliter uideatur fortasse cum Ernesto Stein [*Histoire du Bas-Empire* II. 257.— Bieler's note], scriptore rerum illius aetatis peritissimo, Boethium haud minus de innocentia sua dubitasse [Cf. Cons. I. 4, 20 sqq.— Bieler's note] quam regem de Boethii crimine dicemus. Dubium quidem non est quin incolae oppidi Pauiae Boethii mortem pro martyrio habuerint eumque inde a priscis temporibus ut sanctum coluerint. Inter eos scriptores qui Boethium pro confessione fidei catholicae interfectum esse testantur primus fuit Ado Viennensis (ob. a. 875) idque inde a saeculo XIII. multis uiris doctis persuasum est.

This is indeed a masterly summary. It is, as Bieler writes, certain that Boethius was a strenuous defender of the dignity of the senate and of the Catholic faith and that he had made enemies in government circles. It is also probable that Theodoric became increasingly suspicious of him during the years between his consulship and the healing of the Acacian schism. However, the healing of the schism (517–519), the consulship of Eutharic (519), the most exceptional joint consulships of the two sons of Boethius, Boethius' panegyric of Theodoric on the occasion of their installation as consuls, and, finally, the appointment of Boethius as *magister officiorum* — all these events seem to indicate a sincere ac-

ceptance, both by Theodoric and by the more conservative
Roman aristocracy and by the emperor, of the new situation
created by the healing of the schism: Theodoric would rule
his kingdom (and, presumably, so would his son-in-law
Eutharic after him) with the full recognition of the emperor and with the cooperation, instead of the mere ac-
quiescence, of the more conservative senatorial families. The
fact — if, as I think, it is one — that the old king had laid
his suspicions aside, would of course increase his bitterness
when they were reawakened by the charges against Albinus
and Boethius.

As to chronology, rereading my paper after many years,
I am inclined to accept the conventional dates (arrest of
Boethius in 523, his execution in 524), not as a certainty, but
as a probability. It is difficult in the extreme, as many have
pointed out and as Bieler implies, to believe that Marius
Aventicensis, who made use of the lost chronicles of Ravenna,
should have been mistaken. Further, I took *Cons. Phil.* 3.4.4
Bieler ("Tu quoque num tandem tot periculis adduci potuisti ut cum Decorato gerere magistratum putares, cum in
eo mentem nequissimi scurrae delatorisque respiceres?") to
mean that Boethius had thought of holding office in the same
administration as Decoratus but (prevented by the death of
Decoratus) had not done so. (This would have made Boethius *magister* in 525 instead of 523.) Such an interpretation
of the passage, though, now seems to me perhaps to place
too great a strain upon the Latin.[94]

Coming to the question of the guilt or innocence of Boe-

---

[94] Cf. Boezio *Philosophiae Consolatio,* Testo con Introduzione e Traduzione, di
Emanuele Rapisarda (Catania 1961) 81, and the Loeb edition, 241.

thius, it may be that Bieler slightly simplifies the issue. There can be no doubt that Theodoric thought Boethius guilty: the king would not antagonize the Roman aristocracy, the Catholic church, and the emperor for the mere pleasure of doing so. There is no doubt either — or at least, I have no doubt, and have given my reasons above — that Boethius was not guilty of magic or of conspiring against the king. But, to use the very words of Boethius himself:

> At cuius criminis arguimur summam quaeres. Senatum dicimur saluum esse uoluisse. Modum desideras. Delatorem, ne documenta deferret quibus senatum maiestatis reum faceret, impedisse criminamur. Quid igitur, o magistra, censes? Infitiabimur crimen, ne tibi pudor simus? At uolui nec umquam uelle desistam. *Fatebimur? Sed impediendi delatoris opera cessauit* . . . Cuius dignitatem reatus ipsi etiam qui detulere uiderunt; quam uti alicuius sceleris ammixtione fuscarent, ob ambitum dignitatis sacrilegio me conscientiam polluisse mentiti sunt. (Italics ours.)[95]

Boethius, then, expressly admitted that he had tried to suppress evidence in connection with a charge of major importance to the government, and so he cannot have considered himself innocent so far as his duty to Theodoric was concerned. Rather, he felt himself morally released from his duty to Theodoric by his overriding obligation to the senate.

A. H. M. Jones's article, "The Constitutional Position of Odoacer and Theodoric," [96] describes a situation which helps us to understand the position of Boethius as well. Jones reminds us of Mommsen's belief that Odoacer and Theodoric were kings of their German followers but ruled their Roman

---

[95] *Cons. Phil.* 1.4.20–22, 37 (Bieler).
[96] As above, chap. 2, n. 26.

subjects as commissaries of the emperors, holding the office of *magister militum* with certain precisely defined additional powers. He continues that Stein and Ensslin considerably modified this theory, holding that Theodoric was king of all his subjects. They nevertheless held that he was *magister militum* at the same time as king, and that his powers were limited in certain respects by a formal concordat with the emperor. Jones then states that, in his opinion, "Odoacer and Theodoric were kings pure and simple, in the same position as the other barbarian kings." He tells us that Theodoric bestowed one of the consulships (citing Cass. *Var.* 6.1; 2.2 and 3; 9.22 and 23) and that these appointments were generally acknowledged by the emperors. But, citing Procopius for the Gothic claim that they "allowed the Romans each year to obtain the rank of consuls from the Emperor of the East," Jones says that this can only mean that the men appointed by Theodoric were not *ipso facto* acknowledged as such by the emperors, but had to obtain *codicilli* from them before they were recognized as consuls in the East. Some agreement, Jones felt, must have been reached between Theodoric and the emperor to the effect that the emperor would leave one of the consulships open and give favorable consideration to persons nominated for the office by Theodoric. The emperor, though, Jones insisted, did not give Theodoric authority to appoint one of the consuls but, on the contrary, appointed both himself. This is not the place to discuss the very persuasive arguments advanced by Jones, but it does seem pertinent to call attention to two senatorial inscriptions cited by him which imply that the senators who erected them wished to believe that they were still living within the Empire. Caecina Mavortius Basilius Decius set up an inscription in which Theodoric was styled: "d. n. gloriosissimus adque inclytus rex Theodericus victor ac triumfator semper Augustus." An inscription set up by Valerius Florianus began: "salvis dominis nostris Anastasio perpetuo Augusto et gloriosissimo ac triumfali viro Theoderico." The situation reminds me of a remark made to me by an Italian friend during the early days of the Mussolini regime, before the Vatican Treaty: "We Italians are a subtle people, and disinclined to push things to extremes. Like a juggler keeping several balls in the air at once, we are quite able to keep several apparently inconsistent ideas in our minds at the same time. We are loyal to the Pope in the Vatican, to the King in the Quirinal, and we could easily be loyal too to a Mussolini in the Palazzo Venezia, and perhaps, if we had to, to a commissar in the Lateran."

It was just this sort of ambiguity, Theodoric considering himself an independent king, the emperor claiming, not too overtly, a shadowy suzereignty which might become more definite if opportunity should offer, some at least of the senators sympathizing with the claims of the emperor, but careful not to offend the feelings of Theodoric — it was just this ambiguity that made possible the situation leading to the downfall of Boethius.

As to the claim of Boethius to martyrdom, it seems very difficult to consider him technically a martyr when the *Anonymus Valesianus,* Procopius, and especially Boethius himself all agree that the charges against him were based on political grounds. The fact remains, though, that, whatever chronology may be adopted, whatever the nature of the charges against him, the fate of Boethius was inextricably entwined with the conflict between the Arian Goths and the Catholics of Italy and the East. According to the chronology which I previously advocated, his death would have been due to the suspicions and anger aroused in Theodoric and the Goths by Justin's persecution of the Arians in the East; on the basis of the conventional chronology, which I am now more inclined to accept, the execution of Boethius and Symmachus and, presumably, Albinus destroyed all possibility of a genuine acceptance of Theodoric's rule by the Catholic church and the great Roman families, was the prelude to the persecution of the Arians in the East, and, in spite of the efforts of Cassiodorus and Amalasuntha, to the Gothic wars when Justinian at last felt that the time was ripe for the reconquest of Italy.

Finally, a few words about recent Boethian studies. Bieler (pp. xvi–xxvi) prints an excellent *bibliographia selecta* through 1957, the year of the publication of his work. We have already referred to Rapisarda's valuable edition of the *Philosophiae Consolatio,* with an exceptionally beautiful and careful translation into Italian. Reference should also be made to his excellent text of the theological works, also with translation: E. Rapisarda, *Opuscoli Teologici* Testo con Introduzione e Traduzione (2nd ed., Catania 1960). L. M. de Rijk has given us a most interesting and — to my scant understanding of this subject — persuasive article in two parts on the extremely complicated and controversial problem of the sequence of Boethius' works on logic: "On the chronology of Boethius' works on logic," *Vivarium* 2 (1964), 1–49, 125–62. Lastly, M. Geymonat has recently published a palimpsest of about the year 500 from the capitulary library of Verona: *Euclidis Latine Facti Fragmenta Veronensia,* ed. Marius Geymonat (Istituto Editoriale Cisalpino, Milan and Varese 1964). This manuscript appears to be a fragment, not of the pseudo-Boethian geometry with which we are all familiar, but of the actual text of Boethius. I am indebted to the late Professor Ullman for the reference, and to Dr. Geymonat for a copy of the work.

CHAPTER V

THE ECONOMIC POSITION OF CYRENAICA IN CLASSICAL TIMES

ON THE MAP Cyrenaica (the Libyan Pentapolis)[1] looks like a knob on the north coast of Africa, southwest of Crete, facing toward the ball of the foot of Italy. But the apparent connection with Africa is misleading: Cyrenaica is essentially an island, sundered from Africa by deserts more impassable than the sea.[2] Indeed, the desert was a far greater obstacle in ancient times than it is now. Even the camel was not a factor in transportation until late in the classical era, not being really common in Egypt until the Ptolemaic period or in Libya, so far as we have evidence, until the second half of the fourth century after Christ.[3] Not until Vandal

---

This article is reprinted from *Studies in Roman Economic and Social History in Honor of Allan Chester Johnson,* ed. P. R. Coleman-Norton (Princeton: Princeton University Press, 1951).

[1] Roughly from the corner of the Syrtis to the Gulf of Bomba. Marmarica was at some periods included in Cyrenaica; it was a strip of desert, important only for its ports and for the Oasis of Siwa, the land gate of Egypt. See *RE* XIX 509ff, XIV 1881ff.

[2] Cf. the remarks of E. F. Gautier on the Djezirat-el-Maghreb: *Le passé de l'Afrique du Nord* (Paris 1937) 9.

[3] See M. Rostovtzeff, *The Social and Economic History of the Roman Empire* (Oxford 1926, 2nd ed. 1957, hereafter referred to as *SEHRE*) 260; *RE* X 1824ff; Daremberg-Saglio, *Dictionnaire des Antiquités Grecques et Romaines* (hereafter cited as DS) II 856ff; Gautier (above, n. 2) 190–97. As Gautier indicates, Arnobius writes as one familiar with the beast, but the first evidence we have for camels in quantity west of Egypt is the well-known demand for 4,000 camels made by Count Romanus as a condition for repelling a barbarian attack

times do we encounter what Gautier calls "les grands nomades chameliers" [4] — tribes capable of dominating the desert routes and of conquering the settled country as distinct from raiding it. The late introduction of the camel is of capital importance: during the period under consideration Cyrenaica was approachable by sea, not, on a serious scale, by land.

Let us consider, however, the land approaches, such as they are.

The easiest is the route along the Marmarican coast. But it is comparatively easy only because a succession of small harbors, such as Mersa Matruh (Paraetonium), Solum (Catabathmus), Tobruk (Antipyrgos), Derna (Darnis), Marsa Suza (Apollonia, Sozousa), Tolmeita (Ptolemais), Tokra (Tauchira, Arsinoe), Bengasi (Euhesperides, Berenice), make it (and always have made it) possible to use the sea to supply invaders marching overland. [5]

on Leptis (Ammianus Marcellinus 28.6.5). If camels existed in quantity in Tripolitania, they must have been common also in Cyrenaica. For a not much later period we have proof: Synesius writes that camels comprised a great part of his wealth, *Epist.* 130 in R. Hercher's *Epistolographi Graeci* (Paris 1873) and in A. FitzGerald's excellent translation, *The Letters of Synesius of Cyrene* (London 1926). In subsequent citations of Synesius, I refer to his *Letters,* unless otherwise specified, and I give the numbers as in Herscher and FitzGerald; the numbering in the *Patr. Gr.* varies, because Migne printed letter 80 as 79 *bis* and letter 130 as 129*, omitted letters 157 and 158, and counted letter 159 as 156. (See FitzGerald, 6f). But even in the time of Synesius the nomads used not camels but horses on their raids (104). (Cf., however, chap. 9, n. 31 below.)

[4] See Procopius *Hist.* 3.8.14–29, 4.11.17ff. These tactics of the nomads remind us of episodes in the days of the covered wagons of our western plains.

[5] The expedition sent against Barca by Aryandes at the request of Pheretime consisted of both military and naval forces (Herodotus 4.167, 203). Cambyses abandoned his projected expedition against Carthage because the Phoenician fleet refused to help him (Herod. 3.19). Cyrene, having submitted to Persian suzerainty, appears to have recovered its independence with Greek recovery of the command of the sea (Thucydides 1.110.1). It may well be also that a relation could be established between the vicissitudes of Ptolemaic sea power and the periods of independence of Cyrenaica from the Ptolemaic empire. In 1805 a small

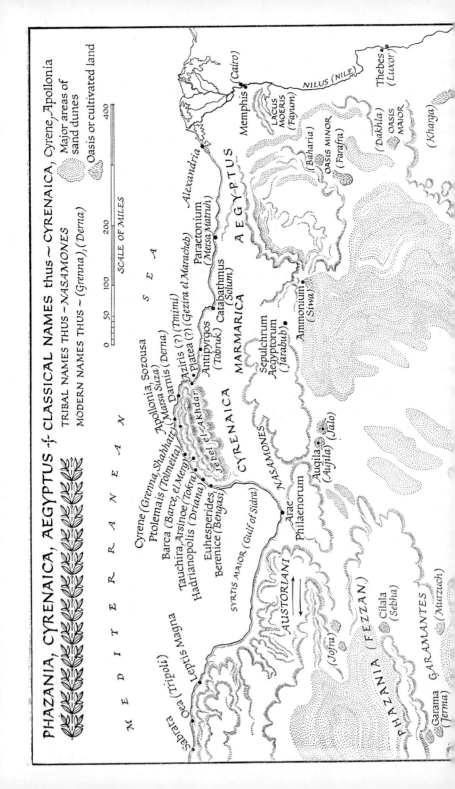

PHAZANIA, CYRENAICA, AEGYPTUS & CLASSICAL NAMES thus ~ CYRENAICA, Cyrene, Apollonia
TRIBAL NAMES THUS ~ NASAMONES
MODERN NAMES THUS ~ (Grenna), (Derna.)

Major areas of sand dunes

Oasis or cultivated land

M E D I T E R R A N E A N   S E A

SCALE OF MILES
0   50   100   200   400

Cyrene (Grenna, Shahhat)
Ptolemais (Tolmeita)
Apollonia, Sozousa (Marsa Suza)
Barca (Barce el Merge)
Darnis (Derna)
Tauchira, Arsinoe (Tokra)
Hadrianopolis (Driana)
Aziris (?) (Tmimi)
Euhesperides, Platea (?) (Gezira el Maraheb)
Berenice (Bengasi)
Antipyrgos (Tobruk)
Paraetonium (Mersa Matruh)
Alexandria
Catabathmus (Solum)

Jebel el Akhdar
CYRENAICA
MARMARICA
AEGYPTUS

Sepulchrum Aegyptorum (Jarabub)
Ammonium (Siwa)

Memphis (Cairo)
Lacus Moeris (Fayum)
Bahariá
OASIS MINOR (Farafra)
(Dakhla)
OASIS MAIOR
(Kharga)
Thebes (Luxor)

NASAMONES
Augila (Aujila) (Jalo)

SYRTIS MAIOR (Gulf of Sidra)

Arae Philaenorum

AUSTORIANI

Sabrata
Oea (Tripoli)
Leptis Magna

(Jofra)

Cilala (Sebha)

PHAZANIA (FEZZAN.)

Garama (Jerma)
GARAMANTES
(Murzuch)

NILUS (NILE)

Then, there is a desert route from Upper Egypt: Thebes, the Oases of Kharga, of Dakhla, of Farafra and Baharia, of Siwa, of Jarabub. From Jarabub the traveler may go northward to the Jebel and the Mediterranean or westward to Augila, from Augila either northwestward to the coast of the Syrtis or by a series of inland water-points to the Fezzan.[6] (And it is from the Fezzan that it is easiest to cross the Sahara.) If this route was not practicable for armies — we know of the attempt of Cambyses and that it failed,[7] it probably was of great importance to culture and to commerce,[8] especially when for any reason the coastal route was blocked or dangerous. Of course, for the reasons already given, bulky articles cannot have been carried over it in any quantity.

Next, there is a direct route southward from Augila through Kufra to Dar-Fur and the Sudan. But this is one of the most difficult crossings of the whole Sahara (the Senussi established their headquarters at Kufra precisely because of its inaccessibility): it cannot have been used at all at the time of which we write; any crossing of the eastern Sahara which did take place must have been by way of the Fezzan. In this

---

orce under William Eaton, American consul at Alexandria, succeeded in marching across the Marmarican desert. It reached Derna, but was so exhausted that it went no farther and, indeed, captured that place only with the aid of American warships. (*Encycl. Britannica* [11th ed.] and *Dictionary of American Biography, s.v.* Eaton, William). Cf. the importance of Tobruk and Bengasi and (to a lesser extent) Mersa Matruh in the desert campaign in World War II.

[6] Herod. 4.172, 181ff; 2.32. I do not agree with the note in the Loeb edition of Herodotus that the starting point of this route was exclusively Memphis, not Thebes. When Cambyses attempted to conquer Siwa, he marched his troops from Memphis to Thebes and from Thebes sent them across the desert by the oasis route of which we are speaking. To be sure, Cambyses was mad and his expedition vanished (Herod. 3.26).

[7] *Ibid.*

[8] The head of Zeus Ammon is constantly represented on Cyrenaican coins. See authorities cited in nn. 53 and 116 below.

connection we recall that Herodotus, when he wanted to
learn about the lands beyond the desert, was able to find
some Cyrenaeans who had heard from Etearchus, king of
the Ammonians (the ruler of Siwa), that he once had been
visited by some Nasimonians (Libyan tribesmen from the
region of the Syrtis, near the Fezzan), who told him that
five of their young men once had made their way to a country of swamps, a great river, crocodiles, and a city inhabited
by small black men.[9] It is evident that, even before the camel
was known in these parts, men made their way across the
desert, but only rarely. Any commerce must have been restricted to small objects of great value.[10]

Lastly, there is the route along the Syrtis to Leptis and
Tripoli. Pomponius Mela[11] and Sallust[12] tell us of the ex-
hausting boundary wars between the Carthaginians and the
Greeks of Cyrenaica; Sallust mentions also that the fighting
took place both on land and at sea. We have no other knowledge of such wars, unless these passages echo the attempt
of the Spartan prince Doreius to found a colony at the mouth
of the river Cinyps (near the later Leptis), an attempt in
which he may have been helped by the Cyrenaeans. After
his expulsion by the Carthaginians in 510 B.C. (or there-
abouts) the boundary was established at Arae Philaenorum
just west of the southernmost point of the Syrtis — an ar-

---

[9] Herod. 2.32.
[10] This state of affairs came to an end in Tripolitania in the time of the Severi.
Leptis certainly grew not merely by favor of its most prominent son but also by
trans-Saharan trade by way of the Fezzan. S. Gsell is inclined to assume (in order
to account for this) a somewhat earlier introduction of the camel (*Histoire an
cienne de l'Afrique du Nord* [Paris 1920] IV 3, and, for a more detailed ac
count of this trade, the same author's study there cited).
[11] 1.7.
[12] *Bell. Iug.* 79.

rangement which has remained without substantial change to this day.[13] Our only sure evidence of trade along this coast is by sea — and that, smuggling rather than legitimate trade.[14] On one occasion we hear of an army's march along the coast of the Syrtis: Ophellas of Cyrene followed the coast when he went to join Agathocles in his campaign against Carthage; but he found it most difficult to get supplies, and for some time his troops were reduced to living on the fruit of a tree which they took to be the Homeric lotus.[15] If much of this coast is not quite so forbidding as the extremely dry Marmarican desert, yet the great distance to the nearest habitable region made Cyrenaica practically secure from invasion from that quarter, the more so as, unlike the Marmarican shore, this coast was almost harborless and faced a notoriously treacherous sea.

So much for the approaches to Cyrenaica. The region itself consists of three parts.

A coastal plain, broad along the Syrtis, narrows rapidly after Bengasi but persists with insignificant interruptions to beyond Derna. Inland the Jebel-el-Akhdar forms a curve following the line of the coast, running from the vicinity of Bengasi to the Gulf of Bomba. (It is continued to the southeast by the lower and far more arid highlands of Marmarica, which also follow the line of the coast a slight distance in-

[13] Herod. 5.42. See also *RE* V 1558ff; E. Meyer, *Geschichte des Altertums* (2nd ed., Stuttgart 1937) III 748f; *CAH* III 684; IV 112, 258f. Another passage in Herodotus (5.47) gives great plausibility to Hackforth's suggestion that Cyrene supported the attempt of Doreius and, therefore, to my suggestion that it may have been this expedition which Pomponius and Sallust had in mind, when they wrote of boundary wars between the Carthaginians and the Greeks of Cyrenaica.

[14] Strabo 17.3.20. But see below, p. 125, for other evidence of possible trade with Carthage.

[15] Theophrastus *Hist. Plant.* 4.3.1–2.

land.) It rises in two sharp shelves: the plateau of Barca, some 300 meters high, and that of Cyrene, about 500 meters in altitude. Farther inland, in the neighborhood of Slonta, the eroded remains of a third shelf reach a maximum elevation of 868 meters. These shelves comprise the second region. The third (and by far the largest) consists of the southern slope of the mountain, which descends in a very gradual decline to the lowlands of the Libyan desert.

It is the Jebel-el-Akhdar that has created Cyrenaica. Its southern crests partly shelter the plateaus and the coast from the desert winds, and it is high enough to catch the rain. The rainfall averages at Bengasi 276 mm. (almost 11 in.) a year and is concentrated in a period of some fifty days between November and January; at Barca 403 mm. (almost 16 in.), concentrated in about sixty-seven days; at Cyrene, where the rainy season lasts from October to April, it averages 405 mm. but exceeds a meter in exceptional years; at Derna the rainfall is about 202 mm., the season being from October through February. Aridity increases very rapidly south of Bengasi and east of Derna.[16] (In Attica, one of the driest regions of Greece, the average rainfall is 16.1 in.,[17] that is, very slightly higher than on the Jebel, but one doubts that Attica has anything comparable to the extremely heavy Libyan dew.) With irrigation and wells and springs the coastal plain and the northern shelves of the Jebel were capable of supporting a considerable urban population. We have proof — for later times at least — that excellent use was

---

[16] See F. Beguinot's excellent article on Cyrenaica in the *Encicl. italiana* (Rome: Trecani, 1929–1939) X 417ff.

[17] So J. D. Bourchier in the article on Greece in the *Encycl. Britannica* (11th ed., Cambridge 1910).

made of the water supply: numerous large cisterns of Roman date have been found.[18]

In these two parts of the country (the coastal plain and the northern shelves of the Jebel) the Greeks proved successful colonists. Partly by interbreeding with the native Libyans[19] and in part by example they hellenized the natives of these districts,[20] going indeed so far as to incorporate many of those near Cyrene with the descendants of the Theran settlers into one of the tribes by which the people were organized (after the usual Doric model) by Demonax of Mantinea.[21] And Barca seems to have had an even stronger Libyan element than Cyrene itself.[22] There was, then, no serious native problem in the Pentapolis proper.

But the third region (the long southern slope of the Jebel toward the desert) was, especially in its southern parts, too arid for Greek settlement on a serious scale. Synesius might have an estate (as an English settler might have a plantation in Kenya), but it would be worked by natives.[23] And

[18] Beguinot (above, n. 16). In the absence of conclusive evidence I am not inclined to believe in a drastic change in climate. On climatic change in Cyrenaica see C. E. P. Brooks, *Climate through the Ages* (revised ed., London 1949) 371ff and the authorities therein cited.

[19] *RE* XII 156ff; E. Meyer (above, n. 13) III 436ff; *CAH* IV 109; and sources cited by those authorities. Note also that the Cyrenaicans were conspicuously dark-skinned; Athenaeus 8.351c, 352b, c.

[20] Herod. 4.170f.

[21] Herod. 4.161.

[22] See above, n. 19.

[23] 148. We have recent interesting testimony to corroborate this. R. G. Goodchild, whose excellent article on the Roman *limes* in Tripolitania appeared in the *Geographical Journal* 115 (1950) 161–78, spent the summer of 1950 in Cyrenaica. I quote from his letter to me: "We found large numbers of Roman farms throughout the Gebel region and also in the plain which extends southward from Benghazi toward Agedabia. In the desert region on the southern edge of the Gebel, close to the 'baltets' or salt marshes, we found only native Libyan farms of the Roman period, a fact which suggests that the Roman development of the fertile plateau had the effect of pushing the native population into the marginal areas."

in parts not suitable for such fixed estates there was still pasture sufficient to support a very considerable nomadic population, not savages,[24] but not possessing even that tincture of Greek civilization which amused Synesius in his own farmers and herdsmen.[25] Beyond them, again, on the fringes of the desert a wretched and savage population lived by hunting and robbery.[26] These must have been a nuisance, but nothing more; it was not they, but the nomadic herdsmen, who menaced Cyrenaica. In a most interesting letter Synesius tells us that the half-civilized natives of his neighborhood, hearing of the weakness and corruption of the *dux* Cerealis, told the more independent tribes and that there followed an invasion which drove Cerealis into taking refuge on a ship in the harbor (presumably of Ptolemais), while Synesius took his turn in keeping watch on the city's walls.[27] The incident is of slight importance, but it is typical of other raids from the time of the early kings to the very end of the Byzantine period.[28] We have very scanty information concerning Cyrenaica; when we consider how often in the extant haphazard notices this theme of barbarian raids and invasions recurs, we cannot avoid the conclusion that southern Cyrenaica, for all the wealth which it brought to the region,[29] was rather a left-handed blessing to the Greek colony.

[24] Diodorus Siculus 3.49; Herod. 4.172f, 186.

[25] 148 (cf. 130).

[26] Diodorus 3.49.

[27] 130.

[28] Herod. 4.159–60; Thuc. 7.50.2 (cf. Pausanias 4.26.2); Pausanias 1.7.1f; Plutarch *Moral.* 257a-c; Strabo 17.3.22; Synesius *Catastasis* and 107, 108, 113, 122, 125, 130, 133; cf. Joannes Antiochenus, *Frag.* 216, in C. Müller, *Fragmenta Historicorum Graecorum* (Paris 1841–1870) IV 621, and Procopius *Aedif.* 6.1ff.

[29] See below, p. 115 and n. 42.

Only less serious than the barbarians were the locusts. A citation from Pliny is worth quoting, since it shows both how serious this drawback must have been and how energetic in dealing with it were the settlers: "In Cyrenaica regione lex etiam est ter anno debellandi eas, prima ova obterendo, dein fetum, postremo adultas, desertoris poena in eum qui cessaverit." [30]

We have considered the desert approaches to Cyrenaica and the district itself; we must not forget the sea. Evidence of fisheries is so incidental that we may assume these to have been of no more than local importance,[31] with the possible exception of sponge fisheries. Pliny mentions the sponges of the Syrtis;[32] today there are sponge fisheries on the Marmarican coast.[33]

Nor do the ports today seem at all impressive: Bengasi accommodates small vessels; Tokra and Tolmeita are negligible; Derna is a roadstead; nothing that one could call a port exists at Apollonia. Bengasi, Tobruk, Mersa Matruh (to a lesser degree) were of major importance during the last war, but that was due more to their location than to the size or the excellence of their harbors. But the ships of the ancients were very small; time no doubt has destroyed harborworks; finally, the coast in this region has subsided since

[30] Pliny 11.35.105; see also Herod. 4.172; Synesius 58.

[31] Athenaeus 7.284c, 300f, 327b; Synesius 57 (but cf. also 148). Regulations of the postwar British administration divide fisheries into "sponge fishing" and "fishing for sea-creatures other than sponges"; for the former, ships carrying five divers seem normal, for the latter "10 tons or over" is the largest category of ships. See "Reg. #34. Registration and Control of Water-Borne Craft" of 13 June 1947, published in *The Cyrenaica Gazette* on 16 June 1947.

[32] 9.49.149.

[33] Beguinot (as above, n. 16); cf. O. Keller, *Die antike Tierwelt* (Leipzig 1913) II 583ff.

classical days.[34] As we shall see, there can be no doubt of the importance of the seaborne commerce of Cyrenaica.

Such was the country; what did the Greeks make of it? The legends of Battus, of the nymph Cyrene and Aristaeus, of the lotus-eaters, of the Gardens of the Hesperides, all point to an age-old knowledge of this coast.[35] Most interesting, too, is Sir Arthur Evans' hypothesis that Minoan Crete knew of silphium.[36] But we know nothing certain before the Theran settlement — and even then we know all too little. It is evident that Apollo meant the settlers to support themselves by making use of the natural resources of the region: the Pythia seems to have been obstinate in her insistence that the Greeks should settle on the mainland by her emphasis on pastures and sheepfolds.[37] The settlers instead, true islanders, wanted to found a trading post; they chose first the small island of Platea, next the port of Aziris, then (only as their last choice) Cyrene. Both god and man were right: the natural resources of the region were prodigious and very great were the possibilities of trade. More than this: Cyrene, though inland, proved the center of power and of trade. It was a strong position with easy access to the sea, able to dominate both the coastal plain and the northern

[34] *CAH* III 667. Cf. also the famous "Minoan" harbor at Pharos; A. J. Evans, *The Palace of Minos at Knossos* (London 1921) I 292ff; E. M. Forster, *Alexandria: A History and a Guide* (2nd ed., Alexandria 1938) 6.

[35] For an interesting study of the subject see L. Malten, *Kyrene: sagengeschichtliche und historische Untersuchungen* (Berlin 1911).

[36] I 284 (above, n. 34). But cf. Theophrastus *Hist. Plant.* 6.3.3; Pliny 19.41. These authors repeat a Cyrenaean report that silphium first appeared in the neighborhood of Bengasi seven years before the founding of Cyrene. It might, of course, be that silphium had disappeared from the region in post-Minoan times and reappeared there in the seventh century B.C. The plant seems to have been an erratic one.

[37] Herod. 4.155, 157. For a serious analysis of the subject see Malten (above, n. 35) 196ff.

terraces of the Jebel, and (above all) was on the easiest route from the southern plateau to the sea.[38]

By all odds the most important as well as the most distinctive product of Cyrenaica was silphium. Here is not the place to review the many speculations concerning the nature of this plant.[39] It suffices to say that, although somewhat similar species grew in Syria, Armenia, Media, the Hindu-Kush and even on Mount Parnassus, none of these (with the possible exception of the plant found in the Hindu-Kush) was more than a poor substitute for the silphium of Cyrenaica.[40] It grew as a wild plant — it was refractory to cultivation — [41] in a broad strip of territory stretching from the neighborhood of Bengasi to the Gulf of Bomba, the southern slopes of the Jebel, and the steppes bordering the desert on the north.[42] This plant (and especially the

[38] The Barca-Ptolemais route seems to have been the next best. The growth in importance of the ports at the expense of inland cities is (one suspects) due to the loss of regional independence. Barca and Cyrene were in strategic positions superior to their ports; with the loss of independence they no longer were allowed to take advantage of this fact. It should be noted that after its destruction by the Jews in Trajan's time, Cyrene never really recovered, whereas Barca became the chief city of the country (at the expense of Ptolemais and Sozousa) the moment that (under the Arabs) the inland land route from east to west became more important than the route from the interior to the sea. It seems quite possible that the chief centers of the production of silphium lay in the southeast of the country (but cf. n. 36 above), thus giving Cyrene a relative advantage over Barca that disappeared with the disappearance of the silphium itself. Otherwise it becomes difficult to account for the fact that Cyrene never recovered at least its relative importance.

[39] See the excellent articles in DS IV 1337ff, and in *RE* IIIA 103ff.

[40] Arrian's account (*Anab.* 3.28.6–7) of the avidity with which sheep ate the Bactrian plant is reminiscent of Cyrenaican silphium. See also the reports (cited in DS and *RE*) of a plant, which is at least extremely like silphium, found in these regions in modern times. Cf. also Strabo's statement (15.2.10) that Alexander's troops found the silphium of the Hindu-Kush helpful in digesting raw food.

[41] Pliny 19.41–42; Theophrastus *Hist. Plant.* 3.2.1, 6.3.1, but cf. 6.3.5 and Synesius 106.

[42] Arrian *Ind.* 43.13; Strabo 2.5.33, 17.3.22–23; Pliny 5.33; 19.41, 42; Herod. 4.169, 192. Theophrastus (*Hist. Plant.* 6.3.6, 6.5.2) places the silphium district

juice or gum extracted from it) was used as a condiment[43] and as a remedy for every kind of ailment.[44] We have many proofs of the extreme value of the product. The cutting of the root was carefully regulated so as not to diminish the supply.[45] Measures to prevent its being overgrazed were taken by the Cyrenaeans.[46] The famous cup of Arcesilaus shows the king, apparently Arcesilaus II, enthroned on the deck of a sailing ship, supervising both the weighing of bales of silphium and the storing of the bales already weighed below deck.[47] Trade in silphium seems to have been a monopoly in the time of the kings.[48] We know that it was one of the principal exports to Athens;[49] that it was smuggled to Carthage;[50] that a Roman audience of the time of Plautus would find it natural for a Cyrenaean landowner to be shipping silphium to Capua;[51] that a curious legend associates it with Sparta.[52] There is every reason to suppose that the trade covered the whole Mediterranean world. Sil-

---

in the hill country, which sounds more like the northern slopes of the Jebel or its crests than the southern slope. On the whole, one is inclined to think with Rainaud that the plant tended to retreat toward the south as the northern district became more densely cultivated and more heavily grazed. But see Synesius (106) for its survival as a garden plant. That Plautus refers to silphium as growing on the coast (*Rudens* 629ff) is of no weight: he obviously would add local color by representing a Cyrenaican landowner as growing silphium. Theophrastus (*Hist. Plant.* 9.1.7) tells us also that it was gathered by the Libyans — which again points to the south.

[43] Athenaeus 3.100e–f.
[44] See especially the exhaustive and amusing list in Pliny 22.100–106.
[45] Theophrastus *Hist. Plant.* 6.3.2.
[46] Arrian *Anab.* 3.28.6–7.
[47] Illustrated in many works, among others in *CAH*, Vol. of Plates I 379.
[48] The cup itself indicates this — also the fact that it was smuggled to Carthaginian traders (Strabo 17.3.20).
[49] Athenaeus 1.27e; Theophrastus *Hist. Plant.* 6.3.2.
[50] Strabo 17.3.20.
[51] See above, n. 42.
[52] Pausanias 3.16.3.

phium is constantly represented on the coins of Cyrene until the period of Roman domination.[53] Finally, we have three statements of Pliny: (1) in the consulship of C. Valerius and M. Herennius (93 B.C.) thirty pounds of Cyrenaean silphium were transported to Rome on behalf of the State; (2) Caesar took 1,500 pounds of silphium from the treasury at the beginning of the Civil War; (3) silphium was worth its weight in silver *denarii*.[54]

Strabo tells us that invading barbarians cut the roots of the plant through spite and nearly exterminated it.[55] Pliny (writing about half a century later) says that in his time it became quite extinct, because the publicans found it more lucrative to use the silphium-growing lands as sheepwalks.[56] There is no inconsistency. Sheep were so avid of silphium that the Cyrenaeans used to fence them from the silphium-growing regions to prevent overgrazing.[57] Evidently the publicans, having contracted for short periods only, kept their exactions at a point so high that it was impossible for proprietors to fence out sheep and leave the lands idle for the few years needed to give the plant a chance really to re-establish itself after the damage done by the barbarians. Nevertheless, silphium may not have been exterminated entirely at this time; Synesius refers to it in two letters.[58] In the first of these, which is well known, it appears as a garden plant, so that one might infer that it was even rarer than it

[53] E. S. G. Robinson, *Catalogue of the Greek Coins of Cyrenaica* (London 1927); see also *CAH*, Vol. of Plates I 307. For a very fine coin of Barca, see G. F. Hill, *L'art dans les monnaies grecques* (Paris and Brussels 1927) pl. LIII, 2.

[54] 19.38–40.

[55] 17.3.22.

[56] See above, n. 42.

[57] See above, n. 46.

[58] 106, 134.

had been in the old days. But in the second letter, which
seems to have escaped notice, Synesius writes of sending a
great deal of silphium juice (ὀπὸς σιλφίου πολύς) and also
saffron to a friend in Constantinople. That he could write
of a great deal of juice — and associate it with even the best
saffron without bathos — is most surprising; it becomes as-
tonishing when we realize that this is the last which we hear
of the product. Can it be that what Synesius and his friends
took to be the true silphium was merely one of the similar
plants common enough in the Orient?

We have seen the emphasis with which Apollo spoke of
the pastures of Libya. These were the second, the more en-
during, perhaps the no less important, source of the wealth
of Cyrenaica. The Libyan horse had existed from very ancient times. Herodotus tells us that the native Libyans drove
four-horse chariots and that the Garamantes used these to
chase the Ethiopian troglodytes.[59] Fantastically enough, such
manhunts are illustrated in Saharan rock paintings and rock
carvings; the dates of these are uncertain, but the style of
some of them is undoubtedly Aegean.[60] In historical times
the Cyrenaean horse was one of the most famous breeds of
the classical world.[61] It must have been at all periods in great

[59] 4.170, 183.

[60] Gautier (above, n. 2) pl. IV and pp. 36–38. The representations mentioned
by Gautier are found far to the west, but others of a much cruder type, by no
means Aegean in character, are found in the Fezzan. See Graziosi, "Incisioni
rupestri di carri dell' Uadi Zigza nel Fezzan" in *Africa italiana* 6 (1935) 54ff.
One wonders whether the former may have been made by the Garamantes — or
at least some Aegean element that established itself as an aristocracy among their
forebears — and the latter by the unfortunate Ethiopian troglodytes.

[61] See *inter alia* Pindar *Pyth.* 4, 5, 9 (verses 4 and 123); Athenaeus 3.100f;
Pausanias 6.8.3, 6.12.7, 6.18.1, 10.13.5, 10.15.6–7; Keller (above, n. 33) I 221
and the illustration of a Cyrenaean horse there shown. Cf. Xenophon *Cyr.*
6.1.27, 6.2.8; Aeneas Tacticus, 16.14–16.

demand for the chariot races so loved by the ancients,[62] and it received particular care in its breeding.[63] Rostovtzeff no doubt is right in supposing that horses were sent in large quantities from Cyrenaica to Egypt.[64] In later times the raising of camels became of comparable importance with that of horses.[65] Cattle also were raised in large quantities and hides were one of the principal exports from Cyrenaica.[66] Sheep-raising, as we have seen, preceded the Theran settlement, and it continued throughout the history of the colony. Cyrenaican mutton acquired an exceptionally fine flavor when the sheep were pastured on silphium — a pasturage, however, which was restricted until the Roman period because of the intrinsic value of the plant.[67] Wool or woolen cloth doubtlessly was exported in great quantities, though I have not found any classical text in evidence of this statement.[68]

The whole country (except for the forested parts of the Jebel) was excellent pastureland; but, as colonization proceeded and the better-watered districts were used for agricultural purposes, stock-raising in the north must have become restricted, while the southern slopes of the Jebel [69] and those parts of Marmarica and the coast of the Syrtis[70]

---

[62] Note the constant appearance of the *quadriga* on Cyrenaean coins (Robinson; above, n. 53). When we find Synesius sending a horse as a present to a friend abroad, we cannot doubt that a regular export continued in his time (40).

[63] Synesius 40, 133; Pausanias 6.12.7.

[64] M. Rostovtzeff, *The Social and Economic History of the Hellenistic World,* hereafter referred to as *SEHHW,* I (Oxford 1941) 293, 385, 396.

[65] See above, n. 3

[66] Athenaeus 1.27e; Synesius 130, 148.

[67] Pliny (above, n. 54); Theophrastus 6.3.2, 6: Arrian *Anab.* 3.28.6–7.

[68] But see *RE* XII 168. And note that the rebel Jonathan, the contemporary of Josephus, was a weaver by trade. Josephus *Bell.* 7.437.

[69] Cf. Synesius 130.

[70] For the coast of the Syrtis, see Herod. 4.172–73. From Pausanias 1.7.1–2,

which were not too dry must have become the centers of
the industry. (It is interesting to note that before the last war
it was estimated that the native tribes in Cyrenaica were
pasturing about 1,000,000 sheep, 100,000 goats, 40,000 camels,
15,000 cattle.)[71]

And in parts, at least, of this southern country agriculture
was possible. Synesius, writing of his estate there, tells us
that it produced wheat, barley, honey, olive oil, figs,[72] though
its real wealth lay in its herds of horses and camels and
cattle.[73]

Here, too, and to the south, where the pastures became
scarcer but the land was not yet full desert, was the country
of the wild beasts. These must have been exported for the
amphitheater; certainly ostriches and ostrich eggs were exported.[74]

The same region produced salt and soda;[75] the dates of
Augila and Siwa were famous.[76] Presumably all three were
exported, although the only text which I have discovered
tells us merely that the priests of Ammon took salt with
them when they went to Egypt and that this salt was used
for hieratic purposes.[77]

Actual trans-Saharan trade, for reasons already given, must

---

we see that Marmarica managed to support enough Libyans to constitute a
serious threat to the expedition of Magas against Ptolemy Lagus. One presumes
that these tribesmen lived by herding, perhaps growing a little barley where
conditions permitted it, and by robbery.

[71] Beguinot (as above, n. 16).

[72] 148.

[73] 130.

[74] Synesius 129, 134. See also Keller (above, n. 33) II 166ff.

[75] Synesius 148; Arrian *Anab.* 3.4.3. For soda see Diodorus 3.50.

[76] Strabo 17.3.23; Herodotus 4.172; cf. Pliny 13.4.9.

[77] Arrian *Anab.* 3.4.3.

have been secondary until the camel became common. However, Pliny mentions jewels in great numbers brought from Ethiopia, and, though the text is not very clear, it seems likely that this commerce found its outlet through Cyrenaica, not Leptis.[78] The real importance of Leptis dates from later times; it seems to have been the heir, rather than the rival, of Cyrene.

So much for the south. The coastal plain and the terraces of the Jebel were one of the granaries of the ancient world; reference to the region is seldom made without mention of its fertility.[79] During the great famine in Greece in Alexander's time Cyrene gave no less than 805,000 medimni of wheat (including 100,000 medimni to Athens) to alleviate the distress.[80] When one considers the small area of Cyrenaica (especially of the agricultural part of the country) and when one takes into account that the inhabitants had to keep on hand enough for their own needs and, moreover, that they probably sold in other markets, this contribution of a round million bushels is extremely impressive. One realizes that the classical authors did not exaggerate in their accounts of the fertility of the Pentapolis and that grain must have been exported on a considerable scale.[81]

The olives of Cyrenaica were famous for their excellence

[78] Pliny 5.34. Cf. above, n. 10.
[79] (*Inter alia*) Herod. 4.198–99; Arrian *Ind.* 43.13; Diodorus 3.50; Strabo 2.5.33; Pliny 5.33.
[80] S. Ferri, *Alcune iscrizioni di Cirene,* no. 3 (cited by W. W. Tarn in *CAH* VI 448 n. 1. The Attic medimnus of this period equaled 40.36 liters, and the Spartan 57.65. The former would be equal to slightly more than 1.1 bushels, the latter more than 1.5 bushels. For the medimnus see *RE* XV 86ff.
[81] Pompey gathered stores of grain from Cyrenaica in preparation for his war with Caesar (Caesar *Bell. Civ.* 3.5).

and for the abundance of their oil; we hear of the export of olive oil from Cyrenaica.[82] Its saffron, too, was of especially good quality; and again we are told that it was exported.[83] We read of the import of wine in early times and of its export later in Cyrenaican history.[84] The flowers of Cyrenaica were exceptionally sweet-scented and perfumes made from its roses especially were esteemed.[85] No doubt these also were exported.

Timber, always an important article in the ancient world, was in good supply, though in the absence of specific authority one dares not hazard that it was abundant enough for export. Particularly mentioned are palm, cypress, a cypress-like cedar (θύον), which furnished exceptionally fine timber, olive, fig, myrtle, varieties of acacia-like trees and thorns (λωτός, παλίουρος).[86] To this day the more remote parts of the Jebel are wooded with myrtle, viburnum, bay, juniper, ilex, carob, pine.[87]

Minor products of Cyrenaica, we are specifically told, included an esteemed variety of truffle (μίσυ),[88] figs,[89] cucumbers,[90] honey.[91] No doubt most other typically Mediterranean products also grew there, though particular mention of these seems not to have survived. Our list is already long;

[82] Theophrastus *Hist. Plant.* 4.3.1; Pliny 17.133; Synesius 134, 148. Roman oil-presses have been found in Cyrenaica according to Beguinot (as above, n. 16).
[83] Theophrastus *Hist. Plant.* 6.6.5; Synesius 134.
[84] Strabo 17.3.20; Synesius 134; cf. Herod. 4.199.
[85] Theophrastus (as above, n. 83).
[86] Herod. 2.96, 4.157; Theophrastus *Hist. Plant.* 3.1.6, 4.3.1–5, 5.3.7; Pliny 12.104–6, 16.143. Diodorus 3.50; Synesius 108, 114, 122, 148.
[87] Beguinot (above, n. 16).   [88] Pliny 19.36; Athenaeus 2.62a.
[89] Synesius 148.
[90] Pliny 20.7.
[91] Synesius 148.

Pindar might well sing of Cyrene as "the choicest garden of Zeus." [92]

Cyrene and its rival Barca and the smaller but not negligible towns of Euhesperides (later Berenice), Tauchira (later Arsinoe), Apollonia (later Sozousa), which constituted the Cyrenaican Pentapolis (Darnis was a later foundation; Ptolemais, which rose in later times to be a very considerable city and the capital of the province, was originally merely the port of Barca), had thus a solid foundation on which Cyrenaicans could build a prosperous urban life. That they did so is evident, not only from the references already given, but also from their achievements in science, philosophy, and art, and from the very considerable remains still to be seen, especially at Cyrene and Ptolemais. These are fields, however, which lie beyond the scope of this paper.

When we endeavor to establish what goods were imported into Cyrenaica, with what regions economic connections were closest, what were the economic vicissitudes of the region through a period of some 1,200 years — when we consider these questions, we find ourselves utterly without statistics, reduced to making from the few hints available what deductions we can.

The connection with Egypt was at all times very close, as the whole political and artistic history of the region shows. We have seen that Rostovtzeff believed, unquestionably rightly, that Egypt relied heavily on Cyrenaica for its supply of horses. [93] Egypt may well have taken Cyrenaican perfumes

---

[92] *Pyth.* 9.57.
[93] See above, n. 64.

also and in return sent linen (we do not hear of flax in Cyrenaica), papyrus, glass, ivory, etc.

Herodotus tells us that a special friendship with Samos existed from the very founding of the colony;[94] and indeed a specifically Samian influence is noted in early Cyrenaean art.[95] There is besides numismatic evidence of early connections with Rhodes.[96] We note also the part played by Crete in the foundation of the settlement[97] and the fact that Crete and Cyrenaica were united by the Romans to form a single province. We have seen that silphium and hides were exported to the Piraeus,[98] and silphium to Capua.[99]

Laconia deserves special mention; its connection with Cyrenaica was extremely intimate. We have indicated already an instance in the field of politics,[100] and we have seen too that there is some evidence of a very early trade in silphium.[101] Pottery was an article of commerce of great importance between them. The cup of Arcesilaus is a particularly fine specimen of a ware which used to be called "Cyrenaican," but is now known to have originated in Laconia. It is all the more striking proof of the intimacy of relations that there should be so much specifically Cyrenaican in this ware's subject and design. It seems possible, as many sup-

[94] 4.152, 162–63.
[95] *CAH* III 668.
[96] *CAH*, Vol. of Plates I 306.
[97] Herod. 4.151.
[98] See above, nn. 49 and 66.
[99] See above, n. 51.
[100] See p. 108 above. There were many others, but we are not concerned here with the political history of Cyrenaica. For a recent and excellent resume of Cyrene's political and social history see K. Freeman, *Greek City-States* (London 1950) 181–201.
[101] See above, n. 52.

pose, that, though this type of pottery first was produced in Laconia, it was imitated later in Cyrenaica.[102]

What of Carthage? We have seen that there was a clandestine exchange of wine and of silphium.[103] Gsell thinks that certain Tanagra-like figurines found in graves at Carthage and in ports with which Carthage traded may well have been made in Cyrene and spread by Punic merchants.[104] That is all we know; and it is true that Cyrene and Carthage, both serving as outlets of the interior of Africa, would not be likely to have many products supplementary to each other. But in addition to political connections, some of which we already have noticed, our attention is struck by the fact that Hannibal, when he wished to persuade the Carthaginians to join Antiochus in making war on Rome, proceeded to Cyrenaica.[105] Of course, he may have received communications across the land frontier, but one suspects that he met Punic merchants.

[102] See *RE* XII 168ff; Meyer (above, n. 13) III 504. But note that pottery, dating from many periods, undoubtedly not Cyrenaican in origin has been found in excavations at Cyrene and elsewhere in the Pentapolis. See L. Pernier, "Campagna de scavi a Cirene nell'estate di 1925" in *Africa italiana* I (1927) 126ff; also in the same issue G. Oliviero, "Documenti epigrafici del santuario di Apollo," 156ff, and in the second volume (1928) of the same publication his article on the excavations in 1927 (111ff, esp. 148), and his article in the third volume (1930) on the excavations in 1928 (141ff), and Pernier's "L'artemision di Cirene" in the fourth volume (1931), esp. 190. See also *SEHHW* I 368 (pl. XLI) for a very fine Alexandrian jar, representing Queen Berenice, found at Berenice. But this was probably used for cult purposes, as Rostovtzeff explains, and so is scarcely evidence of the commercial import of pottery. Another bit of evidence tending to show that the Cyrenaicans were not potters, at least in early times, is the remark of Theophrastus (*Hist. Plant.* 5.3.7) that there were still alive men who remembered roofs in Cyrene made of thyon wood (practically, cedar shingles). On the other hand, see Pernier (as above) for evidence of Cyrenaean imitations of proto-Corinthian *skyphoi*. And see below, n. 104.

[103] See above, n. 14.   [104] IV 68 (above, n. 10).   [105] Nepos *Hann.* 8.1.

Metals must have been the most important imports of Cyrenaica; we hear nothing of any mines in the region in either ancient or modern times. Nor does marble exist there; a glance at the excavations and the museums and the archaeological publications will convince us that this must have been imported in great quantities at all periods.[106] Striking proof of its value in Cyrene is furnished by a statue found there of an enthroned Hades with Cerberus beside him. The face and the hands and the feet of the god are made of Pentelic marble, but all the rest is of common stone.[107]

There are indications that Cyrene maintained both a merchant fleet and a navy. The cup of Arcesilaus has been mentioned.[108] Many centuries later the historian Josephus, shipwrecked in the Adriatic Sea, was rescued by a Cyrenaean ship and taken to Puteoli.[109] As to their navy: we have already noted Sallust's passage in which he wrote of wars with the Carthaginians by land and sea, and, even if his words should apply to the settlement of Doreius, this passage is not wholly to be disregarded.[110] We have marked also that the Cyrenaeans gave two triremes and pilots to Peloponnesian forces which had been driven from their course on their way to Sicily.[111] And the Cyrenaeans, too, are said to have been the first to develop the *lembus*,[112] a small and swift war

[106] See especially the issues of *Africa italiana* and also M. Berenson, *A Vicarious Trip to the Barbary Coast* (London 1938) pls. VIII, X, XII, XIII, XIV, XVI.

[107] C. Anti, "Campagna di scavi a Cirene nell'estate di 1926" in *Africa italiana* I (1927) 308.

[108] See above, p. 116 and n. 47.

[109] Josephus *Vita* 15–16.

[110] See above, n. 12. Cf. Herodotus 5.47.

[111] Thuc. 7.50.2 (cited in n. 28 above).

[112] Pliny 7.208.

vessel, serviceable for scouting or convoy,[113] just the kind of ship that would be useful to them for protecting their merchant fleets from pirates. Apollonia is mentioned as their naval base (ἐπίνειον).[114]

We have mentioned what seem to us the physical foundations on which the economic life of Cyrenaica was based, and we have demonstrated how the Cyrenaicans developed these to form a region wealthy both because of agricultural and pastoral resources and because of manufactures and trade. However, since the history of the Pentapolis covers some 1,200 years, we cannot suppose that it enjoyed an even prosperity throughout that time. We know very little of its vicissitudes, but we must make the most of what evidence we have. Cyrene rose to power and commercial importance in the time of the third king, Battus II. Supported by Delphi, he invited new immigrants from all over Hellas, established them in the land, and proved sufficiently strong to defeat the combined reaction of the natives and the pharaoh Apries about 570.[115] The coinage of Cyrene, which dates from about this time (a period when coinage was still rare and confined to the great centers of trade), is conclusive proof of the position achieved by the young colony.[116] And its treasury at Olympia seems to have dated from an even earlier era.[117]

---

[113] *RE* XII 1894ff.

[114] Strabo 17.3.20.

[115] Herod. 4.159. For the date see *RE* XII 160.

[116] See G. F. Hill in *CAH* IV 128ff. See also authorities cited above in n. 53; in addition to the plate there cited from *L'art dans les monnaies grecques*, see also pl. VI, 2.

[117] Broholm in *RE* XII 168, quoting Pausanias 6.19. The passage in Pausanias does not seem to establish the date, but reliefs from this treasury are well known (Broholm, *ibid.*, 154) and presumably place it to the satisfaction of the archaeologists.

The loss of 7,000 hoplites in an attempt to subdue Barca and the revolting Libyans toward the end of the reign of Arcesilaus II must have been a very serious blow to Cyrene itself, but it was perhaps compensated, if one considers Cyrenaica as a whole, by the new city's rapid increase in wealth and by the Barcans' hellenization of additional groups of Libyans.[118] This Arcesilaus is presumably the ruler represented on the cup to which we have referred so often; its subject, its workmanship, the elegance and richness with which the king is dressed, are all evidence of the prosperity of Cyrenaica in his time. The almost complete depopulation of Barca in 512[119] by the Persians and by Pheretime, the vengeful queen of Cyrene, certainly weakened the Greek settlements as a whole, but even so the Persians did not dare to attack Cyrene itself, though they were tempted to do so.[120] And Pheretime's grandson, Arcesilaus IV, was the ruler to whom Pindar addressed his fourth and fifth *Pythian Odes* (the latter opening with the words: ὁ πλοῦτος εὐρυσθενής . . .). Politics might be (and were) disorderly, but wealth remained.

Much the same may be said of the republican period which followed and of the Ptolemaic period which succeeded that. We have noted already the generous contribution of Cyrene to famine relief in the time of Alexander;[121] it was also Alexander who boasted to his soldiers of the wealth which they received from Cyrene.[122] The changing of the names of Euhesperides to Berenice and of Tauchira to Arsinoe as well

---

[118] See p. 111 above.
[119] Herod. 4.202–3. For date see *RE* III 20.
[120] Herod. (as in preceding note).
[121] See p. 121 above.
[122] Arrian *Anab.* 7.9.8.

as the practical removal of Barca to its port (henceforth called Ptolemais) may imply active measures taken by the Ptolemaic dynasty to further the prosperity of this region, but a desire to weaken the position of Cyrene itself also may have had to do with measures favoring the ports; we know that it was at this time that Apollonia was made an independent commune.[123] We know also that the Ptolemies encouraged Jewish settlement in Cyrenaica; in this case we are told that it was for military reasons.[124]

Broholm believes that Cyrene suffered from the competition of Alexandria, thinking apparently that the latter enjoyed a more favorable position than the former as an outlet for products from the interior of Africa.[125] Of course it did so far as the Nile Valley was concerned, in that respect succeeding the earlier Naucratis (and the still earlier "Minoan" harbor at Pharos), but not so far as concerned the hinterland of Cyrene, from which Alexandria and the Nile Valley were severed by particularly impassable stretches of desert.[126] We have for this two pieces of evidence in the texts. When Pliny tells us of the important trade in precious stones received from the Ethiopians by way of the Fezzan,[127] he does so in connection with Cyrenaica, not Alexandria. Florus, referring to the boldness of the Cilician pirates during the Mithridatic Wars (at a time, that is, when Cyrenaica had newly become a Roman province), writes: "Ac primum duce Isidoro contenti proximo mari Cretam inter atque Cyrenas et Achaiam sinumque Maleum, quod ab spoliis aureum ipsi

---

[123] *RE* XII 163 and authorities there cited.
[124] Josephus *Contra Apion.* 2.14. See also *SEHHW* I 333 and n. 128.
[125] *RE* XII 166.
[126] See pp. 105–6 above.
[127] See p. 121 and n. 78 above.

vocavere, latrocinabantur." [128] Alexandrian commerce would remain unaffected by this barrier in any case, for with the Orient and with Greece it would pass east of Crete and with Rome it could avoid the pirates by hugging the coast of Cyrenaica to Bengasi and by taking refuge in the coastal ports. But it would close the routes between Cyrenaica and the Aegean (and Rome and the Aegean, but the southern barrier would not have been necessary for this); that must have constituted a great part of the trade which led the pirates to call it the "Golden Sea." Piracy, of course, is a great inconvenience to commerce; but it is a parasite which does not exist where commerce is not important.

However that may be, a very serious decline began with the Roman occupation. If the Romans benefited the Cyrenaicans by clearing the seas of pirates, they also (as we have seen) caused the practical disappearance of silphium, a product which had been a major (if not the major) source of the wealth of Cyrenaica. Perhaps this led to the creation, certainly to the increase, of an indigent class. At any rate, as early as the reign of Vespasian we learn of such a class at Cyrene for the first time: a Jewish fanatic, named Jonathan, persuaded some 2,000 ἄποροι to revolt. They were destroyed easily enough, and in addition all the well-to-do Jews of Cyrene (to the number of 3,000) thereupon were executed by the Roman governor on the pretext that they were accomplices.[129] From the implication of Alexandrian

---

[128] 1.41.3.

[129] Josephus *Bell.* 7.437ff. In the *Vita* 424ff, Josephus refers to the same rebellion and gives the number of rebels killed.

On the presence of Jews in Cyrenaica consult R. D. Barnett's account of "Tombs at Tocra" in *Journal of Hellenic Studies* 65 (1945) 105–6. These tombs, which had contained Jewish corpses, at Tocra (the ancient Taucheira or

and Roman Jews, including Josephus, in this alleged plot we may deduce that many of the victims were merchants or bankers; their execution hardly can have helped the economic life of a commercial community.

"Qui mange du pape ou du juif en meurt"; nowhere was this more quickly or more violently illustrated than in Cyrenaica. The great Jewish revolt of A.D. 115 was particularly hideous in the province and in Cyrene itself. Before the rule of Hitler no one would have supposed that civilized men could have committed atrocities such as we are told the Jews perpetrated during this furious rebellion. We hear that 220,-000 persons perished in Cyrenaica alone.[130] And the city of Cyrene was destroyed. From this blow it never recovered; Ammianus described Cyrene as a deserted city[131] and even Synesius spoke of it (to be sure, he was asking for a reduction in taxes) as "now poor and downcast, a vast ruin . . ."[132] Of course, they exaggerated: Hadrian repopulated the region and rebuilt the cities;[133] the ruins of his buildings at Cyrene and Apollonia are impressive. Nevertheless, the great metropolis, only just not of the first rank among the cities of the classical world, the intellectual and artistic life, the commerce on a major scale — all that was gone forever.

The region remained (despite raids such as those deplored

Teucheira) were investigated by personnel of the Royal Air Force during World War II. I owe this reference to the late Professor A. J. B. Wace.

[130] Dio Cassius 68.32.1–2; Eusebius *Hist. Eccl.* 4.2; Orosius *Hist. adv. Pag.* 7.12.6.

[131] 22.16.4.

[132] The opening of the *De Regno*.

[133] See Orosius (above, n. 130); also *SEHRE* 317, 589, and sources there cited. Of exceptional interest are the inscriptions of this period found by Italian archaeologists. See *Africa italiana* 1 (1927) 134, 145, 298, 318, and esp. fig. 5 on p. 321; 2 (1928) 118f.

by Synesius) a reasonably prosperous agricultural province (with its life chiefly concentrated in the ports of Ptolemais and Sozousa) until the Arab conquest — and, indeed, for some time longer. The picture painted by Synesius must have been more or less typical of the whole period. But Synesius and his time, if fascinating, are too well known to be reviewed here,[134] and we have no other serious data. We find Zeno addressing the *Henoticon* to the bishops and the clergy, the monks and the laity of Alexandria, Egypt, Libya, and the Pentapolis;[135] we find Anastasius reorganizing the defense of the province against the barbarians;[136] we find under Justinian something of a revival, for he appointed Cyrus, nephew of the great Solomon and apparently a young man whom he wished to advance, to govern Cyrenaica.[137] Ptolemais, too, had lost in population owing to its poor water supply, evidently to the advantage of Arsinoe and Berenice; we find Justinian repairing the aqueduct of Ptolemais, constructing walls (indeed most imposing at Arsinoe), building a new bath at Berenice, and castles against the barbarians.[138] Almost at the very last (in 608) Heraclius, rebelling against Phocas, was able to raise 3,000 men in the Pentapolis, and Libyan auxiliaries in addition.[139] Chosroes overran the region in 616 [140] and left it in such a weakened state that it fell to the

---

[134] See the introductions to FitzGerald's translations (cited above, n. 3) and the authorities there listed. Also my article in *Byzantion* 15 (1940–1941) 10–38, reprinted in chap. 6 below.

[135] *CMH* I 516.

[136] Joannes Antiochenus (as above, n. 28).

[137] Procopius *Hist.* 4.21.1; cf. Justinian's protection of Sergius, son of Solomon and cousin of Cyrus (*ibid.*, 4.22.11).

[138] Procopius *Aedif.* 6.2.1ff.

[139] *CMH* II 287.

[140] Gibbon, *The History of the Decline and Fall of the Roman Empire* (ed. Bury, London 1896–1900) V 71.

Arabs without resistance in the winter of 642/43,[141] thus breaking its age-old connection with the western world.

But such data are mere shadows and merely shadows of the shell of what had once been Cyrenaica, the last wretched grains of sand in the hourglass. They are gone, and Cyrene is gone, gone but immortal as Lesbia's kisses, of which Catullus sang:

> Quam magnus numerus Libyssae harenae
> laserpiciferis iacet Cyrenis,
> oraclum Iovis inter aestuosi
> et Batti veteris sacrum sepulcrum.[142]

Postscript

A SURPRISING OMISSION in the foregoing article is any reference to A. H. M. Jones's excellent chapter on Cyrenaica in his *Cities of the Eastern Roman Provinces* (Oxford 1937) 351–64. It deals in part with political and administrative matters outside the scope of my study, but also has much to say that would have helped, supported, and enlarged it.

During a visit to Cyrenaica a few years ago, I noticed at Apollonia old foundations, some awash, some completely under water, very tangible evidence of the subsidence of this coast, mentioned on page 113 above.

A reviewer — I have unfortunately mislaid my reference — well pointed out that I had made no mention of the Etesian winds. He referred, I take it, to my remark on page 130 above that Alexandrian shipping bound for Rome could avoid the Cilician pirates by hugging the African coast. It would indeed have been extremely imprudent to have kept

[141] *CMH* II 351.
[142] 7.3–6.

close to that almost harborless coast during the summer
gales: the voyage described by Synesius in *Epist.* 4 ought to
have been enough to remind me of the danger.

Discussing the uses of silphium, a friend once remarked
to me that there could have been only one explanation of
the great value attached to the product: it must have been
an aphrodisiac. If so, though, it is odd that Pliny should not
have mentioned this in his long list of its uses[143] and that
Plautus should not have made some joke about it in *Rudens,*[144] when one of the characters mentioned shipments
of silphium to Capua. The hypothesis, though, perhaps gains
some support from the story told us by Pausanias[145] of the
kidnapping of the daughter of Phormio by Castor and Pollux. The demigods told Phormio, who at that time was living in the house in Sparta that they had inhabited as mortals,
that they had come from Cyrene and would like to sleep in
their old room. He replied that they were welcome to any
other room in the house, but that that one was occupied by
his unmarried daughter. In the morning, the daughter and
her maids had disappeared, and in the empty room were
found statues of the Dioscuri and a little silphium. Certainly,
too, the verses of Catullus with which I ended the preceding
paper take on added pungency if read with my friend's suggestion in mind.

"Le chameau et l'Afrique du Nord romaine," *Annales
(Economies Sociétés Civilisations)* 15 (1960) 209–47, by
Emilienne Demougeot, assembles evidence which proves that,
although the camel was not known in North Africa in the

[143] See above, n. 44.
[144] See above, n. 42.
[145] See above, n. 52.

time of Carthage, it made its appearance in the region sooner than I, following Gsell and Gautier,[146] had believed. Some representations of the beast in the eastern Sahara, the article continues, indicate its existence in the more remote parts of that region in pre-Roman times. The authoress is not sure, though, whether it was a recent importation or a survival, in those isolated areas, of the neolithic camel of Africa, long believed to have become extinct. The first text referring to the camel in North Africa west of the Nile Valley tells us of its alleged use by Alexander to carry water on his visit to Siwa. The source of this account, though, is Quintus Curtius; Demougeot points out that he lived in the time of Claudius, and was not always accurate. (I should, though, be inclined to give him the benefit of the doubt in this instance: Alexander was a man of great imagination, and he had gone to Egypt from Syria, where the camel abounded, so that he may well have attached many to the supply train of his armies. We know that his successors, the Ptolemies, used them extensively in Egypt.[147] Undisputed is the statement by the anonymous author of the *Bellum Africum* that Caesar captured twenty-two camels from Juba I in 46 B.C. (The number strikes us precisely because it is so small: the animal must have been introduced into the region very shortly before this time, perhaps by Juba himself.) It is to be noted that Cato the Younger, marching along the shores of the Syrtis, is reported by Plutarch to have carried a supply of water on donkeys, not camels. Only a few years later, though, in 39 B.C., M. Lollius minted a coin in Cyrenaica

[146] See pp. 104–5 above, and also nn. 3 and 10.
[147] *SEHRE* 699, n. 44.

on the reverse of which a camel was represented.[148] It may well be that Lollius had himself introduced the camel into Cyrenaica, and that he struck the coin to commemorate this. Whether that be so or not, Demougeot is unquestionably right in taking the passage in the *Bellum Africum* and the minting of the coin, and of a somewhat later coin, also with a camel on the reverse, minted by a descendant of Lollius, as definite proofs of the presence of the camel in North Africa as early as the closing years of the pre-Christian era.

The camel, once introduced, increased greatly in numbers, being used both as a draught animal and as a beast of burden, and serving for communication between the trading cities of the coast and the interior of Africa, perhaps more especially the Fezzan.[149] Rostovtzeff believed that after the introduction of the camel, trade with equatorial Africa ("the Congo region") reached great proportions.[150] It may be so, but we should remember that ivory, wild beasts, ostrich feathers, negro slaves, etc., could all be obtained in abundance at the time of which we are speaking from the fringes of the desert, from the Fezzan, and from the nearer oases. If the North African elephant was becoming somewhat rarer by the fourth century after Christ,[151] it had certainly been an abundant source of ivory — some also was obtained from

---

[148] It seems probable that Lollius Palicanus is meant. He was proconsul of Crete and Cyrenaica, and there is some reason to believe that his *praenomen* was Marcus. If so, though, and if the date of the minting of the coin is given correctly, then we must suppose that he held this office earlier than 22 B.C., the earliest date hitherto considered probable. See *RE* XIII 1391–92.

[149] *SEHRE* 66, 324, 335–39; Demougeot, "Le chameau," 41; Sir Mortimer Wheeler, *Rome Beyond the Imperial Frontiers* (New York 1955) 95–111.

[150] *SEHRE* 335.

[151] *RE* V 2356.

India and from the Sudan by way of Egypt — until then.[152] As for negro slaves, it is horribly certain that in the nineteenth century Arab traders marched many from Central Africa to the ports on the Barbary Coast — less certain, we Americans may reflect, that the desert marches were more horrible or more often fatal than the amenities of the middle passage — but in late classical times the Berbers, pressing southwards into the nearer oases, would have found negroid populations there that would more easily have served their purposes.[153] We need not look further than the letters of Synesius[154] to read of the hunting and export of ostriches, and I myself remember seeing as a child specimens of the "Numidian lion" kept, in cruelly small cages, in the zoo in Central Park in New York. Nevertheless, if Herodotus, long before the appearance of the camel in North Africa, was able to obtain by hearsay correct, if limited, information about the region that lay south of the great desert,[155] it stands to reason that the crossing should have been made with increasing frequency as camels became more numerous, and as the cameleers learned the desert routes and waterpoints.

Sir Mortimer Wheeler[156] calls our attention to a very curious discovery that points in this direction. At the western end of the wild mountains of the Hoggar, not far from the

---

[152] *RE* V 2358.

[153] *RE* XVII 1230–34; *Encicl. Ital.* XXX 448.

[154] *Epist.* 129, 133.

[155] See above, p. 108 and n. 9.

[156] *Rome Beyond the Imperial Frontiers*, 107–11. I have unfortunately not been able to consult the works cited by him: E. M. Gautier and M. Reygasse, "Le Monument de Tin-Hinan," *Annales de l'Académie des Sciences coloniales* 7 (Paris 1934), and M. Reygasse, *Monuments funéraires préislamiques de l'Afrique du Nord* (Paris 1950) 88ff.

oasis of Abalessa, and just about halfway between the Fezzan and Timbuktoo, the remains of a small fortified edifice crown a low hill between two wadis. The Tuaregs say that this was the residence of their ancestress Tin Hinan, a lady of noble birth who came to this region from Tafilalet — an oasis south of the Great Atlas in far-off Morocco — on a superb white camel, accompanied by a resourceful and faithful serving woman and a number of slaves. Excavation brought to light, under the floor of one of the rooms or courts (the roofs have vanished), a tomb containing a female skeleton lying on a bed or couch of carved wood. There were remains of matting, and two iron pins which had perhaps pinned some cloth by the left shoulder; unfortunately, the cloth crumbled to dust upon exposure. There were quantities of beads of gold, silver, agate and other hard stones, antimony, glass, etc., that had evidently, from the positions in which they were found, been parts of bracelets, anklets, and necklaces. There were also baskets that had contained dates and grain, together with two wooden bowls. There was a gold ring, and there was a statue of polished gypsum in the form of a grotesquely developed woman, evidently a fertility charm. None of these objects seems to have been of identifiable date or place of origin. But there were also some fragments of glass cut in a geometric pattern characteristic of the third or fourth centuries, and there were "traces of a coin of Constantine the Great." In another chamber, there was a pottery lamp of the type of Roman lamps of the third century after Christ. In one place, a camel and some other animal were scratched on an interior surface.

The bones and the other relics from the site are now to be found at the Museum of the Bardo in Algiers.

Of this discovery, Sir Mortimer writes: "In the absence of comparable relics within hundreds of miles of Tin Hinan, it is impossible at present to put her fortlet and tomb into a wider context. The Fezzan is the nearest known spot whence Roman goods such as the lamp and glass could have been obtained, but reason — if such be expected for an isolated occurrence — is lacking. To postulate that the structure may have been a rather superior blockhouse on a supposititious trade-route is a mere guess. We may be content to leave Tin Hinan in geographical suspense midway between the Roman provinces and Timbuktoo, and to think of her, perhaps, as a Lady Hester Stanhope of another age." Sir Mortimer is right. Still, building, skeleton, and legend all exist, and with them objects of unmistakenly Mediterranean origin.

So much for the use of camels for peaceful purposes. The introduction of the animal was also of great military importance: possession of herds of camels greatly strengthened the position of the nomadic tribes beyond the frontiers. Able to migrate more easily over wider ranges, the nomads could, we may feel certain, take control of more oases and exact more food and other tribute from those who cultivated them, and so increase their own numbers either by natural growth or by amalgamation. These growing tribes, too, coming from greater distances, could fall upon the settled countryside without warning and, if resistance developed, vanish into the desert far beyond pursuit by cavalry or foot soldiers. Obviously, the coming of the camel to North Africa was not to be without drawbacks for the settled population.

When, though, did the "grands nomades chameliers" first become a serious scourge? An inscription near Thebes of the time of Hadrian tells us of a Sulpicius Serenus who made war against the Agriophages, a tribe living between Thebes and Berenice. He slew most of them, and captured their camels.[157] This, though, was in the far south of Egypt between the valley of the Nile and the Red Sea, a very long way from Cyrenaica and North Africa.

Christian Courtois writes[158] that the "nomades chameliers" appeared in North Africa as early as the extreme end of the third century after Christ, citing Corippus' mention of the wars of the emperor Maximian against the Laguantan or Ilaguas.[159] Corippus does indeed refer to the wars of Maximian against the Laguantan in the passages cited — the Laguantan of a later day are encouraging themselves by remembering the victories of their ancestors — but he does not mention the use of the camel at that time by either side. It is in his accounts of the wars, two and a half centuries later — between Iohannes, the *magister militum* of Justinian and the Laguantan and other native tribes — that he writes of the nomads encamping within a circle formed by their camels and defending themselves from their attackers from between the legs of these living ramparts.[160] One supposes

[157] Demougeot, "Le chameau," 243. See also *RE* I 896; IV A 862–63.

[158] *Les Vandales et l'Afrique du Nord* (Paris 1955) 103–4.

[159] *Iohannidos* I 480–82, IV–V 822–24, VII 530ff, in *MGHAA* III pars posterio 14, 56, 94. The citations are those of Courtois.

[160] *Iohannidos* II 93; IV–V 598, 1021. Cf. Procopius, *Hist.* 3.8.25–28 4.11.17–54. It is from Procopius that we hear in detail about these tactics, how effective they were against cavalry, how vulnerable to infantry.

that the camels were protected from arrows and darts by heavy coverings of hides or woven materials such as nomads would use for their tents or for carrying their belongings.[161]

The beginnings of such a change would of course be gradual, and perhaps not immediately noticed by contemporary historians. Nevertheless, we do have some hints. Ammianus Marcellinus refers to the Austoriani as a Mauritanian tribe,[162] and tells us[163] that during the reign of Jovian, they raided the countryside near Leptis for three days but did not dare to approach the city. At the beginning of the reign of Valentinian and Valens — that is, very shortly afterward — he tells us[164] that they were ravaging Africa.[165] A little later,[166] Ammianus tells us that they raided the territories of Leptis and Oea for the second time. Not being seriously opposed, they soon returned a third time, apparently in greater numbers, since they now felt strong enough to blockade Leptis itself for eight days and actually to assault the walls of the city. Their mobility, their increasing strength, and the ease with which they seem to have escaped

---

[161] Cf. *Encycl. Brit.* V (11th ed. 1910), Plate I opposite p. 392, figures 1 and 2. It must be admitted, though, that Procopius (see preceding note) says nothing of the camels' being protected in any way.

[162] 26.4.5.

[163] 28.6.4.

[164] 26.4.5.

[165] It is true that Leptis was within the old province of Africa Proconsularis and was still within the Diocese of Africa, but Ammianus would scarcely have used this general term to designate the region around the city. Cf. 28.6.4, just cited, the use of *Tripolitani* in 28.6.7, of *Tripolitanis, Lepcitanoque agro et Oeensi, Tripolim,* and *militi disperso per Africam,* all in 28.6.10–12, *Tripolitanae legationis* in 15.5.36, and, finally, the contrast between the general and the particular at the opening of the account of the suicide of Remigius: ". . . Africanas clades et legatorum Tripoleos manes, inultos etiam tum et errantes, sempiternus vindicavit Iustitiae vigor . . ." in 30.2.9.

[166] 28.6.10–11, 13–15.

after their raids, all imply that the barbarians were using camels.

We have further evidence in the demand made by the notorious Count Romanus upon the people of Leptis after the first raid.[167] They had called on him for help and he had come with his troops, but the barbarians had withdrawn before his arrival. He remained for forty days but refused to pursue the raiders unless the provincials would supply his forces and furnish four thousand camels. Count Romanus may have been as corrupt as he is painted by Ammianus and have intended to keep a good part of the camels for himself. Yet, if we assume that the Austoriani were *nomades chameliers,* his demand, though perhaps grossly excessive, was not without sense. The nomads had withdrawn into the desert; the Roman cavalry and infantry could not hope to follow them without water and provisions, and camels to carry both. If enough camels and supplies could be amassed, the general was ready to lead an expedition into the desert to attack the barbarians in whatever oasis they had made their refuge; if not, he would withdraw, since he could neither follow the nomads nor keep his forces in Libya indefinitely.

At the beginning of the next century, Synesius wrote of the repeated attacks of the same tribe (Αὐσουριανοί) upon Cyrenaica. For a number of years they ravaged the countryside, retiring after one such expedition with their booty loaded on five thousand camels. They besieged Cyrene, and even the capital and port of Ptolemais, so terrifying the governor that he took refuge on board a ship in the harbor.

[167] 28.6.5–6.

In a moment of discouragement, Synesius himself wrote that he was considering fleeing across the sea because even Egypt was not safe: there was nothing to prevent an "Ausurian hoplite" from crossing the desert on his camel.[168] It has been acutely remarked that the round number of five thousand camels is open to suspicion.[169] Perhaps few statistics, ancient or modern, are above suspicion, but even so the figure given by Synesius is proof enough that the tribe had a good supply of camels, and his remark about the "hoplite" is evidence that the Ausurians used the animals to transport their fighting men as well as supplies. Finally, in spite of our skepticism of the figures, it is interesting to compare the five thousand camels reported by Synesius with the four thousand demanded by Count Romanus.

The same tribe (personified as *Austur*) is known to Corippus as an ally of the Laguantan, and as, like them, assembling its camels into circles for the defense of its camps.[170] They seem, though, also to have made use of cavalry:[171]

> cornipedum saevus laxatis Austur habenis
>
> . . . quo victus ab hoste,
> Austur equo fidens, tanta formidine curris?

We should note that this tribe, called Mauritanian by Ammianus,[172] is now referred to by Corippus as coming from the extremes of Libya.[173]

---

[168] See chapter 9 below, especially pp. 231–32, 246, 260 and n. 31, already cited, and n. 79.

[169] The Rev. Joseph C. Pando, *The Life and Times of Synesius of Cyrene as Revealed in his Works* (Washington, D. C. 1940) 139, n. 445.

[170] *Iohannidos* II 91–95, 209–10, 344–45; IV–V 814–20.

[171] Corippus, *Iohannidos* II 89; IV–V 815–16. See also Procopius, *Hist.* 4.11.19; 4.12.9, 22, 24; 4.13.14–16.

[172] See p. 141 above and n. 162.

[173] *Iohannidos* II 85–91.

It has seemed worth while to go into these problems in some detail not only because of their intrinsic interest, but also because of their bearing on the comparative isolation of Cyrenaica from the rest of Africa, a factor of the greatest importance in the economic, the political, and the military history of the region.

Among the more interesting works about Cyrenaica in recent years, we may cite: P. Romanelli, *La Cirenaica Romana* (Verbania 1943); Alan Rowe, *A History of Ancient Cyrenaica* (Cairo 1948), this work being *Supplément aux Annales du Service des Antiquités de l'Egypte* 12; Gennaro Pesce, "Il 'Gran Tempio' in Cirene," *Bulletin de Correspondance Hellénique* 71–72 (1947–1948) 307–58; R. Goodchild, "Roman Milestones in Cyrenaica," *British School of Rome Papers* 18 (new series, 5) (1950) 83–91, and *Cyrene and Apollonia, an Historical Guide* (Antiquities Department of Cyrenaica 1959); François Chamoux, *Cyrène sous la monarchie des Battiades* (Paris 1953), this work being fasc. 177 of the Bibliothèque des Ecoles Françaises d'Athènes et de Rome, série 1; *Cyrenaican Expedition of the University of Manchester, 1952* (Manchester 1956). In listing here J. Ward Perkins, "Christian Antiquities of the Cyrenaican Pentapolis," *Bulletin de la Société d'archéologie copte* 9 (1943) 123–39, I wish to call attention to its relevance to the subsequent chapters concerning Synesius.

CHAPTER VI

SYNESIUS, A *CURIALIS*
OF THE TIME
OF THE EMPEROR ARCADIUS

T HERE ARE certain persons who have great influence upon history, not so much because of their genius — indeed, genius is rare in the category of which we speak — as because they embody the spirit of the age in which they live; they crystallize its latent possibilities and create an era. Such were Augustus, Diocletian, Louis XIV. Ford, it may be, and perhaps Roosevelt, will be seen by our descendants to belong to this group. Synesius, on the other hand, not only occupies a far less important position than these men in the history of the world, but his relationship to his own time was fundamentally different in character. He seems at once an echo of an era that had already passed when he was alive, and a pioneer of times that were yet to come.[1]

This paper, which the author had the honor of reading before the Classical Club of Yale on November 18, 1940, is reprinted from *Byzantion* 15 (1940–1941) 10–38. In the notes advantage was taken of some very helpful suggestions made by members of his audience, and of references very kindly given by them.

[1] The translations of Synesius which appear in the text and in these notes are from Augustine FitzGerald (above, chap. 5, n. 3) and from the same author's *The Essays and Hymns of Synesius of Cyrene* (2 vols., London 1930). When references are made to letters, essays, hymns, etc., without mention of the author, those of Synesius are meant. The works of Synesius are published in J. P. Migne, *Patr. Gr.* LXVI, but the numbering of the letters in Migne is not in all cases the same as that in Hercher's *Epistolographi Graeci*, the text followed by Fitz-Gerald. See FitzGerald, *The Letters of Synesius*, pp. 6–7, but note also a variation from letters 80 (79 bis) through 101 (100). For the convenience of the

But every man is in large measure the child of his own day, and if anyone seems to posterity not to have been so, that is (at least in part) because posterity views the past in broad perspective. It sees currents of history that were destined to prevail, but it does not so easily notice counter-currents and eddies that still were strong, it does not observe weak spots in the bank, through which the stream, in some flood that was yet to come, was to carve itself a new channel. One ought not to make the mistake of over-emphasizing figures apparently out of harmony with the age in which they lived, but if one can succeed in taking them into account without exaggeration, a somewhat truer picture of the past will emerge.

By no means was every *curialis* a Synesius, but the central fact in the life of Synesius was that he was a *curialis:*[2] he consistently looked at the world from the point of view of

---

reader, the numbering of Migne is given in parentheses when it differs from that of Hercher and FitzGerald. Cf. above, chap. 5, n. 3.

[2] Cf. *De Regno* 2: "Cyrene sends me to crown your head with gold . . ." Such missions were curial functions. See *Digest* 1.7.8–9; also, the *Paratitlon* of Gothofridus to *Cod. Theod.* 12.12. The passages in the *Digest* and some of the laws cited by Gothofridus (*Cod. Theod.* 6.22.1; 8.5.23; 12.1.25, 36) show us that it was customary to grant such emissaries exemption from curial duties, at least for two years. This is consistent with the statement (in allegorical form) of Synesius in *De Providentia* 1.18, that the philosopher (Synesius) had received from Osiris (the praetorian prefect Aurelian) exemption from public services. It is also consistent with *Epist.* 100 (99). Synesius there wrote that he had been exempted from curial obligations by the emperor as a reward for the mission which he had undertaken, but that he had voluntarily resumed them, and now wished to be released a second time because they left him too little leisure. From *Cod. Theod.* 12.1.172, 177, we see that those who became *curiales* voluntarily, remained bound to that order. These statutes, however, date from 410 and 413 respectively; Synesius is generally thought to have become Bishop of Ptolemais in 410 or 411 (see below, n. 18, for the authorities on his life), so that *Epist.* 100 may have been written somewhat earlier. Synesius and the other texts cited, apart from the *Digest,* say nothing of a restriction of the immunity from curial service to two years; it may well be that, at least in earlier times, rescripts conferring immunity on legates were not, or not necessarily, limited to this term.

a *curialis* of Cyrene. If we study some aspects of his life and writings with that fact in mind, it may well be that his activities and his opinions will shed some light on the position and on the opinions of the *curiales* of his time.

Rostovtzeff, in his epoch-making book, *The Social and Economic History of the Roman Empire,*[3] has some most interesting remarks concerning the fate that overtook this class after the third century. He writes:

> The social revolution of the third century had been directed against the cities and the self-government of the cities, which had practically been concentrated in the hands of the city *bourgeoisie* . . . Diocletian made no effort to change the conditions which he inherited from the military anarchy of the third century . . . He took over the legislation of his predecessors, which tended to transform the *bourgeoisie* into a group of unpaid hereditary servants of the state, and developed it in the same spirit. The *curiales* (those who were eligible for the municipal council and the magistracies) formed a group of richer citizens . . . responsible to the state through the magistrates and the council both for the welfare, peace and order of the city and for the fulfillment by the population of all its obligations towards the state . . . An army of officials was on the spot to keep close watch on them, and to use compulsion and violence if any of them tried to break away from the enchanted circle in which he was included . . . It is no wonder, therefore, that the reforms of Diocletian and of Constantine . . . brought no relief to the people of the Empire and did not lead to any revival of economic life and restoration of prosperity . . . Oppressive and unjust taxation . . . the immobilization of economic life . . . the cruel annihilation, consciously pursued and gradually effected, of the most active and the most educated class of the Roman Empire, the city *bourgeoisie;* the steady growth of dishonesty and of violence among the members of the imperial

[3] 1st English ed. (Oxford 1926) 460, 468–70.

administration, both high and low; the impotence of the emperors . . . to check lawlessness and corruption, and their boundless conservatism as regards the fundamental principles of the reforms of Diocletian and Constantine — all these factors did not fail to produce their natural effect. The spirit of the population remained as crushed as it had been in the times of the civil war. The only difference was that a wave of resignation spread over the Roman Empire.

Ernst Stein, Ferdinand Lot, Otto Seeck, Bury, Gibbon, all paint the same picture. And rightly, because it is a true picture. We shall think of these words again when we deal with the relations between Synesius and Andronicus. But they present a panoramic view, and therefore necessarily lose details of topographical relief, thus giving us, perhaps, a somewhat one-sided impression. We should remember four things. First, it is unanimously agreed that the chief drawback to membership in the curial class was that its responsibilities were extremely burdensome from the financial point of view. Now, the people of the turn of the fifth century after Christ were neither the first nor the last to complain of excessive and unequal taxation — which was in effect what those burdens amounted to — and people who complain of the taxes are likely, even when their complaints are justified, to exaggerate and to refer to themselves as ruined long before they are so. Second, most of our information concerning the *curiales* during the later Empire comes from legal texts — the Codes of Theodosius and Justinian, the Breviary of Alaric, the Edict of Theodoric, and various passages in the official correspondence of Cassiodorus. But laws tend to deal with exceptional rather than normal cases. In America, our countless statutes do not mean that every contract is broken or that every American is a criminal; our laws, taken alone, would give a very revealing picture of American society, but one gloomier than would be drawn if other sources were available. Third, the later Empire strove to form a rigid system of castes, and of these castes, the curial class was one. But at all times, in every society, there is a tendency toward change. Some men have the ability to rise, and do so whatever the obstacles; others cannot hold their position in society, and can hardly be prevented from sinking to a more humble condition. A system that tries to stop such natural movements will always encounter difficulties; we cannot assume that all attempts to escape from the curial class imply that the position of the members of that class was, necessarily and always, intolerable to the mass of its members. Fourth and last, the curial class did in fact survive the reforms of Diocletian by many centuries. When Leo the Wise abolished it by his Novel 46, he was no doubt not so much making an innovation as recognizing an accomplished fact.[4] Still, if the position of the *curiales* had been so hopeless as it has been painted as early as the time of Diocletian, the class would scarcely have survived even nominally until the end of the ninth century. In Gaul, Pirenne believed the curias to have disappeared in the confusion of the eighth century,[5] and Ernst Mayer tells us[6] of their continuance and gradual

---

[4] *RE* IV 2351. But see also G. I. Bratianu, *Etudes Byzantines d'Histoire Economique et Sociale* (Paris 1938) 122.

[5] Henri Pirenne, *Mahomet et Charlemagne* (3rd ed., Paris & Brussels 1937) 175.

[6] *Zeitschrift der Savigny-Stiftung für Rechtsgeschichte,* germ. Abt., 24 (1903) (1903) 211ff. On the question of the survival of the *curiae*, see also "Les curies municipales et le clergé au Bas-Empire," by J. Déclareuil, in *Revue historique de droit français et étranger* 14 (4th series, 1935) 26ff. A very illuminating

modification in Istria and Dalmatia until they insensibly merged into the form of municipal government prevalent in Italy between the eleventh and thirteenth centuries.

All this, though, does not affect the fundamental truth of the picture given us by Rostovtzeff; neither the cities nor, where they survived, the *curiales* of the later Empire or the Dark Ages could be compared with the brilliant municipalities or with the prosperous, cultivated, and patriotic *curiales* of earlier times. It does, however, go a long way to explain Synesius, to explain how it is possible that in the time of Arcadius we come across a figure that we might almost have expected to find in the age of the Antonines.

Synesius was a direct descendant of Herakles, through Eurysthenes, who led the Dorians into Sparta and founded one of the lines of the Spartan kings, and this august lineage was engraved on the public monuments of Cyrene.[7] If the family was no longer divine or even royal, it was still wealthy and well-considered.[8] Synesius himself, though not

---

analysis of the position of the *curiales* in the Empire in the East is contained in *The Greek City from Alexander to Justinian* (Oxford 1940) by A. H. M. Jones. Chapters 12 and 18 in particular bear on the aspects of the subject discussed in this paper. I must gratefully acknowledge my debt to the late Professor Rostovtzeff for his kindness in calling this most valuable work to the attention of the author.

[7] *Epist.* 57, at p. 135 FitzGerald and p. 1393 Migne. This "letter," as Fitz-Gerald rightly points out, is not a letter at all, but an address by Synesius to his congregation. See also *Catastasis,* at p. 367 FitzGerald and 1572 Migne. The Catastasis, conversely, seems to be, not an address, but a letter. See FitzGerald, *Essays and Hymns of Synesius,* II 475–76.

[8] Euoptius, the brother of Synesius, owned a property, perhaps near the port of Phycus, which was famous for its garden, in which silphium was still grown. See *Epist.* 106, 114, 132 (131). He evidently took a considerable part in the political life of Cyrene. See *Epist.* 50, 93 (92), and 95 (94). He was made a *decurio,* but was not willing to accept office unless his mother-in-law was excused from certain obligations not very clearly defined by Synesius. He left the province while Synesius tried to arrange the matter for him. See *Epist.* 93 (92). To judge from the tone of Synesius, no very serious difficulty was to be expected. This letter is a most curious commentary on the operation of such laws as *Cod. Theod.*

extremely rich, was at least very well off: he certainly had

12.1.16 (*Cod. Iust.* 10.32.18); 12.1.161 (*Cod. Iust.* 10.32.51), etc. It is probable that Euoptius, like his brother, became bishop of Ptolemais; a Euoptius, bishop of Ptolemais, took a prominent part in the Council of Ephesus, and enjoyed the esteem of Cyril of Alexandria. See Smith and Wace, *A Dictionary of Christian Biography* (London 1880) II 430; H. Druon, *Oeuvres de Synésius* (Paris 1878) 10.

Stratonice, a sister of Synesius, was married to a member of the imperial guard (ὑπασπιστής). See *Epist.* 75.

Herodes, a cousin, was born of parents of senatorial rank, and himself, while still young, held the office of *praeses*. It has often been said that the family of Herodes was of curial rank. See *RE* VIII 921; Druon (as above) 455 and note; George Grützmacher, *Synesios von Kyrene, ein Charakterbild aus dem Untergang des Hellenentums* (Leipzig 1913) 112. This seems quite inconsistent with the Greek of *Epist.* 38. Synesius writes: ὅστις ἐκ προγόνων λαμπρότατος ὤν, καὶ τὴν πατρῴαν βῶλον ὑποτελῆ τῇ συγκλήτῳ διαδεξάμενος, ἐπειδὴ γέγονεν ἡγεμών, ἀξιοῦται συντελεῖν ὥσπερ οἱ νεόβουλαι, καὶ γενέσθαι διπλοῦς λειτουργός· τὸ μέν τι διὰ τὴν οὐσίαν, τὸ δὲ δι' ἣν ἦρξεν ἀρχήν. The word λαμπρότατος is a clear translation of *clarissimus,* and means of senatorial, not of curial, rank. Συγκλήτῳ, also, can refer only to the imperial senate, not to the *curia* of Cyrene. In *Epist.* 19 and 21, for example, Synesius refers to the *curia* of Alexandria as τοῦ βουλευτηρίου and as τῷ τῆς μεγάλης Ἀλεξανδρείας βουλευτηρίῳ. As for the office held by Herodes, the Greek word used is ἡγεμών. FitzGerald, *Letters of Synesius,* 110 n. 1, following Petavius, takes this to mean *dux. Epist.* 21 is headed τῷ ἡγεμόνι, and in this instance, FitzGerald translates "To the Governor." In *Epist.* 62, the same heading occurs again, and this time FitzGerald is uncertain whether to render it "To the General" or "To the Governor." The normal usage of the time is probably shown by the Greek heading of the *Catastasis* (Migne, *Patr. Gr.* LXVI 1565): ΣΥΝΕΣΙΟΥ ΤΟΥ ΚΥΡΗΝΑΙΟΥ ΚΑΤΑΣΤΑΣΙΣ ῥηθεῖσα ἐπὶ τῇ μεγίστῃ τῶν βαρβάρων ἐφόδῳ, ἡγεμονεύοντος Γενναδίου, καὶ Δουκὸς ὄντος Ἰννοκεντίου. But this of course cannot be relied upon to show the usage of Synesius himself, since it was obviously by the publisher of the address. Difficulty arises only from *Epist.* 62. This was written in praise of a certain Marcellinus, and apparently addressed to him, under, as we have seen, the heading τῷ ἡγεμόνι. Seeck and Ensslin, perhaps influenced by this heading, state that Marcellinus held the office of *praeses.* See *RE* XIV 1444, and Seeck, "Studien zu Synesios," *Philologus* 52 (1894) 442–83, especially 471 and 479. But the contents of the letter seem to establish that Marcellinus was a military, not a civil, officer. But even if Seeck was mistaken, and Marcellinus held the office of *dux* and not of *praeses,* the heading of this letter would not establish *dux* as the proper translation of ἡγεμών in Synesius. As Seeck very rightly remarks (as above, 466), such headings as that of *Epist.* 62, were obviously added by the publisher of the letters when Synesius had not preserved the superscriptions among his papers. From some other passages in Synesius (see *Epist.* 94 (93); *Constitutio*), one is inclined to think that Synesius used στρατηγός to translate *dux,* though it is hard to feel certain that the word was used in a technical, not a general, sense.

For the ill-timed magnificence of another relation, see *Epist.* 3.

one large and productive estate in the Pentapolis; he probably had two;[9] he may also have owned lands in Egypt.[10] In Alexandria, he was the student and lifelong friend of Hypatia; he was the disciple and friend of the great bishop, Theophilus; he was highly considered by the senate of the city; he was on excellent terms with the *praefectus augustalis,* Pentadius.[11] When he went to Constantinople, he delivered an oration before the emperor; he was on terms of close friendship with such outstanding figures as the praetorian prefect and consul, Aurelian, who was later elevated to the rank of patrician; with Simplicius, *comes et magister utriusque militiae per orientem,* who seems later to have risen to even higher rank; with Constans, perhaps the Constans who was *magister militum per Thracias* in 412 and consul in 414; with the count Paeonius; with Marcian, the former

[9] The estate of which Synesius wrote so delightfully in *Epist.* 148 (147), was in the remote country at the southern extremity of Cyrenaica. The place was apparently named Anchemachus. See *RE* IV A 1362, but cf. FitzGerald, *Letters of Synesius,* 245 n. 1; the passage in the letter of Synesius might just as well be, as FitzGerald thinks, an obscure literary allusion. Whatever its name, this place, as FitzGerald points out (43 n. 1) can scarcely be the property spoken of in *Epist.* 95 (94), since that was so near Cyrene that the enemy were using the house as a base from which to menace the city. Perhaps a particle of corroborative evidence, apparently unnoticed hitherto, is found in *Epist.* 125. In that letter, Synesius urged his brother to enroll his peasants to resist the barbarian invaders of the Pentapolis. He added: "I myself enrolled companies and officers with the resources I had at my disposal. I am collecting a very considerable body at Asusamas also . . ." It seems probable that Synesius was writing from Anchemachus or a camp nearby and that Asusamas was the name or the location of his other estate.

[10] The second part of *Homily* 2 is clearly a defense of the water rights of an agricultural community against the inhabitants of Leontopolis. There were several communities of that name in Egypt. See *RE* XII 2054ff. The wife of Synesius came from Alexandria, and he and his brother spent much time there. For Euoptius in Alexandria, see *Epist.* 4 and 105. From *Epist.* 93 (92), we learn that Euoptius was not in the Pentapolis at the time it was written, but we do not know that he had gone to Alexandria.

[11] See *Epist.* 10, 15, 16, 33, 81 (80), 124, 154 (153); 9, 66–69, 76, 80 (79), 90 (89), 105; 18–19, 21, 29–30, 127.

corrector of Paphlagonia; and with many others of whom we know less, though they seem to have been considerable figures in the worlds of culture and of politics.[12] In his own province of the Pentapolis, he was a great personage, playing an important part in the political life of Cyrene and of the province, supporting imperial officials, both civil and military, when they were honest and capable, and having much to do with the removal of others who were neither the one nor the other.[13] When marauding tribes invaded the province, and the imperial troops retired to the fortified cities,[14] it was Synesius who, taking the law into his own hands,[15] assumed the lead in organizing the resistance of the provincials.[16] When the situation became still more desperate, owing to incompetence and corruption among the military and civil rulers of the province, it was Synesius who was chosen bishop of Ptolemais; who led the fight on behalf of the *curiales* against the oppressive governor, Andronicus; Synesius who appealed, through his powerful friends, to the *consistorium*[17] for help against the invading barbarians.

[12] *De Regno; Epist.* 31, 34, 38; *RE* II 2428ff; *Epist.* 24, 28, 130 (129*), 134 (133); *RE* III A 203 (from the dates given here for the term of Simplicius as *comes et magister utriusque militiae per orientem,* it is evident that *Epist.* 24 refers to a subsequent promotion); *Epist.* 27; *RE* IV 952; *Epist.* 154 (153); *Sermo De Dono Astrolabii* (FitzGerald, *Letters of Synesius* 258ff, Migne, *Patr. Gr.* LXVI 1577ff); *Epist.* 101 (100) and 119; *RE* XIV 1514; cf. Grützmacher (above, n. 8) 61–72.

[13] See *Epist.* 37, 47, 57, 58, 62, 72, 73, 77, 78, 79, 90 (89), 91 (90), 93 (92), 94 (93), 95 (94), 100 (99), 110, 130 (129*), 135 (134), and 144 (143).

[14] *Catastasis,* at p. 1568 Migne, and cf. *Epist.* 130 (129*) and 133 (132).

[15] See *Epist.* 107.

[16] See *Epist.* 113, 125, 108. It is difficult to establish the order of the letters of Synesius dealing with the barbarian invasions, but these three and the account of the spirited resistance of the priests of Axomis (*Epist.* 122) appear to mark the opening stage of the first campaign.

[17] In the opening paragraph of the *Catastasis,* Synesius writes: ". . . since they who wield the sceptre of the Romans ought, themselves also, to know this,

In short, Synesius was a provincial nobleman of considerable wealth, extremely active, and successfully so, in the political life of his province, and of such culture and rank in society that wherever he went he was well received by the most important and interesting people of his time. He was far better born than Montaigne; his literary and philosophic works, though distinguished, were by no means on a par with the essays of the great Frenchman; otherwise, allowing for the great differences of time and place, the two men occupied comparable positions.

Without going in greater detail into the life of Synesius, the facts of which are sufficiently well known,[18] it is evident that he was a *curialis* who was not ruined, one who, though he passed through moments of profound depression,[19] was not crushed in spirit, one who spent his whole life in the active and successful service of his native town and province. Let us now turn to a closer analysis of two episodes in his life, which, we think, will prove particularly illuminating: his address to the emperor Arcadius, his contest with Andronicus.

The speech of Synesius before Arcadius was certainly one

do you write to whomsoever you may of those empowered to bring a statement before the council of the emperor. Let some one announce to this body, in brief, that until the other day Pentapolis was still a province valuable to an emperor."

[18] For brief summaries of the life of Synesius, see *RE* IV A 1362ff, and Bury's Gibbon's *Decline and Fall of the Roman Empire* (J. B. Bury, 5th ed., London 1912) III 482. An excellent bibliography will be found in FitzGerald's *Letters of Synesius,* and an even more complete one in the first volume of the same author's *Essays and Hymns of Synesius* (see above, n. 1). The introductions to these works are also of great value. For the chronology of the life of Synesius, two works are indispensable: O. Seeck, "Studien zu Synesios," and Georg Grützmacher, *Synesios von Kyrene* . . . (both cited above in n. 8). But even with the aid of these works, it remains impossible definitely to establish more than a few dates in the life of Synesius.

[19] Cf. *Catastasis;* also *Epist.* 10, 16, 46, 57, and 69.

of the most extraordinary, one of the frankest addresses that a monarch has ever been called upon to listen to. So much so that it has been doubted that it was ever delivered in the form in which it has come down to us.[20] But Synesius was a man of rare honesty and courage; we must believe, with Gibbon[21] and with Seeck,[22] that he did deliver the address in substantially the form in which it was published. The more so since, in a later work, Synesius wrote of his undaunted conduct in the presence of the emperor.[23] In any case, the speech as published was, we hope to show, no mere exposition of the personal ideas of Synesius but a political program of the first importance. To establish this fully, it will be necessary to quote from it and to comment on it at some length.[24]

[20] See FitzGerald, *Letters of Synesius,* 22. FitzGerald himself is not inclined to accept the criticism cited by him. Cf. also Grützmacher (above, n. 8) 38. Synesius was not, of course, independent of earlier authors. See *RE* V 874 and IV A 1364, and the authorities cited in those articles, especially J. R. Asmus, "Synesius und Dio Chrysostomus," *BZ* 9 (1900) 85–151. But it is no belittlement of the proven courage of Dio if one remarks that it was one thing to praise the military virtues before Trajan, and another to praise them before Arcadius. Seeck goes so far as to say that the frankness of Synesius was proof of the contempt in which Arcadius was held. See *Geschichte des Untergangs der antiken Welt* (2nd ed., Stuttgart 1921) V 266ff. And this point of view is shared by E. Stein. See Stein I 345. But it is perhaps easier to treat Arcadius with contempt at the safe interval of almost a millennium and a half than it would have been to do so in his presence. And the speech of Synesius, however it may have affected Arcadius himself, must have been extremely offensive to a party powerful at his court. See above, pp. 160–62 and cf. *De Providentia* 1.18.

[21] Bury's Gibbon's *Decline and Fall of the Roman Empire,* III 246–47.

[22] See n. 20 above.

[23] *De Insomniis* 9.

[24] The *De Regno* is published in English in FitzGerald, *Essays and Hymns of Synesius,* I 108ff, and in Latin and Greek in Migne, *Patr. Gr.* LXVI 1053ff. Since the quotations from the *De Regno* in this article are many, and since they follow the order of the speech, it would only weary the reader to give the exact page of each quotation; it will be easier for anyone wishing to check the quotations, direct or indirect, to follow the speech through. The author, as has already been stated, follows the English text of FitzGerald.

"Must a man abase his glance in entering here," Synesius opens, "if he carry not with him his city's prestige, as though he had no freedom even to open his mouth in a royal palace unless he has come from a community great and wealthy . . . ? . . . Freedom of speech should be of great price in the ears of a monarch. Praise at every step is seductive, but it is injurious . . . Cyrene sends me to you to crown your head with gold and your spirit with philosophy, Cyrene, a Greek city of ancient and holy name, sung in a thousand odes by the wise men of the past, but now poor and downcast, a vast ruin, and in need of a king, if perchance she is to do something that may be worthy of her ancient history. This very need you can remedy whenever you so desire, and it is for you to decide whether I shall bring back to you a second crown from my great and then happy city." Synesius then goes on to describe the greatness of the Empire and to praise the military virtues of Theodosius. "For him the soldier's art procured the control of Empire, you that Empire enlists as a soldier and virtue is your debt to Fortune . . . He whom the Divinity has most largely endowed with fortune, and whom, when still a mere boy, He has made to be called a great king, must choose all labour and abandon all ease . . . In truth the tale of his sheep makes not the shepherd more than the butcher who drives the sheep before him to the slaughter, . . . he who does not fatten his flock, but himself desires to be fattened by it, that man I call a butcher amongst his cattle, and I declare him to be tyrant whenever that which he rules over is a people endowed with reason." The "houses, cities, peoples, races and continents" of his empire will "have the benefit of earnest solicitude and forethought" from the true king; the true king will be in contact with his friends and neighbors. He will live and toil with his army, "so that not merely in semblance shall he call them fellow soldiers . . . What could be more shameful than to be a king who is recognized only through the painters by the very men who war in his defense? . . . how . . . shall the king understand how to use his tools, namely soldiers, when he does not know these tools? . . . nothing has done the Romans more harm in past days than the protection and attention given to the sovereign's person, of which they make a secret as though they were priests, and their public exposure in barbarian fashion of the things that pertain to you . . . Accordingly, this majesty and the fear of being brought to the level of man by becoming an accustomed sight, causes you to be cloistered and besieged by your very self, seeing very little, hearing very little of those things by which the wisdom of action is accumulated . . . Consider as ancestral institutions of the Romans not the things which yesterday or the day before came into the commonwealth when it was already changed in its habits, but those by which they won their empire . . . at what period do you esteem the affairs of the Romans to have been in the most flourishing condition? Is it from the time in which you have been robed with purple, and bedecked with gold, when you wear gems from foreign mountains and seas, placing them, now on your brow, now on your feet, now round your waist, now suspended from your person, now buckled on your garments, now used as a seat? . . . Or was it then when men living in the throng, blackened by the sun, led armies to battle . . . bearing themselves . . . simply and artlessly . . . ?"

Synesius, in these biting words, was making a direct attack on what used to be called "the orientalizing of the monarchy," [25] on this treating the emperor as a god, on his costly magnificence and seclusion, on the consequent passing of power into the hands of corrupt officials, responsible neither to the people of the Empire nor to an informed and active emperor, but only held in check by the intrigues of rival candidates for office. Rostovtzeff, speaking of the reforms of Diocletian, has well written: "The idea of the ruler as first magistrate of the Roman citizens, whose authority was based on the conception of duty and on consecration by the great Divine Power ruling the universe, was one which did not reach, and was not comprehensible to, the mass of semi-barbarians and barbarians who now formed the staff of officials, the army, and the class which supplied both — the peasant population of the Empire." [26] That is true. But its truth only makes it the more interesting that, almost a

[25] This theory has been much modified by later research. See A. Alföldi, "Die Ausgestaltung des monarchischen Zeremoniells am römischen Kaiserhofe," *Mitt. d. Deutschen Archäol. Inst., röm. Abt.*, 49 (1934) 1–118, and, in the same publication, *röm. Abt.*, 50 (1935) 1–158, the same author's "Insignien und Tracht der röm. Kaiser." Also, O. Treitinger, *Die oströmische Kaiser- und Reichsidee nach ihrer Gestaltung im höfischen Zeremoniell* (Jena 1938). I am much indebted to Professor Grégoire and Professor Rostovtzeff for these citations, which are particularly valuable in this connection.

Alföldi, in the second article cited, writes (58ff): "Dass das römische Selbstbewusstsein sich noch im 3. Jahrhundert gegen diesen barbarischen Prunk empörte, erweist die einmütig ablehnende Stellungnahme der Schriftsteller . . Sie verurteilen die barbarische Gold- und Edelsteinpracht in der Kleidung des Macrinus, empören sich über die nicht minder prunkvollen syrischen Priesterkleider des Elagabal, rügen sowohl Aurelianus, wie Diocletianus und Constantinus wegen der 'Erfindung' des edelstein- und goldstrotzenden orientalisch-autokratischen Herrscherkostüms." Synesius, in his criticisms, was as usual remaining true to the classical tradition.

[26] *SEHRE* (1st ed.) 455.

hundred years after the abdication of Diocletian, more than half a century after the death of Constantine, we should find a *curialis* who, speaking in his official capacity of envoy to the emperor, advocated in unmistakable terms that very idea. It is evident that the idea died hard, harder than we had supposed, and that even at the beginning of the fifth century, the *curiales* had not resigned themselves to its abandonment.

The true king, continued Synesius, would choose his soldiers and his officials from the natives of his kingdom, not from barbarians: ". . . the shepherd must not mix wolves with his dogs, even if caught as whelps they may seem to be tamed, or in an evil hour he will entrust his flock to them; for the moment that they notice any weakness or slackness in the dogs, they will attack these and the flock and the shepherds likewise . . . Even now some skirmishings of this sort are manifest." Gainas was fighting with very doubtful loyalty in Asia Minor against the revolting Gothic leader, Tribigild; Alaric was for the moment more or less quiescent as *magister militum per Illyricum*; the ambitions of Stilicho had resulted in extremely strained relations between the two halves of the Empire.[27] "Even now some skirmishings of this sort are manifest and certain parts of the Empire are becoming inflamed, as though it were a human body in which alien portions are incapable of mingling in a healthy state of harmony . . . Rather than to allow the Scythians to be under arms here, we ought to seek from the agriculture so dear to them the men who would fight to defend it, and we ought to . . . summon the

[27] *RE* I 1287; II 1147–48, 2429; VII 487; VIII 2280.

philosopher from his study, the craftsman from his lowlier calling, and from the shop its salesman. As to the crowd of drones who pass their lives in the theatres by reason of their unlimited leisure, we should beg of them to make haste for once in their lives, before they should be turned to tears from their laughter . . ." (We are reminded of Salvian's description of the sieges of Carthage and Cirta — the shouts of the soldiers battling outside the walls mingled with those of the crowds applauding at the games within.[28]) The barbarians should be excluded, said Synesius, not only from the armies, but from the high magistracies and from the imperial council. This infiltration of barbarians into high offices existed "in face of the fact that every house, however humble, has a Scythian for slave . . . that these fair-haired men . . . should be slaves in private to the same men whom they govern in public, this is strange, perhaps the most incredible feature of the spectacle . . . Remember that . . . there are . . . great and pernicious armies who, kinsmen of our own slaves, have by evil destiny poured into the Roman Empire, and furnished generals of great repute both amongst themselves and amongst us . . . Consider also that in addition to what forces they already possess, they may, whenever they will, have the slaves as soldiers . . . This fortress of theirs you must pull down; you must remove the foreign cause of the disease before the festering abscess actually declares itself, before the ill-will of these dwellers in our country is exposed."

Synesius, to use the modern jargon, was protesting against the "fifth column" and against "appeasement." More seri-

[28] *De Gub. Dei* 6.69 and 71.

ously, in asking for a citizen army, in protesting against the barbarization of the military and high civil offices, Synesius was once more faithful to an earlier point of view, again asking for the return to a state of things to which any permanent return was probably impossible. Indeed, some years later, we find him grateful and loud in his praises of the Unnigardae, barbarian mercenaries who had distinguished themselves in the defense of the Pentapolis. Even then, however, he emphasizes that they should be kept in hand and that it is important that for this reason they should remain under the command of a certain Anysius,[29] who, to judge by his name, was no barbarian. More important than the personal views of Synesius is the fact that, in demanding a citizen army, he was not merely voicing his own opinion; he was acting in accordance with a formal vote taken, apparently, in the *curia* of Cyrene.[30]

More still, this demand must have had wide general support: it was actually accepted, and an anti-barbarian policy was instituted in the East, which lasted throughout the administrations of Aurelian and Anthemius, some fifteen years. As Seeck points out,[31] with the exception of a few Armenian or Persian names, we know of no military officers in the Empire in the East during this period with barbarian names — they are all Roman or Greek. If, as we have seen from the evidence of Synesius himself,[32] the barbarian troops

[29] *Epist.* 78; *Constitutio.*
[30] *Epist.* 95 (94). Synesius does not tell us that the vote took place in the *curia* of Cyrene nor how it came out, but he has just been speaking of his embassy, so that one supposes the vote to have taken place in the *curia* and to have concerned the instructions of Synesius as envoy.
[31] *RE* II 1151. See also Stein I 362ff.
[32] See n. 29 above; cf. also Stein I 377.

were not done away with, we may at least deduce that the high-ranking barbarian officers were generally replaced and that the proportion of barbarian troops in the eastern armies was reduced. Seeck, in the passage cited, comments on the disastrous results of this policy in Cyrenaica itself and elsewhere, but it may be that these disasters were trivial and transient in comparison with what would have taken place if the pro-barbarian policy of Stilicho and Caesarius, the brother and rival of Aurelian, had been continued. If some Gothic leader had taken it into his head to adopt the policy later followed by Gaiseric, had seized some strategic point, and held it as the open foe, not as the restive ally, of the Empire, it might well have been that the Roman Empire would have disintegrated in the East as it did in the West, that there would have been no Byzantine Empire to preserve a large part of classical civilization and law and letters and to transmit them to later ages.

The reaction against the barbarians, indeed, was not confined to the East. It spread to the West somewhat later and resulted in the execution of Stilicho and the overthrow of his regime.[33] But the western portion of the Empire lacked the intrinsic strength of the East; its frontiers had been forever broken, and not even the repeated victories of Constantius, the brilliant general of Honorius, were sufficient permanently to restore the situation.

To return, however, to our subject, Synesius continued his speech with an analysis of the duties of the king in time of peace. "He will visit again and again in his tours as many races and as many cities as possible; and whatever portion

[33] *RE* VIII 2284; Stein I 386–87.

of his Empire he does not reach, even to that he will devote his attention in what is apparently an effective and excellent way." This way, said Synesius, the ambassador from Cyrene, was by receiving embassies from his subjects. By rendering himself accessible to embassies and conferring with them, he would familiarize himself with the needs of the most distant of his peoples.

Synesius then turned to the needs of the subjects which the true king would set himself to satisfy. "First of all, let the soldiers be enjoined to show consideration to the city populations, and to the rural also, and to be as little as possible a burden to them, remembering the duties they have undertaken on their account . . . Whosoever . . . keeps the foreign enemy from me, but does not himself treat me with justice, such a man as this seems to me in no wise to differ from a dog who pursues wolves as far away as possible for no other reason than that he may himself slaughter the flock at his leisure, whereas in his fill of milk he has received the due reward of his guardianship."

It is needless to emphasize that this is the point of view of a *curialis.* We see from countless sources, including other writings of Synesius himself,[34] how oppressive the soldiery could be in their treatment of the citizenry when the armies were commanded by lax or indifferent officers.

No less naturally does the next point come from the mouth of a *curialis.* "It is by no means a kingly trait to exhaust cities by levying taxes . . . the good king . . . can become a most harmless collector of these revenues by cancelling the inevitable deficits and by being satisfied with the imposition

---

[34] *Epist.* 130 (129*). Cf. also *Epist.* 62; *Constitutio.*

of such amounts as are commensurate with the means of the taxpayers . . ." It would be possible, argued Synesius, for the king to do this because, by pursuing the policy previously outlined, he would reduce his expenses both in war and peace.

The good king will order everything well so far as he himself reaches, and he will extend his beneficent influence further by making suitable choices for subordinate positions. "Let his choice of those who are to rule be of the best, and not of the richest, as it now is . . . the . . . man who has become rich by hook or by crook, and has thereby purchased his office, could never know what manner of man a dispenser of justice might be. For it is evident, for example, that such a one would not easily hate injustice, or show a contempt for possessions, nor would he fail to make the magistrate's house a place of sale for decisions in the courts.[35] It is little likely that he should look gold in the face with stern eyes, and pass on.'"

We shall have more to do with this topic when we come to the struggle between Synesius and the corrupt and tyran-

[35] Cf. *Cod. Theod.* I.20.1, of February 3, 408: "Honorati, qui lites habere noscuntur, his horis, quibus causarum merita vel fata penduntur, residendi cum iudice non habeant facultatem: nec meridianis horis a litigatoribus iudices videantur. Quina itaque pondo auri tam iudici quam eius officio atque honoratis parem multam adscribendam esse cognoscas, si quis contra praeceptum huiusmodi venire temptaverit."

This law, as far as through the word *facultatem,* appears also as *Cod. Iust.* I.45.1, and it is repeated integrally in the Breviary as I.7.1. The *Interpretatio* in the *Breviary* is particularly interesting: "Honorati provinciarum, id est ex curiae corpore, si et ipsi in lite sunt constituti, tempore, quo causae a iudicibus ventilantur, cum iudice non resideant, et litigatores meridianis horis iudicem non salutent. Si aliud praesumpserint, multam supra scriptae legis exsolvant." The *curiales,* far from having been ruined in the Visigothic dominions, remain so powerful that the governor is not expected to withstand without difficulty the corrupting influence of those of them that are actually holding office as municipal councillors.

nical governor, Andronicus. For the moment, it is enough
to say that such officials were one of the greatest plagues of
the *curiales*.[36]

Finally, Synesius prayed, "May you, my liege, be enam-
oured of Philosophy and real education . . . Would that I
might see you take to yourself Philosophy in addition to
Kingship . . . in this one word, I have summed up all."

In asking for a philosopher-king, Synesius had indeed
"summed up all." At the extreme end of the fourth century,
we find a *curialis* who is still hoping for the return of a
Marcus Aurelius to the throne.

It has been suggested that Synesius in this speech was
expressing the views of his patron, the praetorian prefect
Aurelian.[37] That is true. Synesius had advocated that the
emperor should abandon his hieratical seclusion and splendor, and return to classical standards of life. That did not
take place, but in the administrations of Aurelian and
Anthemius, in the practical regency of Pulcheria, in her rule
and that of Marcian, we seem to see at least an attempt to
attain the ideal preached by Synesius. The fifth century
could not return to the second century, but these rulers, too,
do seem to have tried to base their authority, in the words
of Rostovtzeff, "on the conception of duty and on consecration by the great Divine Power ruling the universe." [38]

Synesius had asked that the emperor should familiarize
himself with the needs of his subjects, both by travel and
by facilitating the reception of embassies. Except for an

---

[36] See, for other examples, *Cod. Theod.* 9.27.6 (*Cod. Iust.* 9.27.4); 11.30.32
(*Cod. Iust.* 7.62.24); 12.1.85 (*Cod. Iust.* 10.32.33); 12.1.186 (*Cod. Iust.* 11.59.16).
[37] See Grützmacher (above, n. 8) 38; Stein I 360.
[38] See p. 158 above.

occasional trip to Ancyra during the heat of summer,[39] Arcadius did not travel; but we find Synesius praising Aurelian for his detailed knowledge of the needs of the citizens of the Empire,[40] and we find a law, *Cod. Theod.* 12.12.14, of September 18, 408, addressed by Theodosius II to Anthemius, directing the Prefect to weigh the requests of the provincial legations and to submit to the Emperor all matters worthy of his attention. "Nam remedia fessis quibusque necessaria nostro arbitrio decernentur." Gothofridus, in his commentary to this law, suggests that it was probably made at the request of Anthemius himself, and of his councillor, the philosopher Troilus, the great friend of Synesius.

Synesius had strongly urged the de-barbarization of the army; we have seen that this policy was drastically carried through by Aurelian and Anthemius.[41]

Synesius had asked that civilians should be protected from oppression by the soldiers. His own later writings show that this abuse was not eliminated, but they show, too, that at least some generals would not tolerate it.[42]

Synesius had asked for lower taxes and for cancellation of arrears. Not only did he obtain relief for Cyrene and exemption from curial duties for himself,[43] but Aurelian went so far in his measures for relieving and assisting the municipalities of the Empire[44] as to earn the severe censure

---

[39] See Otto Seeck, *Regesten* . . . (above, chap. 1, n. 34) 291, 293, 295, 309, and sources there cited.

[40] *De Providentia* 1.12.

[41] See pp. 161–62 above.

[42] See n. 34 above.

[43] *De Providentia* 1.18; *Epist.* 100 (99).

[44] *De Providentia* 1.12.

of Otto Seeck.[45] We find his successor, Anthemius, taking steps to assist the *curiae* of the towns in Illyricum and re-mitting arrears of taxes for forty years past throughout the prefecture of the East.[46]

Synesius had asked for the appointment of honest officials and the abolition of the sale of offices. From his own later experiences,[47] we see that no miracle was achieved in this direction, but his praise of the administration of Aurelian,[48] though in exaggerated terms, was probably sincere, and he tells us that Anthemius promulgated a law tending to prevent at least some of these abuses.[49] We also learn from him that Andronicus, the worst official with whom he had to deal, was brought to trial for his crimes.[50]

But if Synesius was the mouthpiece of Aurelian, Aurelian was, at least to a great extent, the mouthpiece of the *curiales*. That the measures advocated by Synesius, as the ambassador of Cyrene, were precisely those which Aurelian and An-themius strove to put into effect, and that they were every one of them favorable to the *curiales* — this cannot have been an accident. And, as we have seen, even the replace-

[45] See *RE* II 1147.

[46] *Cod. Theod.* 12.1.177; 11.28.9. Both laws are cited by J. B. Bury in his *History of the Later Roman Empire* (above, chap. 4, n. 51) I 213. The former law allowed well-disposed persons of means to come to the assistance of the *curiae* of the Illyrian towns without rendering themselves liable to curial duties in the future. It thus constituted an exception to *Cod. Theod.* 12.1.172.

[47] See *Epist.* 130 (129*). Of his relations with Andronicus, the worst of such venal officials, we shall have more to say presently.

[48] *De Providentia* 1.12.

[49] In *Epist.* 73, Synesius tells us that Anthemius had caused a law to be made supplementing an old one which forbade anyone to administer his native province. This was obviously designed to prevent abusive use of the powers of the ad-ministrator. I have not succeeded in finding this law in the Theodosian Code, but *Cod. Iust.* 1.41.1 is obviously to the same effect. Cf. also *Epist.* 72.

[50] *Epist.* 90 (89).

ment of barbarian officers by natives of the Empire — the measure which might be supposed to have interested the *curiales* least directly — had been the subject of a formal vote, apparently in the *curia* of Cyrene.[51] It becomes clear that the two prefects[52] based their power largely on the support of the *curiales*.

Indeed, it would have been difficult for them to do otherwise. The personal power of the notorious eunuch, Eutropius, had been destroyed, and it was as a result of its destruction that Aurelian had come into power.[53] The Germanophile party of Stilicho and Gainas and Caesarius had next been destroyed — the speech of Synesius was an incident in this struggle; his *De Providentia* is a thinly veiled description of its course — and it was as a result of its destruction that Aurelian, after a brief eclipse, had been restored to power.[54] The imperial government in the East had, as Ernst Stein tells us,[55] always striven to avoid falling into the power of the great senatorial landowners, and we see that under Anthemius, and presumably under Aurelian, it was aware of that danger.[56] The power of these two prefects, then, could not have been based on any of the foregoing elements but must of necessity, and presumably from conviction, have been based on the elements that were opposed

[51] See n. 30 above.

[52] Anthemius succeeded Aurelian toward the end of 404, shortly after the death of the empress Eudoxia. But he had held the office of *magister officiorum* under his predecessor, and the philosopher Troilus, the old friend of Synesius, became his advisor. See Stein I 375. Cf. *Epist.* 26, 73, 91 (90), 111, 112, 118, 119, and 123. It is not surprising, therefore, that we find no evidence of any change in policy, at least concerning the matters with which we are dealing in this chapter.

[53] *RE* II 2428.

[54] *Ibid.*

[55] Stein I 101.

[56] *Ibid.*, 375.

to the forces which Aurelian had destroyed: on the support of the empress Eudoxia,[57] herself, amusingly enough, the daughter of a Frankish general; on the support of the Church, which disliked the barbarian officers because they were Arians;[58] and on the support of the well-to-do citizens of the Empire — the *curiales* — who wanted neither the outrageously corrupt bedchamber government of Eutropius nor the barbarian domination of Stilicho and Gainas. It would be an absurd anachronism to insist too strongly on this point, to pretend that the city-state and its dominating class, the *curiales,* played a part in the Empire of Arcadius and Honorius in any way comparable to that which they had played during the Principate. But that does not mean that we should ignore the evidence that as late as the reign of Arcadius the city state remained a reality in the eyes of the *curiales* and that these *curiales,* though harassed, remained an important factor in the Empire, that they held to classical standards, and were at once the agents and the supporters of a vigorous reaction against barbarizing the government of the Empire and shutting off the emperor behind a screen of hieratic splendor.

Perhaps the best way for us to keep our picture of this reaction — if we are right in seeing a reaction — within proper proportions is to examine one other episode in the life of Synesius. His contest with Andronicus forms the true pendant to his address before the emperor Arcadius.

At the time of this contest, Synesius was, it will be remem-

[57] *RE* II 2428.
[58] The downfall of Gainas, and ultimately of Caesarius, appears to have been precipitated by an attempt to assign to the barbarians a church within the City for their Arian services. See *De Providentia* 1.18; Stein I 361.

bered, no longer a *curialis,* but bishop of Ptolemais, the metropolitan see of the Pentapolis. In one aspect, though, and perhaps the most important aspect to Synesius, the episcopate might be considered the proper culmination of the curial career. As the *curiales* became weaker and weaker owing to the oppressive fiscal policy of the Empire, as their field of action became ever more limited owing to the increasing regulation of the *curiae* by the officials of the imperial administration, the bishops came more and more to be the local representatives of the people, their protectors against the abuses of the imperial bureaucracy, against the tyrannical and venal officials of that bureaucracy, and, when occasion arose, against the barbarians. Thus it happened that the people, who still retained a great share in the election of bishops,[59] tended in time of trouble to choose local magnates for the episcopal office, men who knew the local needs, men competent through birth, education, and experience to meet the problems with which they had to deal as the political as well as the religious heads of their communities.[60]

This, at any rate, was certainly the point of view of Synesius. In a letter written to his brother while he was still hesitating to accept the bishopric, he said: "He [the bishop] is a teacher of the law, and must utter that which is approved by law. In addition to all this, he has as many calls upon him as all the rest of the world put together, for the affairs of all

[59] See *Epist.* 67, 96 (95), 105. See, also, Sidonius Apollinaris, *Epist.* 4.25; 7.9. The letters of Sidonius are published in *MGHAA* VIII (Berlin 1887). There is an excellent English translation in two volumes, *The Letters of Sidonius,* translated by O. M. Dalton (above, chap. 2, n. 3). [They now appear as well in the Loeb Classics. For this also see above, chap. 2, n. 3.]

[60] No better illustration of this can be found than in the letters of Sidonius, or than the case of Synesius himself. Cf. also the very significant case of Siderius and Orion, mentioned in *Epist.* 67.

he alone must attend to, or incur the reproaches of all . . .
I know well that there are such men . . . I regard them as
really divine men, whom intercourse with man's affairs does
not separate from God. But I know myself also. I go down
to the town, and from the town I come up again, always
enveloped in thoughts that drag me down to earth . . ." [61]
We see this even more clearly in a very curious address made
by him to his congregation.[62] He did not at the moment
seem to be meeting with success in his contest with Andronicus, he felt himself unable to cope with these political duties,
and he asked his congregation either to accept his resignation as bishop, or else to appoint a coadjutor. "The past ages
made the same men priests and judges . . . Then, later . . .
God separated the two ways of life . . . Why then do you
move backwards, why do you seek to fit together those
things which have been separated by God, you who demand
not that we should govern, but that we should govern badly?
. . . He has need of leisure, who is a bishop and a philosopher. I do not condemn bishops who are occupied with
practical matters, for knowing of myself that I am hardly
equal to one of the two things, I admire all the more those
who are competent in both fields. Power to serve two masters
is not in me. Nevertheless, if there are some who are not in-
jured even by a condescension, they would be able both to
be bishops, and to conduct the affairs of the cities . . .
Therefore you must all choose the most useful man in place
of us . . . Let the man be chosen to succeed us, or chosen
to act with us, but by all means let him be chosen."

[61] *Epist.* 105.
[62] *Epist.* 57.

It is interesting, by the way, to notice that Synesius, who had once been relieved of curial duties but had voluntarily resumed them, and had asked to be again relieved, not because of any expense, but because they interfered with his need for philosophic contemplation,[63] now asked, for the same reason, to be relieved of the political duties inherent in his position as bishop. His was a nature which had profound need of leisure and contemplation, yet one which drove him again and again to active life.

Such, then, was the position of bishop in the time of Synesius, and as understood by him. The governor, on the other hand, was the representative in his province of the imperial government in all civil matters, both administrative and judicial. There were in theory considerable restrictions on his power, but in practice he could do nearly what he liked with the provincials — excepting always the great magnates, with whom he quite often could do nothing at all.[64] In theory, the provincials could appeal, but the vicar or the prefect or the emperor was far away, and a well-placed

[63] See above, n. 2.

[64] A striking example is found in Symmachus *Relationes* 31, printed in *MGHAA* VI (1) 304–5. Here we are told of a Valerianus, *vir clarissimus,* who repeatedly evaded the summons of the authorities, and finally used violence against an *apparitor* of the prefect of the City. I am much indebted to Professor Max Radin for his correction of my serious misunderstanding of one passage in this letter. See his review (as above, chap. 1, n. 1).

In *Nov. Theod.* 15.2, we hear of another Valerianus, a *curialis,* who, fraudulently securing the insignia of a *vir illustris,* and gathering a band of barbarians about him, burst into the *secretarium* of the governor of the province, sat himself at the right hand of the governor, cleared out the governor's staff, and proceeded to run things to his liking. This text is cited by A. H. M. Jones in *The Greek City* (above, n. 6) 201.

Synesius himself tells us of the bold contempt with which a certain Julius treated the governor, Andronicus. See *Epist.* 79. This Julius seems to have been a considerable figure in the political life of Cyrene, and a rival of Synesius. See *Epist.* 50 and 95 (94).

friend or a timely bribe could usually turn matters in such a way as to make an appeal ineffective — and an ineffective appeal could easily be not only expensive but very dangerous for the maker.[65] The situation is dramatically revealed by an edict *ad provinciales* issued on June 22, 386 from Constantinople, an edict of universal and lasting validity, as is proved by its inclusion in the Codes of both Theodosius and Justinian.[66] "Iubemus hortamur," say the emperors, "We order, we urge that if perchance any *honoratus* or *decurio* or landed proprietor, or lastly even any *colonus* or person of any rank whatever shall have been subjected to extortion in any matter by a judge, if anyone knows a judgment of law to have been venal, if anyone shall be able to prove a criminal sentence to have been remitted for a bribe or imposed because of vicious greed, if, finally, anyone shall be able to prove a judge unjust in any matter whatsoever — we urge, we exhort that he come forth publicly, whether during the term of office of the judge or after his administration, that he denounce the crime, that he prove his charge. When he shall have proved it, he will gain both victory and glory." *Iudex* is the word used in this law, which is translated as "judge"; it most emphatically included the provincial governor.[67] The word that we have translated "subjected to ex-

[65] For an instance of official tyranny and corruption, see the well-known story of Count Romanus and the people of Tripolitania, as told us in the *History* of Ammianus Marcellinus, 27.9.1–2; 28.6.1–29; 30.2.9–12; cf. also 29.5.2. An outline of this story is also given in *RE* I A 1065. Count Romanus was of course far more powerful than a provincial governor, but the story is so complete that it is perhaps the best instance that can be given.

For an amusing trick by which an oppressive governor of Lydia escaped the consequences of his misdeeds, see *Epist.* 127.

[66] *Cod. Theod.* 9.27.6; *Cod. Iust.* 9.27.4.

[67] See Heumann-Seckel, *Handlexikon zu den Quellen des römischen Rechts* (9th ed., Jena 1926), under the heading "Iudex" 3. The exception that proves

tortion" is *concussus;* perhaps a better translation would have been "shaken down." That slang expression gives us the true analogy. The emperor is helpless. He cannot bring his corrupt officials to justice for the very same reason that we are having such a hard time in bringing our gangsters to book: the victims do not dare to accuse the malefactors. "Iubemus hortamur," said the emperors, and one feels more than a literary elegance in the words. "Iubemus hortamur" — but it would have taken a bold man to heed them.

Synesius, though, was a bold man, and he knew Andronicus. Andronicus of Berenice[68] was a man of the most obscure origin. He had made his way in politics by, we may presume, not too laudable means: Synesius tells us that he had twice saved him from prison.[69] Now, he had bought the governorship of the Pentapolis,[70] partly with a view to making money and partly to settle old political quarrels.[71] Indeed, even before his arrival in the province, he had started to take his revenge on his opponents: his supporters had imprisoned a man and held him incommunicado until he had

---

the rule is *Cod. Theod.* 12.1.85 (*Cod. Iust.* 10.32.33), a law of July 21, 381. This law, also a good example of the difficulty experienced by the emperors in controlling the tyranny of the provincial governors, opens with the words: "Omnes iudices provinciarumque rectores a consuetudine temerariae usurpationis abstineant sciantque neminem omnino principalium aut decurionum sub qualibet culpae aut erroris offensa plumbatarum cruciatibus esse subdendum." It might seem that the legislator was here referring to two separate categories of officials, *iudices* being the one and *provinciarum rectores* being the other. The law, however, goes on to impose stringent penalties on any *iudex* who may violate it and upon the staff of such a *iudex* if it fails to restrain him, but it says not a word about penalties for its violation by the *provinciarum rectores*. It is evident that the judges include the provincial governors and that the latter are only specifically mentioned for emphasis, presumably because they were the chief offenders.

[68] For the story of Andronicus, see *Epist.* 57, 58, 72, 73, 77, 79, 90 (89); also *RE* I 2164.

[69] *Epist.* 79.

[70] *Epist.* 58 and 72.

[71] *Epist.* 72 and 73.

agreed to bring a charge of embezzlement against Gennadius, the outgoing governor.[72] It is significant that Synesius praised Gennadius for his mild and successful administration;[73] just as Synesius, the *curialis* born, stood for an administration based upon the support of his class, so Andronicus, the son of the fisherman, still hated the *curiales* with all the hate that had found expression in the civil wars of the third century.

If Andronicus did not even wait to arrive in the Pentapolis before commencing to persecute his enemies, Synesius did not wait for his arrival either before taking steps to secure his recall. While the new governor was still at sea, Synesius wrote to his friend Troilus, the advisor of the praetorian prefect Anthemius, setting forth in the strongest language his objections to the appointment.[74] In addition to the reasons we have already mentioned, he emphasized that by a law which had received fresh confirmation from Anthemius himself it was illegal for a man to be appointed governor of his native province.[75]

Andronicus on his arrival fulfilled the worst prognostications of Synesius. *Curiales* were scourged even when they were quite able to pay their taxes.[76] The Governor further used tortures, such as the thumbscrew, and instruments to torture the feet, ears, lips, and nose,[77] which it was illegal to

---

[72] *Epist.* 73.

[73] *Ibid.*

[74] *Ibid.* For the influence of Troilus with Anthemius, see *RE* I 2365 and the authorities (Socrates and Synesius himself) there cited. Cf. also n. 52 above.

[75] See n. 49 above.

[76] *Epist.* 79.

[77] *Epist.* 58 and 79. For an analysis of the laws regulating the punishment of *curiales,* see the *Commentary* of Gothofridus to *Cod. Theod.* 12.1.85, a law which we have already cited, and to *Cod. Theod.* 12.1.39.

use against *curiales* under any circumstances, unless of course they were accused of *crimen maiestatis* or kindred offenses such as magic. It is interesting to notice that Synesius remarks that such practices had not hitherto been known in the Pentapolis,[78] though adding that he wished he could say that Andronicus alone had made use of them — from which it is evident that he had heard of similar abuses elsewhere.

Among other specific cases of which Synesius tells us, was that of Leucippus. This man had had ten thousand staters of public funds stolen from him. He had repaid nine thousand, and wished to sell some property to repay the rest from the proceeds. But Andronicus, who was a personal enemy of Leucippus,[79] held off possible purchasers by threat and kept his unfortunate victim in prison and without food for five days, alleging that he was afraid that Synesius would try to carry him away.[80]

At about this time, Synesius received a letter from his influential friend Anastasius, in Constantinople,[81] asking help

[78] *Epist.* 58.
[79] *Ibid.* Leucippus is named only in *Epist.* 79, but he seems clearly to be the unfortunate man referred to in *Epist.* 57 and 58; in *Epist.* 79, it is said that Andronicus keeps off prospective purchasers of the property of Leucippus by threatening them; the same is true of the victim mentioned in *Epist.* 57; in *Epist.* 57, we are told of the theft of public funds from the victim, and in *Epist.* 58, it is said that the victim got into difficulties through misfortune, not misfeasance.
[80] *Epist.* 57. We must remember that we have only Synesius' account of these events. We do not know what happened to Leucippus, and there may have been some justification for the fear of Andronicus. Later, when Andronicus himself was in danger of condemnation, Synesius, wishing to help him, seems to have spirited him off to Alexandria. See *Epist.* 90.
[81] See *Epist.* 79. It is often said, on the authority of *Epist.* 22, that this Anastasius was tutor to the children of the emperor Arcadius. See FitzGerald, *Letters of Synesius,* 102 n. 1, and the authorities there cited. Seeck, however, takes *Epist.* 22 to mean that Anastasius had secured permission to legitimize his own illegitimate children. See *RE* I 2067. In fact, *Epist.* 22 does not seem necessarily

on behalf of the priest Evagrius, whom Andronicus was
attempting to compel to take up curial duties. Synesius, in
answering, took the opportunity to complain of the outra-
geous behavior of Andronicus and to say that the latter had
told Evagrius himself that it would be useless to attempt a
legal defense, since he, Andronicus, would give his opinion
against him. The letter ended with a moving appeal for help
against the Governor.

The letter to Anastasius, like the earlier letter to Troilus,
may, as we shall see, have had a material effect on the out-
come of the struggle, but in the meantime that struggle went
on. The unhappy Leucippus was taken out of prison, but
only that he might be tortured in the full glare of an African
noon. When Synesius heard of this, he went at once to comfort his friend. This is the last we hear of Leucippus.[82] The
silence concerning him, though, may be construed favorably:
Synesius tells us more about the misdeeds of Andronicus, he
tells of other victims; he would not have forborne to tell us
more of Leucippus if his affairs had not taken a turn for the
better.

But if the affairs of Leucippus did take a turn for the
better, the struggle between Synesius and Andronicus did
not. On the contrary, it entered upon an even more acute
phase. Andronicus, when he heard of the intervention of the

---

to imply more than this. But even so, it is evident that Anastasius was a person
of considerable influence at Court. Besides the two letters just cited, see *Epist.*
43, 46, 100 (99).

It seems reasonable to date the letter from Anastasius to Synesius at this point
because Synesius in his reply mentions only the facts that Leucippus is not allowed to sell his property and that Andronicus tends not to respect the Church.
If Andronicus had already uttered the blasphemous words that were to lead to his
excommunication, Synesius would certainly not have kept silence about it.

[82] See *Epist.* 58, for Synesius' account of these events.

Bishop, flew into a rage. In his fury, he called out three times that Leucippus had placed his hope in the Church in vain and that no one should be torn from the hand of Andronicus, "not even should he be embracing the foot of Christ Himself." Not only that, but he nailed to the door of the church edicts of his own, denying his victims the right of sanctuary at the altar and threatening the priests in case they should attempt to give sanctuary to them.[83]

This was blasphemy, and Synesius was a bishop; the Governor had afforded him an opportunity to carry the struggle into a new field. Perhaps encouraged by St. Isidore of Pelusium,[84] he drew up a decree of excommunication.[85] When Andronicus heard of this, he at once promised to reform. Synesius had little belief in his protestations of repentance, but his clergy were unanimous in urging moderation. Synesius therefore suspended publication of the decree.[86]

Synesius was right. Andronicus construed his moderation as an act of weakness and proceeded anew upon his course of tyranny. He demanded money of a certain Magnus, the son of a man of senatorial rank, but himself a *curialis*.[87]

[83] *Ibid.*

[84] Four letters of St. Isidore of Pelusium are addressed to Synesius: 1.232, 241, 418, 483. His letters are published in Migne, *Patr. Gr.* LXXVIII. No. 483 concerns a Cappadocian of whom we know nothing more than appears in the letter itself. No. 241 defines a point of theology, apparently in connection with Synesius' campaign against Eunomianism. Cf. Synesius, *Epist.* 5 and, perhaps, 45. Nos. 232 and 418 encourage Synesius to action. They might well have been written in connection with the Eunomian controversy, but they are perhaps applicable, as Grützmacher suggests (142; see above, n. 8), to the excommunication of Andronicus.

[85] See *Epist.* 58.

[86] See *Epist.* 72.

[87] *Epist.* 72, speaking of Magnus, says: παῖς ἀνδρὸς λαμπροτάτου, and again, ἅπασι τοῖς οὖσι λελειτουργηκὼς τῇ πόλει. We need not take the ἅπασι quite literally: the letter of Synesius shows us that Magnus still had an estate to sell.

There are many laws forbidding *curiales* to become members of the senate or

Magnus, who had spent much of his fortune on public objects, wished to sell an estate to raise the amount requested. A *curialis,* however, was forbidden by law to sell his lands without the consent of the governor of the province.[88] Perhaps by pure intimidation, perhaps under color of this law — if so, then a perversion of the law amounting almost to genius — Andronicus was compelling Magnus to sell the property, not to a friend who would give him a good price, but to a certain general, evidently a man acting in collusion with the Governor. But before the sale could go through, the unfortunate Magnus, who had been repeatedly flogged, died,

---

to acquire senatorial rank, before the completion of their curial duties. But such advancement was not, except for a few short intervals, forbidden to *curiales* who had fulfilled all their curial duties. If, though, it was legal under certain circumstances for a *curialis* to become a senator, it was the deliberate policy of the emperor (never very successfully pursued, as the constant repetitions of statutes and constant condoning of old evasions show) to make such advancement difficult. As Constantius very frankly says in *Cod. Theod.* 12.1.48: "Qui [former *decuriones*] vero praetorum honore perfuncti sunt residentes in senatu, redhibere debebunt quae ex rationibus fisci aut urbium visceribus abstulerunt, ita ut omnibus deinceps adipiscendi honoris huiusce aditus obstruatur." One method of making such advancement difficult and of protecting the interests of the *curiae* was the insistence, as a general rule, that if a *curialis* became a senator, his son, or all but one if he had several, should remain bound to the *curia*. In all probability, Magnus, though the son of a *vir clarissimus,* remained bound to the *curia* under these laws. For citations and analyses of the many laws on this subject, see the *Paratitlon* of Gothofridus to *Cod. Theod.* 12.1, and the excellent treatment of the subject in A. H. M. Jones, *The Greek City,* 193–96.

[88] *Cod. Theod.* 12.3.1 of November 24, 386, and *Cod. Theod.* 12.3.2 of August 9, 423, both substantially incorporated in *Cod. Iust.* 10.34.1. It has been stated by A. H. M. Jones (*The Greek City* 199) that for many years it was assumed that the provisions of the earlier of these two laws applied only in case of a sale by a *curialis* to a *principalis,* not to sales to persons exempt from curial connections, and that it was to remedy this defect that the second law was promulgated. The terms of the second law leave no doubt that such an assumption had been made and that the second law was promulgated in order to do away with it. But the terms of the first law were general, and there seems no need to suppose that the abusive interpretation was made long before the case which gave rise to the promulgation of the later one. The situation of Magnus would be somewhat affected by this, since the period we are discussing is precisely the time between the first law and the second.

apparently as a result of the tortures to which he had been subjected. "Up to that moment," said Synesius, "confiscation of property had not been ventured upon, and murder had not been taken in hand."

But now they had, and Synesius issued his decree of excommunication against Andronicus: "Andronicus of Berenice let no man call a Christian . . . but rather as accursed of God, let him with his whole household be turned out of every church." [89] The decree goes on to recount his violence and misdeeds in the field of politics but says that it is not for these that he is excommunicated. "The reason for this condemnation is, that first amongst us, and alone of our number, he blasphemed Christ both in word and deed." The decree then recites his outburst against Leucippus and his nailing of edicts to the church door. It concludes: "For these reasons the church of Ptolemais enjoins her sister churches everywhere in these terms: Let the precincts of no house of God be open to Andronicus and his associates, or to Thoas [a creature of Andronicus] [90] and his associates. Let every holy sanctuary and enclosure be shut in their faces. There is no part in Paradise for the Devil: even if he has secretly crept in, he is cast out. I exhort, therefore, every private individual and ruler not to be under the same roof with them, nor to be seated at the same table, particularly priests, for these shall neither speak to them while living, nor join in their funeral processions when dead. Furthermore, if any one shall flout the authority of this church on the ground

[89] The decree appears as *Epist.* 58; the covering letter to the bishops, with which it was finally issued, is *Epist.* 72.

[90] See *Epist.* 58 and 79.

that it represents a small town only, and shall receive those who have been excommunicated by it, for that he need not obey that which is without wealth, let such a one know that he is creating a schism in the Church which Christ wishes to be one. Such a man, whether he be deacon, presbyter, or bishop, shall share the fate of Andronicus at our hands, and neither shall we give him our right hand, nor ever eat at the same table with him, and far be it from us to hold communion in the holy mysteries with those desiring to take part with Andronicus and Thoas."

Here this paper ought to end. We have seen a *curialis* of the beginning of the fifth century, prosperous, well educated, still full of the local patriotism of the cities of ancient Greece. We have seen him stand in the presence of the emperor Arcadius and advocate — unsuccessfully of course, but perhaps not altogether unsuccessfully — a return to the ideals of the time of Marcus Aurelius. Now, this same man is confronted at home with the incarnation of the evils against which he has protested, with a tyrannical and venal governor bent on enforcing and exceeding the harsh laws which control and crush the *curiales*. What happens? This *curialis* born, Synesius, is not crushed. This embodiment of classical patriotism and culture has become a Christian bishop; this pupil of Hypatia, while yet her friend, is the disciple of Theophilus; this mitred descendant of Herakles thunders against the oppressor with the voice that, in the fullness of the centuries, is destined to bring an emperor to Canossa.

But Synesius was too civilized, too classical, too pleasant a man for us to take our leave of him on any such note of hyperbole. We have still space, perhaps, for one more letter, a short one, and in need of little explanation.[91] Synesius has triumphed. His letters to his friends in Constantinople, or his decree of excommunication, or both, have been effective. He is writing to his ecclesiastical superior, Theophilus, bishop of Alexandria:

> Justice has gone from out mankind. In the past Andronicus did injustice, but now he in turn is treated with injustice. Nevertheless it is the character of the Church to exalt the humble and to humble the proud. The Church detested this man Andronicus on account of his actions, wherefore she pressed for this result, but now she pities him for that his experiences have exceeded the measure of her malediction. On his account, we have incurred the displeasure of those now in power.[92]
>
> After all, it were dreadful if we could never take our stand with those that are prosperous, and if we were ever weeping with them that weep. So we have snatched him from the fell tribunal here, and have in other respects greatly mitigated his sufferings. If your sacred person judges that this man is worthy of any interest, I shall welcome this as a signal proof that God has not yet entirely abandoned him.

[91] *Epist.* 90 (89).

[92] It is evident that, just as Synesius' opposition to Andronicus must have offended the latter's supporters, so his rescue of Andronicus must have offended the latter's enemies. Now, *Epist.* 79 shows that Anastasius had at one time been a supporter of Andronicus (σὺ γὰρ δὴ φήμην ἔχεις προστατεῖν ἀνδρὸς λυσσῶντος). And cf. Seeck (above, n. 39) 480, and Grützmacher (141; see above, n. 8). But this same letter shows that he had then found it necessary to ask the help of Synesius against Andronicus on behalf of Evagrius (see pp. 176–77 above). He may well, then, have yielded to the appeal of Synesius and have taken an active part in bringing about the trial of Andronicus. If so, the break in the friendship of Synesius and Anastasius (see *Epist.* 46) was caused not, as Seeck and Grützmacher supposed, by Synesius' attack upon Andronicus but because Synesius rescued Andronicus from the tribunal which Anastasius had helped to set up.

CHAPTER VII

CHRISTIANITY
AND THE INVASIONS:
PAULINUS OF NOLA

🮖🮖🮖🮖🮖🮖🮖🮖🮖🮖🮖🮖🮖🮖🮖🮖🮖🮖🮖🮖🮖🮖🮖🮖🮖🮖🮖🮖🮖🮖🮖🮖🮖🮖🮖

O N AUGUST 9, 378 the emperor Valens was crushingly
defeated by the Goths and their allies near Hadri-
anople. Two thirds of his army fell, including the *magistri
militum* Sebastianus and Traianus, and Valens himself was
never seen again. His nephew, the emperor Gratian, had
been hurrying with his own army to the help of Valens and
had begged him to avoid a battle until their forces could be
united. Now, unable to cope with the cares of the whole
Empire in this crisis — the infant Valentinian II and his
mother Justina were of no help to him; indeed, the Arian
inclinations of Justina must, if anything, have caused him
difficulties — Gratian soon selected the Spaniard Theodosius
to be co-emperor in place of Valens.

This was an extremely bold choice: almost the opening
act of the reign of Gratian had been the execution of the
father of the new emperor, though it seems unlikely that
Gratian himself had been responsible for it.[1] Gratian's bold-

---

This article and the following one are reprinted from *Classical Journal* 54
(1959) 146–59.
[1] N. H. Baynes is inclined to hold Gratian's minister, Merobaudes, responsible,
though he suspects that his plans may have been supported by the eastern administration; CMH I 228–29. F. H. Dudden suspects the empress Justina, but cites
no authority; *The Life and Times of St. Ambrose* (Oxford 1935) I 172. W.

ness proved amply justified: Theodosius collaborated loyally with Gratian as long as the latter lived, and if he recognized Maximus after the murder of Gratian, there was probably little else he could do. At any rate, he protected the young Valentinian when Maximus occupied Italy and restored him to power when, having defeated Maximus, he might have kept the West for himself or ruled through a lieutenant. More important than questions of loyalty, Theodosius was certainly the greatest Roman emperor between Constantine and Justinian, a period of one hundred and ninety years.

Yet even Theodosius, though he defeated the Goths in a series of difficult campaigns, could not wholly undo the effects of their decisive victory. He was obliged to accept the Visigoths and their allies as *foederati* and to settle them in Pannonia and northern Thrace.[2] To be sure, there was nothing new in accepting barbarian tribes as *foederati* and settling them in Roman territory: at the time of which we are writing, a very great part of the Roman armies was recruited from *foederati,* and many of the commanders and lesser officers were barbarians too.[3] These Goths, though, and their allies were so numerous, so restive, and so strategically placed that they remained a most dangerous threat to the security of the Empire. If flatterers declared that Theodosius had strengthened the Roman State by swelling his armies with

---

Ensslin suggests, with great probability, that this execution had been ordered by Valentinian I at the very end of his life and carried out shortly after his death; *RE* V A 1944.

[2] See Stein I 292–99 for a concise account of these events and for references to the sources.

[3] For a review of the position of the *foederati,* see G. Humbert in DS II (2) 1210ff. The actual term *foederati,* however, does not occur in this connection till 406; cf. Baynes (see above, n. 1) 237 n. 1.

Gothic recruits and by finding new peasants to till the fields,[4] the emptiness of their boasts was shown when, after his death, the Empire was divided between his two weak sons, Arcadius reigning in Constantinople, and Honorius reigning in Rome. Discord between them, or rather between their domineering ministers, set the two governments by the ears.

The Goths took full advantage of their opportunity:

> Non patiar. Semperne Getis discordia nostra
> proderit? En iterum belli civilis imago? [5]

Alaric, the Gothic leader, plundered the Balkans and Greece. The Huns, too, crossed the Danube, made their way to Asia Minor, and even plundered Syria. Gainas, an Ostrogothic leader in the service of Arcadius, rebelled, and compelled the Emperor to allow him to occupy Constantinople itself with his barbarian followers. Nevertheless, these disturbances produced no permanent effect in the East: the eunuch Eutropius drove the Huns back across the Caucasus; Gainas was killed and his followers dispersed; Alaric and his Visigoths were maneuvered into attacking the western portion of the Empire, whence they never returned.

In the West, though, the consequences were profound and lasting. If the sack of Rome by Alaric in 410 was dramatic rather than fatal, yet the Rhine frontier had been denuded of its garrisons to gather troops to withstand his attacks and those of Radagaisus, another Gothic chieftain who in 405

---

[4] *Dicamne ego receptos servitum Gothos castris tuis militem, terris sufficere cultorem? . . . quaecumque natio barbarorum robore ferocia numero gravis umquam nobis fuit, aut boni consulit ut quiescat aut laetatur quasi amica, si serviat;* Latinius Pacatus Drepanius, *Panegyricus Theodosio Augusto Dictus* 22 (Baehrens, *XII Panegyrici Latini* [Leipzig 1874] 291).

[5] Claudian *In Rufinum* 2. 235f.

took advantage of the weakness of the Empire to descend upon Italy with a mixed and savage horde of barbarians from across the Alps. To be sure, Radagaisus was defeated, and his army perished in the mountains back of Fiesole, but on December 31, 406, great numbers of Alans, Vandals, Swabians, and Burgundians crossed the Rhine in spite of the opposition of Frankish *foederati*. Neither they nor the Visigoths nor the other Germanic tribes that followed them were evermore to leave the West. They produced few great conquerors — even Clovis, Gaiseric, and Theodoric are not of the first rank — but they were a corrosive acid which ate away the cement, already weakened, which held the Empire together: within a couple of generations they split western Europe and northern Africa (except of course Egypt and Cyrenaica) into barbarian kingdoms. Though the Empire in the East overcame the crisis, the Empire in the West fell.

The purpose of this chapter and the two following ones is to show how these events appeared to three well-educated and intelligent contemporaries, figures well known in their own times, but nevertheless not of the first order, and to describe their reactions to the crisis of the Empire.

Talleyrand once remarked that only those who had lived under the *Ancien Régime* could know what was meant by *la douceur de vivre*. The soldier-peasant emperors of the fourth century cannot have had much of the elegance and grace of the Bourbons,[6] but they did defend the frontiers, and they did establish and maintain internal peace.[7] The

[6] Magnificence they did have, as we see from the palace mosaic at Constantinople and from the remains at Spalato and Piazza Armerina.

[7] The not infrequent barbarian incursions, rebellions, and dynastic wars of this period were in no way comparable to the terrible chaos of the preceding century and did not, as a rule, affect very extensive areas.

civil administration was dominated by an opulent, secure, and highly cultivated aristocracy, the great landowning families of senatorial rank, many of which still bore names that had already been famous during the Republic and the Principate.[8] This group, at least, enjoyed a *douceur de vivre* in the fourth century that was in many ways comparable to that of the French nobility in the eighteenth century. To them fell, almost by hereditary right, the great administrative positions in the imperial government. This was especially true in the western, Latin half of the Empire, which was less populous, less urbanized, less deeply civilized than the Greek East, and so less able to supply adequately educated administrators from any but the upper classes.

Meropius Pontius Paulinus was born into this oligarchy in A.D. 353/54, or possibly a year or two sooner.[9] He was probably brought up mainly on his family's estates in Aquitaine,[10] and he was educated at the University of Bordeaux. We are

[8] See J. Sundwall, *Weströmische Studien* (Berlin 1915); Karl Friedrich Stroheker, *Der senatorische Adel im spätantiken Gallien* (Tübingen 1948); Arnaldo Momigliano, "Gli Anici e la Storiografia Latina del VI Secolo Dopo Cristo," *Atti della Accademia Nazionale dei Lincei, Rendiconti*, vol. XI, fasc. 11–12 (Rome 1956) 279–97. See also the excellent articles in *RE* under the names of the great Roman families. Cf. also, for the not always easy relationships between civilian administrators and military emperors, A. Alföldi, *A Conflict of Ideas in the Late Roman Empire* (Oxford 1952); and my *Iud. Quinq.*

[9] On Paulinus of Nola, see, among many other authorities, especially Helm in *RE* XVIII 2331–51; Pierre Fabre, *Saint Paulin de Nole et l'Amitié Chrétienne* (Paris 1949) [this book is fasc. 167 of the Bibliothèque des Ecoles françaises d'Athènes et de Rome]; Gaston Boissier, *La Fin du Paganisme*, written in 1891 (8th ed. Paris, no date) II 49–103. His works are published in vols. XXIX and XXX of the *Corpus Scriptorum Ecclesiasticorum Latinorum* (Vienna 1894).

[10] He tells us that his family took him to Nola in earliest childhood and that he first saw the shrine of St. Felix at that time; *Carmen* 21.349–50, 367–68. We do not know how long he remained there or whether he went there again before his return as governor. Cf. Gino Chierici, "Sant' Ambrogio e le Costruzioni Paoliniane di Cimitile," *Ambrosiana. Scritti di Storia, Archaeologia ed Arte Publicati nel XVI Centenario della Nascita di Sant' Ambrogio, CCCXL–MCMXL* (Milan 1942) 315–31 and plates.

given an excellent account of the pleasant, cultivated, somewhat artificial life at the university in the *Professores* of Ausonius. Indeed, not only was Ausonius himself the most distinguished member of the faculty, but he was a close friend
of the father of our Paulinus and actually seems to have been
the principal teacher of the young man himself.[11] It is perhaps worth noticing that in later life Paulinus deplored his
inadequate knowledge of Greek[12] and that Ausonius wrote
that there was little inclination to serious study of Greek in
Bordeaux:[13] the educated classes were ceasing to be bilingual.

Following the usual career of a young man of his class,
Paulinus was made governor of Campania at an early age.
Young, of very good family, immensely rich, aided by the
patronage of Ausonius, who had himself received every
honor from another even more distinguished pupil, the emperor Gratian — Paulinus seemed to have a most brilliant
career before him, both in politics and in literature. In fact,
his career was to be brilliant — his name and his writings
survive to this day — but it was to be that of a Christian
writer, an ascetic, a bishop, and a saint; not that of a Cicero-
nian, a Roman senator, man of letters, and official. So far
as we know certainly, his governorship was the last official
position he ever held, though there is some reason to believe

[11] His formal teaching cannot have lasted very long, because he was called to
Trier about 365, when Paulinus was still very young, to become the tutor of
Gratian, the future emperor. No doubt, though, he continued to follow the education of Paulinus very closely, by correspondence when they were separated, and
in person when they were both in Bordeaux. Indeed, he took very great pride in
the literary achievements of Paulinus, whom he complimented on having sur-
passed his teacher.

[12] *Epist.* 46.2. ". . . obwohl," says Helm (see above, n. 9), "man die Briefe 46,
47 hat für unecht erklären wollen." We should notice, too, that St. Jerome seems
convinced that St. Paulinus can read Greek easily; Jerome *Epist.* 85.3.

[13] *Prof.* 9.

1 . Consular diptych of Nonius Arrius Manlius Boethius,
consul in 487, father of the great Boethius

11. Capital from the *edicola* of St. Felix at Cimitile

that he may have been *consul suffectus* not long afterward.[14]

St. Felix of Nola, a confessor of the time of the Decian persecution, was one of the most popular saints of southern Italy, and his tomb, just outside Nola, was a great center of pilgrimage. The possessed, the sick, the halt, the blind, peasants who had lost their oxen, wives who wished for children, parents who sought husbands for their daughters, all came to his shrine, and with them came multitudes to marvel, to pray, to give thanks, to feast and be merry. Thither, too, came the new governor, the more naturally as he had estates in the vicinity. His conventional Christianity[15] was utterly different from the warm, indeed fanatical and boisterous, enthusiasm of the Campanian peasants; their living faith and the miracles that he witnessed struck an unsuspected but responsive chord in his being and were to have a decisive effect upon his life.

Not at once, though, or unaided. The revolt of Maximus and the assassination of Gratian in 383 marked the end of the political influence of Ausonius and must have at least

[14] It is often said, on the authority of Ausonius, *Epist.* 24.3 and 25.60, that Paulinus was *consul suffectus* (if *consul* at all, then *suffectus* because his name does not appear on the *fasti*) at some date before A.D. 379, but his governorship was a curule one and entitled him to six lictors, so that that may be sufficient explanation of the passages in Ausonius. Paulinus himself, though in later life he wrote of the days when people referred to him as *senator,* never mentioned having been *consul.* See Helm and also Fabre (above, n. 9) 22–25.

[15] There seems no reason to doubt that Paulinus was a Christian. Prudentius, as Tillemont reminds us (*Histoire des Empéreurs,* V [1st ed., Paris 1701] 304; Prudentius, *Contra Orationem Symmachi* 558), lists the *Paulini* among the great patrician families who were Christians, and our Paulinus, a close relation of Melania the Elder and the owner of estates in Italy, was in all probability a member of this family. Cf. Stroheker (see above, n. 8) 201. His parents were certainly Christians when they died, but we lack positive proof that they were Christians when he was born or that he was educated as a Christian; Fabre, pp. 16f. Unless, indeed, we may accept as such his statement that he was dedicated to St. Felix from his earliest childhood. So far as the writer knows, this has not been advanced as evidence elsewhere, but it does seem important; see above, n. 10.

impaired the immediate prospects of Paulinus. He retired first to Gaul and then to Spain, where he married a very rich lady named Therasia. The violent death of his brother, his fear that he himself would be executed and his property confiscated,[16] the death of his infant son, his associations with St. Martin,[17] St. Ambrose, Sulpicius Severus, Bishop Delphinus of Bordeaux, the encouragement of his wife Therasia, the memory of his experiences at the shrine of St. Felix — all these influenced him towards a more zealous Christianity. He was baptized by Delphinus and, somewhat later, ordained a priest by Bishop Lampius of Barcelona — this, as a result of popular pressure and without having passed through the lower orders. At length, perhaps late in 394, he and his wife renounced all worldly interests, and he began to sell their properties and to devote the proceeds to good works.

The very eminent position of Paulinus caused these steps to be followed with the greatest interest, some approving, many blaming. St. Ambrose wrote:

[16] We do not know the details. One is tempted to think of the revolt of Eugenius and Arbogast in 392, but there is really nothing to go on. Paulinus, moved as he had been by his experience at Nola, would certainly not have been inclined to favor the pagan cause. We know, too, that he later wrote a panegyric of Theodosius, a thing which he, no longer a layman, would have been most unlikely to do unless he had felt a strong admiration for that emperor. These are hints that he and his brother may have favored Theodosius so strongly as to have incurred the hostility of the usurper, but they are at most faint hints, not evidence.

[17] Sulpicius Severus states that St. Martin miraculously cured Paulinus of an illness of the eyes (*Vita S. Mart.* 19.3) and since, in addition to being the biographer of St. Martin, he was the intimate friend of Paulinus, his statement carries great weight. Paulinus, however, ready though he was to see miracles everywhere — or at least at the shrine of St. Felix — tells us nothing of this one. This is the more remarkable as he does refer to having met St. Martin in Vienne (*Epist.* 18.9) and since it is reported by an eyewitness that on his deathbed he called for his brothers St. Martin and St. Januarius (Uranius *De obitu sancti Paulini* 3, in Migne *Patr. Lat.* LIII 861).

I am informed that Paulinus, a member of one of the greatest families in Aquitaine, has sold his possessions and those of his wife, with the intention of bestowing the proceeds on the poor, and, having himself become poor instead of rich, is preparing to bid farewell to his home and country and kindred, in order to serve God more diligently. It is rumoured that he has chosen a retreat in the city of Nola wherein to pass the remainder of his days, away from the tumult of the world. His wife, who resembles him in virtue and zeal, wholeheartedly concurs in his decision. She has parted with her estates and follows her husband; content with the small property which he has reserved at Nola, she will solace herself with religion and charity. They have no children, so their great desire is to leave good deeds behind them. What will the nobles say, when they hear all this? That a man of such exalted family, such famous ancestry, such brilliant genius, such gift of eloquence, should actually quit the Senate and suffer his noble house to become extinct — this, they will cry, is not to be borne! They themselves shave their heads and eyebrows when they consecrate themselves to Isis; but if a Christian, out of zeal for religion, takes to wearing the dress of a monk, they call it a shameful deed.[18]

And St. Jerome, writing to Julianus:

Nec est, quod te excuses nobilitate et divitiarum pondere. Respice sanctum virum Pammachium et ferventissimae fidei Paulinum presbyterum, qui non solum divitias, sed se ipsos domino obtulerunt . . .[19]

Ausonius, most deeply distressed, begs him to reconsider:

ne sparsam raptamque domum lacerataque centum
per dominos veteris Paulini regna fleamus.

Haec precor, hanc vocem, Boeotia numina Musae,
accipite et Latiis vatem revocate camenis.[20]

---

[18] *Epist.* 58.1–3. In view of the length of the quotation, I use the translation given in Dudden (see above, n. 1) II 488.

[19] *Epist.* 118.5.

[20] *Epist.* 24.15f; 29.73f.

No doubt Paulinus himself found it extremely difficult to give up the duties and responsibilities entailed by his birth and position but felt at the same time that his very consciousness of his position, his wealth itself, made it impossible for him to become a true Christian without a complete break. Indeed, he practically expressed this in a letter to his old friend Sulpicius Severus:

> Atque haud scio an fortioris fidei iudicanda sit ista constantia et firmitas tui cordis, qua inter ignes non ureris, inter laqueos non caperis, picem tangis nec inquinaris, quam eorum, quos tu fortes putas, ego autem infirmiores arbitror iudicandos, quia non credentes infirmitati suae festinaverunt alienare omnia, quibus inhaerere timuerunt . . . qua negare non potes fortius esse manentibus quam alienatis rebus carere et spernere quod habeas quam non habere quod spernas.[21]

The very harshness of his farewell to Ausonius is, as Fabre with subtle sensitivity has felt, an indication that he could not feel safe while still remaining in touch with friends and with a way of life that had meant so much to him:

> Si placet hoc, gratare tui spe divite amici;
> si contra est, Christo tantum me linque probari.[22]

Settling with Therasia at the tomb of St. Felix, just outside Nola, Paulinus built a monastery for himself and his companions, a nunnery for her and hers, a basilica for St. Felix; he embellished the tomb and the basilicas that were already there; he built lodgings for pilgrims and strangers; he improved the local water supply; he built a church at Fondi.[23]

[21] *Epist.* 24.4.

[22] *Carmen* 10.330f; Fabre (see above, n. 9) 163. See also *Epist.* 4.3 to St. Augustine: . . . *ut de hoc mundo quasi de naufragio nudus evadam.*

[23] Some of these constructions date from his term as governor; indeed, he seems to have superimposed his monastery on an asylum which he had already built

We follow his new life through his letters and poems. He maintained long correspondences with his old friend Sulpicius Severus, with St. Augustine and very many others, and every year for many years he wrote a poem in honor of the feast of his patron, St. Felix, on January fourteenth. This date was that of the saint's death, so Paulinus called these poems *Natalicia* because they commemorated the birth of St. Felix into the life everlasting.

Not all his writings, of course, have come down to us; but from what he tells us and what we hear from other sources, we have a picture of a true ascetic, but a most urbane and pleasant one, a man who combined practical ability with the greatest devotion to prayer and good works, and added to both a very uncommon gift for friendship. He was extremely superstitious, but also, one suspects, ready to smile — and even, perhaps, to suppose that his beloved St. Felix was amused — at some of the miracles that the latter felt called upon to perform in order to edify peasants who undertook to get the better of the Saint by skimping their vows, by substituting a thin pig for a fat one, or by keeping for themselves animals they had promised to bring to the shrine to feed the poor.

Although coldly treated at first by Pope Siricius (perhaps the Pope disapproved of the irregular haste of his ordination, though that was not uncommon at the time; perhaps he did not approve of the more ascetic type of Christianity which Paulinus represented), Paulinus was welcomed by the people

---

for poor people. He felt that in such a location he and his monks would benefit from the prayers of those living below them; *Epist.* 29.13; *Carmen* 21.390. On the subject of the constructions at Cimitile, cf. especially Chierici (see above, n. 10).

of Nola, by the great fathers of the Church, St. Augustine, St. Jerome, and St. Ambrose, and by at least those that were more devoutly Christian among the members of the great senatorial families of Rome. He was encouraged, too, by the visit of his relation, Melania the Elder, who stopped at Nola to see him on her way back from Jerusalem. Poorly dressed, mounted on a wretched nag, she was accompanied by a large group of the foremost nobles of Rome, who, brilliant with every luxury and ornament of equipment and dress, had gone to meet her when she landed. She brought Paulinus a piece of the True Cross (of which he sent a sliver to Sulpicius Severus) and also, no doubt as a symbol of her approval of the ascetic life he had adopted, a woolen tunic. As Pickman puts it, he "stamped the ascetic life with a prestige it had hitherto lacked." [24]

A very agreeable quality to us is St. Paulinus' lack of interest in the more speculative aspects of theology. Although his letters are full of the dreary, farfetched Biblical exegesis typical of the period, his primary interest is in acquiring strength to lead the Christian life, not in discussing the fine points of the nature of Christ or of predestination and original sin. Indeed, St. Augustine once found it advisable to warn him against Pelagianism, and St. Jerome, who seems to have had the most genuine admiration for him, yet urged him to further study of the Scriptures in order that he might become as great a figure in theology as he was in letters.[25] Paulinus, though, was entirely frank in stating his position. When St. Augustine wrote to him asking him for his opin-

[24] Edward M. Pickman, *The Mind of Latin Christendom,* I (London, New York, Toronto 1937) 462.
[25] Augustine *Epist.* 186; Jerome *Epist.* 58.11. Cf. also Jerome *Epist.* 53.

ion concerning the future life of the blessed, Paulinus calmly
replied:

> Quae vero post resurrectionem carnis in illo saeculo beatorum
> futura sit actio, tu me interrogare dignatus es. At ego de prae-
> senti vitae meae statu ut magistrum et medicum spiritalem con-
> sulo, ut doceas me facere voluntates Dei, tuis vestigiis ambulare
> post Christum et mortem istam evangelicam prius emori, qua
> carnalem resolutionem voluntario praevenimus excessu . . .[26]

Later in the same letter, to be sure, he did consider the cor-
poral resurrection of the blessed, and he referred to the same
subject in another letter,[27] also to St. Augustine. Such speculations, though, were clearly of only secondary interest to
him.

All this seems very far away from the crisis produced by
the barbarian invasions, but now the time was approaching
when these events were to touch Paulinus directly. So far as
we know, the only possible sign of interest in worldly matters that he had shown since his retirement was his action
in writing a panegyric of the emperor Theodosius. That has
now been lost, but Paulinus himself says of it that he had
praised a servant of Jesus Christ rather than an emperor, and
Gennadius comments that Theodosius is shown to have overcome the usurpers (it will be remembered that Eugenius and
Arbogast had favored the pagan party) more by his faith and
prayers than by arms or his own power.[28] In short, what little
we know of the panegyric would seem to indicate that it was
composed entirely from a churchman's point of view and
probably less concerned with the relationship between the

---

[26] *Epist.* 45.4.
[27] *Epist.* 50.14.
[28] Paulinus *Epist.* 28.6; Gennadius, c. 48; cf. Jerome, *Epist.* 48.8.

Empire and the barbarians than with that between the Christians and the pagans.

What, though, when Alaric invaded Italy? When the hordes of Radagaisus threatened Rome? When Rome was sacked? When Nola itself was sacked and Paulinus imprisoned by the barbarians? How did Paulinus feel about these events? What did he think it his duty to do? What in fact did he do?

First, he hoped that the Church would lead the barbarians to the true faith (at this time, many of the Goths and other Germans who had long been in contact with the Empire were Christians to be sure, but Arians; many others, including Radagaisus himself, were heathens) and civilize them. Of his friend and visitor, Nicetas, bishop of Remisiana in Dacia, he wrote:

> orbis in muta regione per te
> barbari discunt resonare Christum
> corde Romano, placidamque casti
> vivere pacem.[29]

Second, he hoped that Italy and Nola and he himself would be delivered from the invaders:

> sancte deo dilecte, dei tu dextera, Felix,
> esto, precor, nobis tu munitissima turris.
>
> effera barbaries Christo frangente dometur.[30]

Third, he felt that under no circumstances whatever should the Christian use force, not even to defend his family or the state:

---

[29] *Carmen* 17.261–63. For an interesting comparison between the Arian Alaric and the heathen Radagaisus, see Orosius *Hist*. 7.37.

[30] *Carmen* 26.233f, 257.

Hoc tamen et repetens iterumque iterumque monebo
ut fugias durae lubrica militiae.

Ideo nec affectum nec patriam nec honores nec divitias Deo prae-
ferre debemus . . . qui militat gladio mortis est minister . . .[31]

Fourth, he felt that the Christian should accept the possibility
of being made prisoner and proclaimed that the soul could
still remain free and Christian.[32]

Not yet, though, was Paulinus called upon to put the full
measure of his preaching into practice: Alaric was turned
back temporarily; Radagaisus was captured and executed,
and his great armies were destroyed. Upon the defeat of
Radagaisus, our Paulinus burst into a paean of joy, attribut-
ing the deliverance of Italy to the intercession, not of course
of Apollo, but to that of St. Peter, St. Paul, and his own beloved St. Felix.[33]

But the principles of Paulinus were to be more sharply
tested. Alaric and his Visigoths sacked Rome in 410, and
then moved south towards Sicily. Melania the Younger and
Pinianus fled before him, accompanied by the aged Rufinus,
as well as by the band of virgins that she had drawn around
her. They stopped to see Paulinus, but this time the danger
was too great for them to stay and they went on to Sicily.
Paulinus must have been tempted to go with them, but no
doubt devotion to St. Felix and loyalty to the community

---

[31] *Epist.* 8.3.11f; 25.2 and 3.

[32] *Epist.* 8.3.22f; *Carmen* 26.20–28.

[33] *Carmen* 31. In this same poem he tells us that a group of the most distinguished Romans of his time had taken refuge with him. They were all connected with him through his close relation, the elder Melania. Enough of the
old patrician remained in Paulinus for him to mention that one of them, Pinianus,
the husband of Melania the younger, was descended from the P. Valerius Pu-
blicola who was consul in the Year I of the Republic.

founded about his tomb restrained him. A greater responsibility too, for it was in all probability just about this time, or a little before, that he had been consecrated bishop of Nola. The new bishop, protected by God and needing no earthly arms, must defend his people:

> nos crucis invictae signum et confessio munit,
> armatique deo mentem non quaerimus arma
> corporis . . .[34]

He himself tells us no more, but we learn from his friend St. Augustine that the Goths besieged Nola and, in spite of the encouragement of the inhabitants by the appearance of St. Felix in a vision, took and sacked the city. Paulinus himself was imprisoned and feared that he would be tortured, as were many other victims of the barbarians, in an attempt to make him reveal hidden riches. His Christian attitude under these trials was wholly consistent with the uncomprising principles he had advocated beforehand, and he earned the lasting praise of St. Augustine as a true citizen of the City of God.[35]

Therasia probably died shortly before the sack. The couple had the touching habit of writing their letters jointly, open-

[34] *Carmen* 26.106ff. The date of the consecration of Paulinus as bishop of Nola is not certain. St. Augustine, in *The City of God* (1.10), begun shortly after the sack of Rome but not finished until many years later, refers to *Paulinus noster, Nolensis episcopus* in describing the behavior of Paulinus during the sack of Nola. One cannot be certain that Augustine meant that Paulinus was already bishop at that time, or whether — which seems much less probable — he refers to him as bishop because, though he was not bishop at the time of the sack, he had become so by the time St. Augustine finished his book.

[35] Augustine (as above, n. 34) and *De cura pro mortuis gerenda* 16. As Fabre says (44; above n. 9), the Goths probably did not stay long at Nola and the damage done by them was probably superficial. We cannot be too sure, though: not much remains above ground at Cimitile today, and Procopius tells us of at least one Italian town, Urbesalvia, which had lain in ruins from the time of Alaric's invasion to his own day; *Hist.* 6.16.27–31.

ing them *Paulinus et Therasia peccatores,* and the last letter beginning with this phrase is thought to have been written in May, 408.[36]

It is pleasant to be able to add that, after this crisis was over, Paulinus lived for another twenty years or so in the exercise of his duties as bishop of Nola. At this period, the bishop was unquestionably the chief figure in the city. He was of course its ecclesiastical head. Not only that, he was also the most important judicial official; he was at the head of civic relief and welfare — of the distribution of alms, of the care of the sick, of the reception of pilgrims and wayfarers; he was the defender by prayer, by encouragement, by negotiation, of the city against the barbarians; he was its protector against rapacious officers of the State, both civil and military.[37] We do not find Paulinus having to defend his people against oppression by the authorities — perhaps his prestige was such as to make that seldom or never necessary; we do know that he successfully came to the help of an old priest of Capua, who had been driven from his house by some powerful neighbors.[38] We have already seen something of his activity in building ecclesiastical structures around the tomb of St. Felix, of his erecting buildings for the poor, for monks and nuns, of improvements made by him in the local water supply. Of his administration of justice, Uranius tells us:

[36] *Epist.* 45. One statement of Gregory of Tours seems to speak of her as still alive after her husband's consecration as bishop; *De Glor. Conf.* 110 (107). This of course is quite possible if Paulinus was consecrated as early as 408 or even earlier, and it is another argument for supposing that he was bishop at the time of the sack.

[37] See Sergio Mochi Onory, *Vescovi e Città* (Bologna 1933), one of the most fascinating books about the period from the fourth to the sixth centuries.

[38] *Epist.* 12.12; 14.4; 15.2–3.

sciens quoniam Spiritus Sanctus quantum aequitati et iustitiae favet, tantum suis gratiam pietatis benignus indulget; et ideo tenebat rigorem in examinatione iustitiae, misericordiam autem in definitione sententiae proferebat.[39]

His charity, as described by Uranius, was such that Onory sees in it no mere haphazard or impulsive giving, but a real organization for the relief of the poor.[40]

On the death of Zosimus in December 418, the succession to the Papacy was disputed. The emperor summoned Paulinus and other bishops to a council to be held at Ravenna to settle the difficulty. Paulinus excused himself on the ground of poor health. An imperial letter to him on the further development of the matter has come down to us:

> Fuit apud nos certa scientia, nihil ab istis sacerdotibus qui ad synodum convenerunt posse definiri, cum Beatitudo tua, de corporis inaequalitate causata, itineris non potuit sustineri iniuriam. Dilatum itaque iudicium nuntiamus, ut divina praecepta ex venerationis tuae ore promantur.

The second council, however, was not held, as the dispute was settled before the date for which it had been summoned. But, as Fabre, who quotes this letter, says, it is evidence that Paulinus had come to be considered the foremost bishop of Italy after the Pope himself.[41]

[39] See *Patr. Lat.* LIII 863.

[40] Uranius; Onory (see above, n. 37) 36f. This seems the more probable because of what we know of the care taken by Paulinus in the disposition of his property. See Jerome, *Epist.* 53 and 58, both addressed to Paulinus. From *Epist.* 58 in particular, it seems probable that Paulinus retained control of part of his property, though using it not for his private convenience, but for good works. Cf. St. Ambrose, *Epist.* 58, already cited. Pickman (see above, n. 24) supposes that Paulinus transferred properties from himself as a private person to himself as bishop of Nola (p. 249). This may well be true of his properties at Nola and Fondi; his estates in Gaul, those of Therasia in Spain, and any others they may have had, had probably been sold before they retired to Nola. See Ambrose, *Epist.* 58, already cited.

[41] Migne, *Patr. Lat.* LXI 137; Fabre (above, n. 9) 48.

In such operations, then, Paulinus spent his last years. No *Natalicia* have come down to us from this period, but that is no reason to suppose that none were composed by him or that he cooled in his devotion to St. Felix. He died on June 22, 431.[42]

In conclusion, one cannot bring oneself to pass over a story told of Paulinus by Gregory the Great.[43] When the Vandals sacked Nola and carried off the inhabitants into captivity, Paulinus spent everything on which he could lay his hands to ransom as many prisoners as possible. Then, when no more money was to be had, a widow came to him and asked his help on behalf of her only son, who had been taken to Africa. Paulinus himself proceeded to Africa to the Vandal court and, not revealing who he was, offered himself as gardener to the son-in-law of the king of the Vandals in return for the release of the widow's son. The offer was accepted, but Paulinus' gift of prophecy soon revealed his identity to the king, who sent him back to Nola, together with all the prisoners who had been taken from that city. The Vandals sacked Nola in 455 — and so far as we know, at no other time —[44] and Paulinus had died more than twenty years before, but the story is so typical both of his teaching and of his practice that one cannot bring oneself to characterize it as essentially untrue.[45]

[42] Uranius 12; Helm.

[43] *Dial.* 3.1, in Migne, *Patr. Lat.* LXXVII 215.

[44] H. Philipp, in *RE* XVII 814.

[45] Helm points out that one of Paulinus' own letters (50.14) tells us, if what he calls a very improbable reading may be accepted, that Paulinus did pass a winter in Carthage. Onory, p. 119, also gives the story some credence, suggesting that it may have befallen not our Paulinus, but a later bishop of Nola of the same name, Paulinus iunior. It seems however that this Paulinus died on September 10, 441, so that we should be forced to assume either a third Bishop Paulinus of Nola or else a sack of Nola by the Vandals of which we hear from no other

Postscript

In the preceding study, I might well have mentioned *Paulinus' Churches at Nola: Text, Translations and Commentary* (Amsterdam 1940), by R. C. Goldschmidt. This work contains a good plan of the excavations at Cimitile, reproduced from *Rivista di archeologia cristiana* 16 (1939), fig. 5. Goldschmidt differs in several respects from Chierici in his interpretation of the ruins; he translates the relevant texts of Paulinus, and he summarizes the *Natalicia*. The notes are elaborate and include comments on all persons referred to in the poems.

Paolino di Nola (Catania 1947; No. 8 of the *Raccolta di Studi di Letteratura Cristiana Antica*) by Giovanni Rizzi and *Humanisme et Christianisme: Ausone et Saint-Paulin, conférence donnée au Grand Théâtre de Bordeaux le 19 Novembre, 1953* (Bordeaux 1954), by Monseigneur Emile Blanchet, are both sensitive studies. Perhaps a more important one is *Paolino di Nola e l'umanesimo cristiano; saggio sopra il suo epistolario* (Bologna 1964) by Serafino Prete. Prete points out the especial influence of the letters of Paulinus on later Christian epistolography. He accepts letters 46 and 47 to Rufinus (the ones in which Paulinus refers to his own inadequate knowledge of Greek) as genuine but attributes these passages to the modesty of Paulinus; Prete

---

source. Another possibility might be that Gregory was mixing the Vandals and the Visigoths and that Paulinus was carried off by the Visigoths — or actually followed them south to secure the release of the widow's son. If so, though, we should have to resign ourselves to the loss of the picturesque episode of his working as gardener: Alaric cannot have done much gardening between the sack of Nola and his death at Cosenza. These pedantries, though, are secondary: we may both doubt that this captivity ever took place and yet feel that the legend, even in the matter of its incredibility, truly embodies the spirit of Paulinus.

believes that Paulinus did know Greek without being a great Greek scholar. Cf. above, p. 188 and note 12.

Chapter 7 and the two following chapters deal with the reactions of three members of the Mediterranean world to the double impact of Christianity and the barbarian invasions. It has not been our task in these papers to consider the effects of the Mediterranean world and of Christianity on the barbarian invaders. These two aspects of the invasions are nevertheless complementary. One is therefore most grateful for *Les Invasions: Les Vagues Germaniques* (Paris 1965) by Lucian Musset. This work, number 12 of the series *Nouvelle Clio,* is a concise but carefully composed history of the migrations, their effects upon the barbarian peoples themselves, upon the peoples and regions through which they passed, and upon those in which they settled. It is the more valuable in that it emphasizes the number of questions to which we still have no reliable answers and because it contains a most impressive bibliography.

The Conflict Between Paganism and Christianity in the Fourth Century, essays edited by Arnaldo Momigliano (Oxford 1963), though cited in the bibliography of *Les Invasions,* should be especially mentioned here both because of its intrinsic interest and because of its special pertinence to our subject. Thinking of Paulinus of Nola and Rutilius Namatianus, one finds a passage (on p. 12) of Momigliano's introduction particularly apt: "Monasticism is the most obvious example of the way in which Christianity built something of its own which undermined the military and political structure of the Roman Empire." It is in no way inconsistent with this to add that in the succeeding centuries, thanks to

Cassiodorus, St. Benedict, St. Columban, and others, the monastic *scriptoria* were to become the principal means of preserving classical literature in the West, and the monasteries themselves centers of comparatively orderly and comparatively civilized life in an age of barbarism.

CHAPTER VIII

CHRISTIANITY
AND THE INVASIONS:
RUTILIUS NAMATIANUS

॥॥

WE HAVE JUST SEEN that Paulinus of Nola, though sentimentally attached to the classical world, felt that no considerations of patriotism, family obligations, or personal inclination should be allowed to stand in the way of the practice of ascetic Christianity. Rutilius Claudius Namatianus[1] was his diametrical opposite. To him, love of Rome and his duty to it came first of all; he felt strongly the ties of family and the responsibilities of property; as to religion, though he wrote elegantly and politely of the gods, his real belief seems to have been pantheistic, the Stoicism common to many of the finer spirits among the pagans of his time; he detested fanaticism.

All that we know about Rutilius we learn from the 712 lines that have survived of a poem written by him — its true name has been lost, but it is often known as *De Reditu Suo,*

[1] Concerning Rutilius, see Vollmer in *RE* I A 1249–54 and authorities there cited. Special mention may be made of Boissier (see above, chap. 7, n. 9) II 197–201; A. Beugnot, *Histoire de la Déstruction du Paganisme en Occident,* II (Paris 1835) 181–86; R. Pichon, *Les Derniers Ecrivains Profanes* (Paris 1906) 260–68; E. S. Duckett, *Latin Writers of the Fifth Century* (New York 1930) 35–44. His poem has been translated, with introduction and notes, both helpful, by J. Wight Duff and Arnold M. Duff, in the Loeb Classical Library (*Minor Latin Poets,* 1935). The translators prefer *Claudius Rutilius Namatianus,* an order often used, to *Rutilius Claudius Namatianus,* which I have followed Vollmer in preferring.

sometimes as *Itinerarium* — concerning his journey from
Rome to Gaul in A.D. 416. He was from Gaul, probably
from the neighborhood of Toulouse. His father had been
*consularis Tusciae et Umbriae, comes sacrarum largitionum,
quaestor sacri palatii,* and finally prefect of the City. Rutilius
himself had been taken to Rome as a young man and had
at least completed his education there. He tells us that he
had held positions no less distinguished than those which
his father had attained, but he mentions only two specifically,
magister officiorum and prefect of the City. He belonged,
then, to at least the second generation of his family to hold
office of cabinet rank, and so was a member of the high
imperial aristocracy. He was returning to Gaul to look after
his estates there, which had been ravaged by the invading
barbarians. He does not tell us that he was in Rome when
the city was sacked by Alaric; considering how much he
speaks of Rome in his poem, and with what feeling, it seems
reasonable to deduce from his silence on the point that he
was not there.

His point of view, that of an extremely patriotic, conservative pagan, was in all probability typical of at least a
very large part of the senate and of the senatorial class.
Four things particularly strike us in his poem: the brilliant
and rich life of Rome such a short time after the sack of
the city by Alaric;[2] the intense patriotism of the poet; his
hatred of Stilicho; his dislike and fear of the Judeo-Christian
point of view, and of Christian asceticism.

It is not so extraordinary that Rome should have recovered
after having been sacked by Alaric. When the city was

---

[2] The striking recovery of Rome is also emphasized by Orosius. See *Hist.* 7.40.

threatened, many of the inhabitants left. Of those that would not or could not go, some starved during the sieges, but surely most survived. The Goths soon evacuated Italy; the rebellion of Heraclian was crushed in 413. Food was brought in again, and no doubt as many refugees as could make their way back did so. The city, with Constantinople, remained one of the two official capitals of the Empire (the real rival of Rome in Italy was not Ravenna but Milan); it was the center from which were spent the vast incomes of the richest senatorial families; it was the seat of the Papacy, and a great center of pilgrimage. What is striking is that the recovery should have taken place so quickly. "All roads lead to Rome," we say, and that was far more true in antiquity than it is now, and it remained true until the greatest road of them all, the Mediterranean, was cut by the Vandals.[3] The particular moment, though, of which we are writing was the exception that proved the rule. Rutilius returned to Gaul by sea.

> postquam Tuscus ager postquamque Aurelius agger,
>   perpessus Geticas ense vel igne manus,
> non silvas domibus, non flumina ponte coercet,
>   incerto satius credere vela mari.[4]

---

[3] H. Pirenne has shown us that the Mediterranean remained of capital importance to the West until command of that sea was lost to the Arabs; *Mohammed and Charlemagne,* transl. by Bernard Miall (New York 1939). But when the western Mediterranean became open again after the Vandal interruption, Rome was no longer a great center of maritime trade, and it never again became one. When so great a ruler as Theodoric wanted to send an embassy to Constantinople in a ship of his own, he had to build one; *Anonymus Valesianus* 14.90. And that was in the Italy of before the Gothic Wars. The Italy that emerged from those wars, the Italy of the exarchs and the Lombards and the popes, was only the wreck of the Italy of Theodoric.

[4] Rutilius Namatianus *De Reditu Suo* 1.39–42. For the rest of this article, our poet will be cited as R. N.

At the time of the voyage of Rutilius, that is, the land routes were still impassable or barely passable, and yet the City had already recovered. Perhaps we should suppose that Orosius, for the purposes of his argument, and Rutilius, because of his intense wish that things might be so, took a somewhat overoptimistic view. But even so, the people for whom they were writing had known Rome before the sack, so that it would have defeated the purposes of these writers if they had exaggerated too greatly. We must believe that Rome recovered with a speed which surprised contemporaries as it does us.

To Rutilius, Stilicho, even more than Alaric, was the enemy. It was Stilicho who defied the gods, the protectors of Rome, by burning the Sibylline Books, *aeterni fatalia pignora regni*.[5] (Rutilius nowhere else shows any tendency toward superstition; one suspects that he resented Stilicho's act, not so much because he really believed that it destroyed the luck of Rome, as because it was a gratuitous insult by the arrogant Christian barbarian to the whole tradition of pagan Rome.) It was the traitor Stilicho who, to further his own ambitions, opened Italy to the Goths. This is not what we hear from Claudian, but it is confirmed, and even carried further, by Orosius: he charges Stilicho, not merely with using Alaric for his own ends, but with deliberately inducing the Alans, Swabians, Vandals, and Burgundians to attack the Rhine frontier.[6]

We need not ourselves accept the extreme view of Orosius, or even suppose that Stilicho consciously intended to betray

[5] R. N. 2.55.
[6] Orosius *Hist.* 7.37–38.

the interests of the Empire. It does though seem clear that, so far as such abstractions meant anything to him, he saw them largely in terms of his own ambitions, that he thought of Alaric and the Goths not primarily as enemies of the Empire to be subdued at the first opportunity but rather as tools that he could use to strengthen his own position, to gain Illyricum for the West, and, very probably, the imperial throne for his son. That he deliberately encouraged the barbarians to attack the Rhine frontier seems improbable in the extreme. The fatal criticism of his policy is not that he had to bribe Alaric, but that he did use him for his own ends and that he finally allowed him to become so strong that, in order to deal with him at all, he had to denude the Rhine frontier, and thus make possible the great and fatal invasions of December 406. This is quite enough to make us understand the hate of Rutilius:

> omnia Tartarei cessent tormenta Neronis;
>   consumat Stygias tristior umbra faces.
>   hic immortalem, mortalem perculit ille;
>   hic mundi matrem perculit, ille suam.[7]

In 416, when Rutilius made his journey, Christianity had been officially tolerated for more than one hundred years: the Rescript of Licinius[8] was promulgated in 313. More than thirty years had passed since Gratian in 382 had deprived the pagan temples and priesthoods of much of their revenues and, in a strikingly symbolic act, had removed the Altar of

[7] R. N. 2.57–60.
[8] The "Edict of Milan" is a familiar but really incorrect expression. See Otto Seeck, *Zeitschr. f. Kirchengesch.* 12 (1891) 381, confirmed in his *Geschichte des Untergangs der antiken Welt* I (4th ed., Stuttgart 1922) 498f. We should do better to speak of the "Rescript of Licinius." Cf. P. Charanis, *Speculum* 33 (1958) 390.

Victory from the senate house. In 391, Theodosius had
solemnly forbidden pagan sacrifices in Rome and had pro-
hibited all from so much as setting foot in pagan sanctuaries
and temples.[9] If paganism had been revived during the
usurpations of Eugenius and Attalus, both usurpations had
been crushed, and in zealous support of the Church,
Honorius followed the example of his father. Rutilius and
a large part of the senate might still be pagans, and the
very large number of the laws directed against paganism
may be taken as an indication that these laws were not
strictly enforced; yet the time had passed for open criticism
of Christianity, especially for such criticism by a man who
had occupied at least two of the highest positions in the
State.

It is not surprising, then, to find that our Rutilius somewhat veils his hatred of the new religion by directing much
of his criticism, at least ostensibly, against the Jews. But
when he writes:

> atque utinam numquam Iudaea subacta fuisset
> Pompeii bellis imperiisque Titi!
> latius excisae pestis contagia serpunt,
> victoresque suos natio victa premit

he is, as both Dill and Beugnot have seen, attacking Christianity under the cover of its parent religion.[10] This becomes,
if possible, even clearer when he calls the Jews *radix stulti-
tiae*; it is evident that he is not confounding the Jews with

---

[9] *Cod. Theod.* 16.10.10. For the temporary abrogation of this law by Eugenius,
and its revival by Theodosius after the overthrow of the usurper, see the comments of Gothofridus, and the sources there cited.

[10] R. N. 1.395–98. Beugnot (see above, n. 1) 183; S. Dill, *Roman Society in
the Last Century of the Western Empire* (London 1906) 47.

the Christians.[11] When it comes to Christian monasticism, Rutilius drops all disguise:

> processu pelagi iam se Capraria tollit
>   squalet lucifugis insula plena viris.
> ipsi se monachos Graio cognomine dicunt
>   quod soli nullo vivere teste volunt.
> munera Fortunae metuunt, dum damna verentur:
>   quisquam sponte miser, ne miser esse queat?
> quaenam perversi rabies tam stulta cerebri,
>   dum mala formides, nec bona posse pati?
> sive suas repetunt factorum ergastula poenas,
>   tristia seu nigro viscera felle tument . . .
>
> aversor scopulos, damni monumenta recentis;
>   perditus hic vivo funere civis erat.
> noster enim nuper iuvenis maioribus amplis,
>   nec censu inferior coniugiove minor,
> impulsus furiis homines terrasque reliquit
>   et turpem latebram credulus exsul adit.
> infelix putat illuvie caelestia pasci
>   seque premit laesis saevior ipse deis.
> num, rogo, deterior Circaeis secta venenis?
>   tunc mutabantur corpora, nunc animi.[12]

As Boissier points out, "Mais Rutilius, derrière les moines, vise le christianisme; il le dit expressément, et tient à nous faire savoir que le monachisme lui semble un produit naturel de la secte 'qui abêtit les âmes.'"[13] The second passage, indeed, is directed not only against the Christians in general, not only against monasticism in general, but against a particular young man comparable in background, family, and wealth to Rutilius himself or to Paulinus of Nola; *mutatis*

[11] R. N. 1.389. See also Beugnot (above, n. 1).
[12] R. N. 1.439–48 and 517–26.
[13] II 201 (above, chap. 7, n. 9).

mutandis, these lines might have been written by Rutilius of Paulinus himself.[14]

It is unfortunate that, after having written of the bitter hatred which Rutilius felt toward Stilicho, of the mingled fear and disgust which he felt for Jews and Christians, and especially for monks — it is unfortunate that we shall not be able to dwell on the gentler, more dominant aspects of his character: his satisfaction that he did not have to pronounce capital sentence against anyone during his period of office as prefect of the City,[15] his devotion to family and friends, his enjoyment of natural beauty, his observant curiosity, his deep feeling for classical literature, his true poetic sense. One must know all these to get a picture of the whole man, but they have no direct bearing on what primarily concerns us here: his reaction to the crisis of the barbarian invasions.

It is quite otherwise with what was, perhaps, his outstanding characteristic, his patriotism: his touching devotion to Rome and to the civilization which Rome had spread throughout the West, which Rome had for so long maintained throughout the whole Empire. Again, his own words express these feelings more clearly and more beautifully than anything we might say:

> exaudi, regina tui pulcherrima mundi,
>   inter sidereos Roma recepta polos,
> exaudi, genetrix hominum genetrixque deorum . . .

[14] This comparison is of course not original; cf. Pichon (see above, n. 1) 267. Miss Duckett (see n. 1), though, is inclined to think that Rutilius felt nothing more than "indifference or silent contempt" for the Christians. She rightly points out that many Christians also disapproved of monks and hermits (p. 43).

[15] R. N. 1.159f. Helm (2334; see chap. 7, n. 9) aptly compares this passage with others in Paulinus (*Carmen* 21.375, 396) in which Paulinus tells us that St. Felix warned him not to shed blood during his term of office.

fecisti patriam diversis gentibus unam:
　　profuit iniustis te dominante capi.
dumque offers victis proprii consortia iuris,
　　urbem fecisti quod prius orbis erat.
mitigat armatas victrix clementia vires.
　　convenit in mores nomen utrumque tuos:
hinc tibi certandi bona parcendique voluptas:
　　quos timuit superat, quos superavit amat.

tu quoque, legiferis mundum complexa triumphis
　　foedere communi vivere cuncta facis.
te, dea, te celebrat Romanus ubique recessus
　　pacificoque gerit libera colla iugo.[16]

It is clear that Rutilius, who prized this Rome, this classical civilization above everything, was bound to detest the man, a barbarian and a Christian at that, whom he felt to have been responsible through treachery for the sack of Rome and the ravaging of Italy and his native Gaul. It is clear too that Rutilius, the devoted public servant, so proud of his career and that of his father, was bound to dislike and fear the religion which led men, even men of his own background and ideals, to abandon the service of Rome when she most needed them. Rutilius, whose whole poem — or rather, all we have of it — is a reflection of the classical spirit, was bound to dislike and fear the new religion because it was essentially incompatible with classicism.[17] The civilization which proclaimed the eternity of Rome could not survive the triumph of the religion which inspired *The City of God*;

[16] R. N. 1.47–49, 63–66, 69–72, 77–80.

[17] It is true that Rome tolerated the worship of Adonis and Mithras: true, even, that Rutilius himself was the pleased spectator of a rustic festival in honor of Osiris (R. N. 1.371–76); these gods, though, if foreign to the true classical spirit — to the Artemis of Euripides who could not defile herself by witnessing the death of Hippolytus — were at least not openly defiant of it or inconsistent with service of the state.

the civilization which proclaimed the ideal of *mens sana in corpore sano* could not survive the triumph of the religion which reverenced St. Simeon Stylites.

These things are clear to us, and it is evident, as we have seen, that Rutilius understood them too. But at no time is the future seen as inevitable by the people living in that time — and indeed it may be that it never is inevitable. The journey of Rutilius took place in 416, and the freshness of his poem leads us to suppose that he composed it shortly afterwards — from notes taken during the voyage, no doubt, but also while his memory was still vivid. If so, he was writing when the emperor Honorius was at the very height of his triumphs. Usurpers had been overthrown one after another in Africa, Gaul, and Spain, and the barbarians, weakened by hunger and by the repeated victories of Constantius, had been driven into Spain, the Vandal king captured, and the Goths compelled, more than induced, to become *foederati* and to surrender Galla Placidia. It would be easy in such circumstances to believe, especially if one most ardently wished to do so, that Rome was once more to rise above all her difficulties. Rutilius writes:

> erige crinales lauros seniumque sacrati
>   verticis in virides, Roma, refinge comas.
>
> porrige victuras Romana in saecula leges,
>   solaque fatales non vereare colos,
> quamvis sedecies denis et mille peractis
>   annus praeterea iam tibi nonus eat.
> quae restant nullis obnoxia tempora metis,
>   dum stabunt terrae, dum polus astra feret!
> illud te reparat quod cetera regna resolvit:
>   ordo renascendi est crescere posse malis.[18]

[18] R. N. 1.115f, 133–40.

And yet . . . yet . . . remembering the bitterness with
which our poet cursed Stilicho, his comparison of Christianity
to the poison of Circe, yet one wonders. The man who
wrote of the sure triumph of Rome may have written in
the optimism, the eager faith of the bright day, but yet one
feels that he had passed many a long night hour facing
courageously the bitter knowledge that his Rome and his
classical world were doomed.[19]

Postscript

It is perhaps not out of place here to compare the bitter
passage of Rutilius about the monks of Capraria with the
letter (*Epist.* 48) written some twenty years earlier by St.
Augustine to Eudoxius, the abbot of the monastery there.
Cf. Smith and Wace, *Dictionary of Christian Biography*
(London 1880) II 267, and the Loeb Classical Library
edition of the letters (selected) of St. Augustine (London
and New York 1940) 110 n. *a*. The saint asks the prayers of
the monks on his behalf and says that he had heard well
of them even before two of the monks, one of whom has
died since, had brought him a letter from Eudoxius. He
warns them, though very politely, against the contrasting
perils of ambition and sloth, saying that they should not
refuse to serve the active church when requested to do so,
but that they should not become proud because of their
services. "Non enim hoc vos monui, quod vos non arbitror
facere; sed credidi me non parum commendari deo a vobis,

---

[19] *Contra,* Duckett (see above, n. 1) 42, 44; Dill (above, n. 10) 310f; and
others. Cf., however, Pichon (above, n. 1) 260f, for a view at least approaching
the one taken in this chapter.

si ea quae munere illius facitis, cum adlocutionis nostrae memoria faciatis."

The two monks of whom Augustine writes were surely the holy men of whom Orosius tells us in *Hist.* 7.36. See the Loeb edition of the letters, *loc. cit.* Mascezel had stopped at Capraria on his way to crush the revolt of Gildo and had taken them with him to Africa. Orosius typically attributed the defeat of Gildo entirely to the prayers and fasting of these holy men and of Mascezel himself, and to the advice given to the latter by St. Ambrose, who had recently died, in a dream. Neither Rutilius nor St. Augustine would have agreed with this theory of history. Rutilius would probably have felt that the idle monks would have done better to fight than to fast, and in any case would have considered it most ironic that they should have prayed to the Christian god for a Roman victory. Augustine, who of course was in northern Africa at the time of these events, surely believed that God was not interested in giving the victory to one party or the other merely because one supported the Church and the other not, but solely as a means of affording the elect the most appropriate means of refining their souls. (Cf. below, chapter 10, pp. 288–89.) For all that, as we can see from his letter, he approved of the action of the monks in obeying the request of the ecclesiastical authorities and accompanying the general and praying for the victory of the Christian forces (perhaps Eudoxius in his letter to St. Augustine had asked him whether he felt that monks should leave their monasteries even for such purposes), but he warned against allowing any feeling of pride to creep in as a result of the success of their missions.

The poem of Rutilius with its strong feeling must not blind us to the fact that the grandsons of the Roman aristocracy of his time had become Christian almost without effort. The process has been well described in older books, notably *La Fin du Paganisme* (see above, chap. 7, n. 9) by Gaston Boissier. A short but interesting study, modifying the views of Boissier in some respects, is "Aspects of the Christianization of the Roman Aristocracy" by P. L. R. Brown, in *Journal of Roman Studies* 51 (1961) 1–11.

CHAPTER IX

CHRISTIANITY
AND THE INVASIONS:
SYNESIUS OF CYRENE

"THE CIVILIZATION which proclaimed the eternity of Rome could not survive the triumph of the religion which inspired *The City of God*; the civilization which proclaimed the ideal of *mens sana in corpore sano* could not survive the triumph of the religion which reverenced St. Simeon Stylites." [1] Yet what more striking proof of the eternity of Rome could there be than the fact that the Popes succeeded the Caesars, that they assumed the venerable title of *Pontifex Maximus,* once rejected as pagan by the emperor Gratian? What greater triumph of the methods of Aristotle than the *Summa* of St. Thomas Aquinas? Classical civilization did indeed die, but not without heirs to inherit very considerable portions of its estate.

The heritage was transmitted to the Europe of the earlier Middle Ages through two main channels. First, in the Mediterranean basin, at a level below that of conscious culture, through the continuity of the daily life and habits of the people. The ruler might be a Roman, an Angevin, or a Savoy; the women of southern Italy would still carry

---

This article is reprinted from *Classical Journal* 55 (1960) 290–312.
[1] See chap. 8, pp. 213–14, above.

their *amphorae* to the village fountains; the shepherds play their pipes in the hills.[2]

The second channel of transmission — the one with which we are here concerned — was the Church. For it was the very Church whose expansion was proof that the classical world was moribund — it was this very Church that was destined to adopt and to hand down much of Roman law, of Greek and Latin literature, the very notions (and the words themselves) of education, orderly administration, urbanity and civilization. If classical civilization could not survive the triumph of the Christian Church, yet neither could the Church become the directing force throughout Europe without first absorbing much of the classical tradition. It had to have leaders, and those leaders, however original, were necessarily men brought up in the classical tradition — what other was there, once the Church had ceased to be merely a Jewish sect? These leaders brought with them much of the background of the only world they knew.

The impregnation of the Church by classical culture began as soon as Christianity sought converts among the upper classes — apart, that is, from the Jews, who, though often very highly educated, generally rejected the classical tradition. The Apologists were cultivated men. If Justin Martyr was not an inspired writer, he was no mean figure; Minutius Felix was one of the most delightful authors of his time;

[2] The peasants of the Abruzzi and Calabria still play the *zampogna* or bagpipe. This name is said to be derived from the Greek συμφωνία; Battisti and Alessio, *Dizionario Etimologico Italiano* (Florence 1957) *s.v.* "Zampogna." It may be much older, but there is no doubt that the instrument was known to the Greeks and Romans; *Encycl. Britannica* (11th ed.) III 205f; Grove's *Dictionary of Music and Musicians* (5th ed., London and New York 1954) I 353.

Tertullian was a genius and a scholar second only to St. Augustine among the Latin Christian writers; Origen was one of the most prolific writers and greatest scholars of all time. He names, by the way, his own teacher, Pantaenus, as an example of a Christian doctor who availed himself of pagan learning.[3] Yet the scathing contempt of Tertullian for the old myths sung by the poets, St. Augustine's severe condemnation of them,[4] the famous dream of St. Jerome, the harshness with which Gregory the Great rebuked Desiderius of Vienne for lecturing on profane literature — [5] there is plenty to prove that the process of absorption was not easy, and of course it was lamentably far from complete.

The barbarian invasions, curiously enough, furthered the process to a marked degree. They were unquestionably one of the major causes of the destruction of classical civilization in the West: the successor-states could not maintain the roads, the schools, the commerce of even the later Empire; the cities shrank to fractions of their former size; law degenerated into custom, history into chronicles; literature, architecture, painting, and sculpture dwindled until they could no longer be said to exist as living arts. Still, though these invasions shared with Christianity the responsibility for killing classical civilization, they also drove many of the members of the senatorial aristocracy, at that time the chief depository of classical culture in the West, into assuming positions of leadership in the Church, thereby increasing both the desire of the Church to assume its new role and its capacity to do so.

[3] Eusebius *H. E.* 6.19.
[4] *Epist.* 101. Cf. *Epist.* 91.
[5] *Epist.* 11.54.

111. Diptych of Stilicho, his wife Serena, and their son Eucherius

IV. Acroterion in the form of a gorgon's head, from Cyrene

At the end of the fourth century the bishop had already become the leading figure in the city: head of the Church, most important judicial officer, leader in all aspects of civic welfare, defender of his flock against predatory soldiers and officials and against barbarian invaders.[6] If this was the position of the bishop under a government still Roman and landlords still indigenous, it is easy to see how much the need for his protection would increase when the Roman governors and prefects were replaced by barbarian kings, when the landlords, though usually left in possession of most of their estates, yet often had to give up parts to Germanic proprietors and, as to the rest, were freed from the restraint, such as it was, of the old authorities.[7] It was natural, therefore, that as the office of bishop became more important from a secular point of view, figures more considerable in the lay world should come to be chosen as bishops with increasing frequency and should be willing, perhaps under a little pressure in some cases, to accept the office. There arose an unmistakable tendency to select men

[6] Cf. Sergio Mochi Onory (above, chap. 7, n. 37).

[7] Most of the civil officers of the new governments were of course Romans and no doubt followed, so far as conditions permitted, the old system of administration: a Goth, wishing to acquire some land near Bordeaux that had been abandoned many years before by Paulinus of Pella, found it necessary to seek him out at Marseilles in order to buy it from him (Paulinus *Eucharisticon* 575). For all that, conditions became steadily more barbarous. The new masters had neither the means nor, probably, often the desire to maintain their administrations at the old level: Alaric II had to simplify the Roman code; Paulinus of Pella could not live near Marseilles (in Roman territory) and still receive income from lands near Bordeaux (in Visigothic territory), although his son, returning to Bordeaux, managed to recover part of the property (*ibid.*, 498). Sidonius Apollinaris, writing to his friend Arbogast, referred to the latter as one of the last upholders of the Latin tongue along the Rhine (Sidonius *Epist.* 4.17). Gregory of Tours, like Sidonius, belonged to a senatorial family from Auvergne, but, writing a century later, he used a Latin that would have scandalized Sidonius. Gregory's contemporary, Venantius Fortunatus, was a good Latinist, but he had been born in northern Italy and educated in Ravenna.

of such capacity, training, and position as to be able to take over the functions that were gradually being abandoned by the lay authorities and also to hold their own under alien rule — to protect the Catholic, Latin population from too great oppression by their new Arian, Germanic masters.[8]

In many cases, such men, though sincere Christians, had not been induced to become bishops so much because of any sudden access of religious zeal as because that seemed to them the best way to help their communities. There was no reason, then, for them to develop any aversion to the Classics which had formed their minds; their admission to the ranks of the higher clergy was undoubtedly a major factor in promoting the absorption of large elements of classical culture by the Church. Even a Paulinus of Nola (and he, converted to a high degree of asceticism, is as difficult an example as one can select), though he might renounce the writing of secular poetry, yet in his *Natalicia*, composed in honor of St. Felix, maintained the same standard — high, but scarcely inspired — that had brought him literary fame as a layman. Sidonius Apollinaris also renounced writing poetry after he became bishop,[9] but he continued to write in the euphuistic style so much admired in his time. St. Ambrose himself, the brilliant prototype of the magnate become bishop, went even further. Though he

[8] One suspects that the particularly bad reputation of the Vandals comes less from their having sacked Rome or from their other raids than from the fact that they treated the Church and the Roman landowners far more harshly than the Goths, Franks, Burgundians, and other barbarians had done. Yet even in Vandal Africa, we find such a bishop as Fulgentius of Ruspe. We note, too, that harsher though the Vandals were than the other barbarians, the father of Fulgentius had been able to recover part of the family property and that the young Fulgentius had received an excellent education in Greek and Latin. See Jülicher in *RE* VII 214f and sources there cited.

[9] *Epist.* 9.12.1.

practiced austerity in his way of living, he continued to
believe in the value of classical education and to introduce
classical allusions into his writings.[10] And, as we have seen,
Desiderius of Vienne was still teaching classical literature a
good two centuries later.

We have just referred to St. Ambrose as the prototype of
the magnate become bishop. Synesius of Cyrene,[11] though
one of the leading figures in his province, was not a magnate
on the imperial scale, as were St. Ambrose himself, Paulinus
of Nola, Rutilius Namatianus, and others whom we have
mentioned. Unlike them, he was not a member of the
immensely rich senatorial class, but was of curial rank, a
member, that is, of the well-to-do provincial nobility.[12]

[10] Dudden (above, chap. 7, n. 1) I 9.

[11] See Christian Lacombrade, *Synésios de Cyrène, Hellène et Chrétien* (Paris
1951) for a recent and most interesting biography, and the very complete bibliography at the back of the volume. Also, Lacombrade, *Le Discours sur la
Royauté de Synésios de Cyrène à l'empereur Arcadios* (Paris 1951). Since we
shall have occasion to refer to the former very frequently, we shall write merely
"Lacombrade" followed by the page number. Of special interest are the introductions to Augustine FitzGerald's translations of the works of Synesius, *The Letters
of Synesius of Cyrene* (above, chap. 5, n. 3) and *The Essays and Hymns of
Synesius* (see chap. 6, n. 1). In citing FitzGerald, we shall write merely "Fitz-
Gerald, *Letters*" or "FitzGerald, *Essays and Hymns*," followed by the volume
and page numbers for the latter and by the page number for the former. When
Synesius is quoted in English, FitzGerald's translations are used. When the letters
are quoted in the original, the text of R. Hercher is used (above, chap. 5, n. 3).
When other works are quoted in the original, we follow Terzaghi (*Hymni*
[Rome 1939]; *Opuscula* [Rome 1944]). In citing the hymns and essays, since
almost all quotations are given in English, the conventional order, used in Fitz-
Gerald, is followed; the order more recently established by Terzaghi is given in
parentheses where different. Another helpful work is Pando's *Synesius,* already
referred to above, chap. 5, n. 169.

[12] At this time the *curiales* were being destroyed by oppressive taxation which,
because of their responsibility for the collection of the full amounts demanded,
fell with especial heaviness upon their group, but nevertheless Synesius and his
family, and doubtless many other *curiales,* were still at least very comfortably
off. Poor people do not send presents of ostriches (*Epist.* 129, 134) or horses
(*Epist.* 40) to their friends overseas, nor would he, if he had not been very well
off, have referred to himself, when the enemy seemed about to conquer the
province, as once a rich man but now about to be driven into poverty-stricken

Nevertheless, the events in which he took part and his re-actions to them made his life a striking illustration of our theme. That he came from the Greek half of the Empire, not the Latin, makes him perhaps the exception that proves the rule. For the barbarian menace became acute in the East some years before it reached the critical stage in the West; it is significant that his reactions to that crisis were so similar to those of the western leaders when they later had to face situations similar to his. That his successors should, for the most part, have been in the West and not in the East is surely due to the fact that the imperial government in the East overcame its crisis, while the imperial government in the West succumbed.

Cyrene had been one of the most prosperous of the Grecian colonies, but it had slowly declined under Roman rule and had been destroyed and the inhabitants decimated by the Jews during their savage revolt in A.D. 115. Dio Cassius, speaking, to be sure, not of Cyrene alone, but of Cyrenaica, tells us that 220,000 Greeks and Romans were killed at this time.[13] Ammianus Marcellinus referred to it as *urbs antiqua sed deserta*.[14] Synesius wrote of it: "Cyrene, a Greek city of ancient and holy name, sung in a thousand odes by the wise men of the past, but now poor and down-cast, a vast ruin . . ." and in another passage he referred

---

exile (*Catastasis* 1572). As to family, he mentions with pride that the public monuments of Cyrene record his descent from Eurysthenes, the Heraclid who led the Dorians to Sparta (*Epist.* 57; *Catastasis* 1572; cf. *Epist.* 124). For the position of the *curiales*, see the masterly summary of Rostovtzeff in *SEHRE* (2nd ed.) I 502–32. For the financial position of Synesius, see Lacombrade 14f; Pando 29ff; chap. 6 above, pp. 150–54.

[13] 68.32.1–2. Cf. Eusebius *H. E.* 4.2 and Orosius *Hist.* 7.12.6.
[14] 22.16.4.

to it as having fallen lower than any of the cities of Pontus.[15] Yet we know that Hadrian had reinvigorated the region with new colonists and that he rebuilt at least the heart of the city — very handsomely, too, as we can still see. Further, Synesius himself often refers to shipping and the sending of goods by sea in a way that implies considerable trade; his letters on local politics reveal an active civic life and prove that there were considerable numbers of well-to-do citizens. The truth would seem to be that the whole region had declined; that the ports, especially Ptolemais and Apollonia or Sozousa, had gained at the expense of the older inland cities of Cyrene and Barca; that the Cyrene of the time of Synesius was a moderately small but lively town, with a very great tradition, concentrated around the temples and shrines that had been the center of the ancient metropolis, but, probably, with large areas of what had been the old city now stretching, ruined and abandoned, beyond the urban limits of his day.[16]

Synesius was born in or near Cyrene, possibly as early as A.D. 360, perhaps as late as 375.[17] He received his early education there. We may get some idea of his school years from a few passages in which Synesius refers to the bringing up of younger members of his family. In one letter, we find

[15] *De Regno* 2; *Epist.* 103. It should be remembered that the object of Synesius' mission to the emperor was to petition for a reduction of taxes, so that in his address he would not be likely to represent conditions in Cyrene as very prosperous.

[16] Rostovtzeff *SEHRE* I 141, 308–11; Broholm, *RE* XII, 156–69; Pando 14–17, 19–25, 29–33, 35–39, 99–120; chap. 5, pp. 131–32 above.

[17] The dates are purely conjectural. N. Crawford (*Synesius the Hellene* [London 1901] 8–11) argues persuasively for 360. Lacombrade (p. 13) presents the case for 370 but makes no claim to certainty. As for place, Synesius alludes to Cyrene as his mother, *Epist.* 4. That, though, can scarcely be taken as precluding the possibility of his having been born in some country place nearby.

him expressing his pleasure at the progress his nephew is making in declaiming verse, and in another praising the boy's assiduity in reading. We find him planning to introduce his own son, as yet unborn, to the great philosophers and other prose writers. He will advise the youth gradually to relax his mind after study of these deeper works by turning to lighter ones, and finally to comedy, "at one moment playing with your books, at another working with them." He refers to the works of Dio Chrysostom as on the border between "preparatory teaching and instruction in the ultimate truth." [18] If we may apply these remarks to his own education, it seems that this must have been about the point that he himself reached before leaving Cyrene for Alexandria. Interestingly enough, we have no evidence whatever that he was familiar with Latin literature.[19]

It would be a serious omission if we were to treat of the education of Synesius without emphasizing further the major part which physical training and games and sports of all kinds played in it. We know that he bought a slave to act as a physical trainer.[20] We are not told whether this was for himself, his nephew, or his sons, but it is obvious that he attached real importance to such training and that he himself had certainly received it as a boy. Indeed, he writes, "When I look up from my books, I like to enter into every sort of sport." Above all, hunting meant a very great deal to him. The earliest of his works that we know of (unfortunately,

---

[18] *Epist.* 53, 60, 111; *Dio* 1124–25.

[19] Synesius used Latin technical expressions four times but in one case apologized to his correspondent for doing so and in the other three explained what he understood the expressions to mean; *Epist.* 67, 79, 144, 145. This certainly implies no real understanding of Latin, but rather the contrary.

[20] *Epist.* 32.

it has not come down to us) was called *Cynegetics*. Near
the end of his life, he wrote: "I feel that I have a good deal
of inclination for amusements. Even as a child, I was charged
with a mania for arms and horses. I shall be grieved, indeed
greatly shall I suffer at seeing my beloved dogs deprived of
their hunting, and my bow eaten up by worms." [21] All in all,
we may be sure that Synesius as a boy and as a youth had
the well-rounded education, physical and mental, of a Greek,
still pagan, of good family, and that it was carried as far
as his age and the resources of the town and of his father's
library[22] permitted.

Cyrene, though, however great its history, was then a
comparatively small town and probably offered only limited
facilities for advanced studies. Further, the parents of
Synesius seem to have died before this time,[23] and perhaps
the young man wanted to see something of the world. At
any rate, he went to Alexandria, then one of the great
centers of living Greek civilization, and there sat under the
great Hypatia, the most famous pagan teacher of her day.

Hypatia was held in esteem as a mathematician and

---

[21] *Epist.* 101, 105, 154. See also *Epist.* 40, 134, 148; *De Insomniis* 9. A good
historical novel often stimulates the imagination more than bits and pieces of
learning. If Kingsley, in spite of the quotation in the text, takes something of a
liberty in putting a theological justification of hunting into the mouth of the
"squire-bishop," he gives a stirring picture of Synesius on an ostrich hunt and
in a skirmish with the barbarians (*Hypatia,* chapter "The Squire-Bishop").

[22] Synesius tells us that he greatly increased the number of books he had in-
herited; *Dio* 13. As he was a younger son, it seems unlikely that the whole of
his father's library passed to him.

[23] None of the letters mentions them as living; he was most closely bound to
his elder brother Euoptius, to whom he addressed 40 of the 159 letters that have
come down to us. In *Epist.* 8, he mentions that they had the same parents, were
brought up together, and received their education together. If their parents had
not died while they were very young, it would surely have been more natural
to say that their parents had brought them up together.

astronomer, and above all as the chief exponent of Neo-Platonism in her time. Dramatic tales of her beauty, her tragic death — these must not deceive us into doubting the solid foundation of her great reputation. Her works have not come down to us, but the very serious respect with which the Christian sources speak of her, the pagan teacher assassinated by a Christian mob, is conclusive evidence that her fame was fully deserved.[24]

This remarkable woman was the outstanding influence in the development of the mental and spiritual capacities of Synesius. He appealed to her for sympathy in his personal sorrows and in his distress at the misfortunes of his beloved Cyrene; he submitted his writings to her judgment; sure of her approval, he wrote of his abhorrence of fanaticism, of his intention to give importance to style even in serious writing, of his wish to mingle the grave with the playful. He was grateful to her above all for her philosophical — or perhaps we ought rather to say, religious — instruction, for having introduced him to the "mystic dogmas," for having taught him to choose the best, ever to strive for the ultimate reunion of his soul, freed from the trammels of debasing matter, with the Divine Being of whom it was, and always had been, a part.[25]

[24] Socrates *Eccl. Hist.* 7.15; Suidas, under the name Hypatia.
[25] *Epist.* 10, 15, 16, 81, 124, 154, 137; Hymns 1, 3, 5. Cf. *Egyptian Tale* 9; *Dio* 7. See Lacombrade (38–71) for an interesting and detailed analysis of the teachings of Hypatia and the studies of Synesius. Lacombrade rightly emphasizes the extent of his scientific knowledge. He also believes him to have been influenced to some extent by Gnostic doctrines and ways of feeling, though Plotinus and Plato himself seem to have been his principal masters. I am inclined to minimize the importance of Synesius' references to esoteric doctrines and mysteries (see especially *Epist.* 105, 137, 143; *Egyptian Tale* 9; *Dio* 5; the preface of *De Insomniis*). They seem to me largely due to his very sound belief that somewhat abstruse doctrines may easily become falsified and vicious through

It cannot be claimed that there was anything very original in the philosophy of Synesius, nor shall we have occasion to analyze it beyond pointing out certain important aspects in which it differed from Christianity. We must always keep in mind, though, that this side of his life was and ever remained of the highest importance to him. We have seen his attachment to sports and hunting, we shall see his devotion to civic duties. These interests must not make us forget that he regarded the one as a necessary relaxation from more serious occupations, and the other, as an indispensable duty to be sure, but also as one that should on no account be allowed to become a burdensome distraction from the pursuit of the highest aim: the redemption of the soul from the bondage of matter, and its reunion with the Divinity whence it came. As he himself expressed it toward the end of his life:

> From childhood, leisure and comfort in life have ever appeared to me a divine blessing which someone has said befits divine natures; and this is naught else but the culture of the intellect, and its reconciliation with God on the part of the man who possesses that leisure and profits by it . . . passing my days as in a sacred festival, I strove throughout all my life to preserve a state of spirit gentle and untroubled by storms.
>
> But, nevertheless, God has not made me useless to men, inasmuch as oftentimes both cities and private individuals made use of my services in time of need. For God gave me the power to do the utmost and to will the fairest. None of these services drew me apart from philosophy, nor cut short my happy leisure . . . I lived with good hopes . . . apportioning my life between

---

injudicious popularization, and partly due to the fact that doctrines and ceremonies not in accord with the legally established Christian usage were poor matter for publicity in Alexandria, where the Serapeum had only recently been destroyed by the very bishop who was before long to consecrate Synesius, where Hypatia herself was to be killed by a Christian mob a few years later.

prayer, books, and the chase. For, that the soul and body may be in health, it is necessary to do some work on the one hand and on the other to make supplication to God.[26]

We have already contrasted the positions of Rutilius Namatianus and Paulinus of Nola.[27] They were diametrically opposite: the one a pagan, the other a Christian; the one believing that man's highest duty was to the state, the other believing that the true Christian should confront even the barbarian invader with nonresistance; the one with real and deep reverence for the classical tradition of moderation and proportion in all things, the other (though he preserved more of the classical than he perhaps realized) an uncompromising ascetic.

It is interesting to find in Synesius, their contemporary, a man who in himself reconciled their contradictions. Like Rutilius, he was born a pagan; like Paulinus, he died a Christian bishop. Like Rutilius, he was intensely patriotic; like Paulinus, he felt that the highest duty of man was the salvation of his soul — but he did not feel that this highest duty entailed asceticism, or that it could be properly performed at the expense of his duty to his country and to his fellow citizens. Like Rutilius, he despised fanaticism; like Paulinus, he was a deeply religious man. We turn now to the mature life of Synesius to witness the manifestation of these qualities.

Sailing to the Pentapolis in 395,[28] Synesius, for all his professed desire to devote himself entirely to philosophy,[29]

---

[26] *Epist.* 57.
[27] See chaps. 7 and 8 above.
[28] The date is established by Lacombrade 24, 55.
[29] *Epist.* 146.

soon found himself actively engaged in war and politics, and yet with leisure to write his *Calvitii Encomium,* an elegant bit of sophistry in avowed imitation of Dio.[30]

Resistance to the barbarian invaders of the Empire was perhaps the dominating external factor in the life of Synesius. Let us, then, look more closely at an aspect of this problem which particularly concerned Cyrenaica and Synesius. Throughout history, the Berbers have constituted the most numerous ethnic element in the population of North Africa west of Egypt. Politically, they have almost always been subject to foreign powers and have adopted the civilizations of the colonizing peoples with considerable success. The Greeks in Cyrenaica, the Phoenicians and Romans further west, the Byzantines, the Arabs and later the Turks (though the Turks seem to have left the Arabic civilization un-disturbed, merely permitting it to sink to a lower stage of degradation), and finally the Spaniards, French, and Italians have all established themselves along these shores; always, though, in long, narrow strips, wherever highlands near the coast have attracted sufficient rainfall to support settled populations. Inland, the highlands fall away to the south, the country becoming ever drier until it merges into the great desert. This region, too dry for permanent settlement, especially before modern machinery made it possible to dig deep wells, has yet always supported nomadic tribes. Until the coming of the camel, these lived more or less wretchedly on their flocks and herds, perhaps on tribute levied from the inhabitants of the smaller oases, to a considerable extent by

[30] Lacombrade (76f) argues very persuasively that letters 104, 113, and 124, describing incidents of a war with the barbarians, belong to this period, and also (78f) that the *Calvitii Encomium* was written about the same time.

hunting and, when driven by hunger or tempted by the weakness of their prospective victims, by raiding the settled areas to the north. The introduction of the camel into Africa west of Egypt seems to have taken place as late as the fourth century after Christ. The animal had already become common in Cyrenaica in the time of Synesius; the nomadic tribes, just beginning to make use of them, were gaining greatly in mobility and in consequence becoming far more dangerous than they ever had been before.[31]

The writings of Synesius are full of allusions to wars with these nomadic raiders from the south, but the dates of many of his letters are uncertain. Two incidents, though, seem surely to apply to the time we have now reached, A.D. 395. The enemy was said to be approaching Cyrene, and local forces, acting on the initiative of Synesius, moved out against them, being joined by others from the neighboring town of Balagrae under their own commander. For five days, Joannes the Phrygian, evidently an officer charged with the defense of the region, was not to be found. At last, though, he came, explaining that he had been fighting the barbarians else-

---

[31] In *Epist.* 104, which Lacombrade dates as of 395, Synesius speaks of the barbarians as riding horses to battle but dismounting to fight. But in the *Catastasis*, which Lacombrade (234f) dates as of 411, Synesius writes that he may flee to an island because "I distrust Egypt. Even there a camel can cross with an Ausurian hoplite on its back." In dating the use of the camel in war by the nomadic tribes at precisely this period, I am slightly modifying the view expressed in chap. 5 above, pp. 104–5. I had there written, "Not until Vandal times do we encounter what Gautier calls 'les grands nomades chameliers,' tribes capable of dominating the desert routes and of conquering the settled country — as distinct from raiding it." I had taken account of the passage in *Epist.* 104, but the passage in the *Catastasis* escaped me. It was evidently during the brief lifetime of Synesius that the transformation began. [These two passages from Synesius do indeed make it probable that the *nomades chameliers* first appeared in Cyrenaica during his lifetime. For evidence concerning their probable appearance elsewhere in North Africa at an earlier date, and for a more recent and detailed discussion of the subject, see above, pp. 134–43.]

where. He assumed the task of whipping the force into shape but caused nothing but confusion. Presently, the enemy appeared, a sorry-looking lot of ruffians on horseback. Following their usual custom, they dismounted in order to fight on foot. Synesius wished to do likewise since the ground did not seem suitable for cavalry maneuvers. Joannes, though, ordered a charge and then, instead of leading it, turned his horse about and galloped off to the shelter of some distant caves. The two forces separated without actually coming to blows.

More heroic was the resistance of the clergy of Axomis. While the professional soldiers were hiding from the enemy, the priests called the peasants of the district together and led them out against the raiders. They surprised the barbarians in a narrow defile — but appear to have been surprised themselves too. The deacon Faustus rose to the emergency: he seized a stone, sprang upon the foremost of the enemy, struck him in the temple with the stone, knocked him down, stripped him of his armor, and followed this by felling other barbarians as they came up, directing the skirmish and putting the raiders to rout. These priests, Synesius tells us, were the first to encourage the people by showing that the barbarians could actually be wounded and killed. Later on, though, Synesius seems to have taken part in actual fighting: he wrote to Hypatia that he saw the enemy and slain men every day and that sooner or later he expected to be killed too.[32]

[32] As we have seen, Lacombrade argues strongly in favor of ascribing *Epist.* 104, 113, and 124 to this period; see above, n. 30. It seems also almost certain that *Epist.* 122 was written at the opening of this campaign: the terms of the letter are such that it could not have been writen after Synesius and the people

If we put this information, scanty as it is, together with what we know of the political activities of Synesius, the pieces fit into a consistent whole. He had declined the offer of his friend Herculian to secure for him an introduction to the commander of the forces in Cyrene. He now accepted the offer after all, on the ground that his friends, both civilians and soldiers, were urging him to take part in local politics. He took his place as a member of the *curia* of Cyrene and there urged that barbarian mercenaries should be excluded from the army and that the Pentapolis should no longer be a separate military command but return to its former status of dependence on the *praefectus Augustalis,* the head of the imperial administration in Egypt.[33] This seems to accord with his experiences as a leader of local levies and with his dissatisfaction with the Phrygian officer Joannes. As to the barbarians, we see from many passages that he felt (though he later somewhat modified his point of view) that they had no real interest in the defense of the country but cared only to make their fortunes. As to the officers responsible to Constantinople, he felt that the authorities there considered Cyrenaica a remote and unimportant province and awarded the command for political reasons or for money, rather than on the ground of merit. Egypt, on

of Cyrenaica had become accustomed to warfare and to seeing enemies slain in battle.

This is as good an occasion as any to remind the reader that all we know about the life of Synesius we know only from his own writings. He was a sincere and admirable character, but we are all inclined to see ourselves as right and our opponents as wrong. Further, Synesius had studied rhetoric and unquestionably used it, partly to present his opponents in an unfavorable light and partly to make his letters more amusing. We need not like him the less for his vitality and exuberance, but we must take them into account.

[33] *Epist.* 144, 95.

the other hand, shared common problems of defense with Cyrenaica and would feel that a threat to the security of that province was a threat to its own security as well.[34]

He seems, though, to have been sharply opposed, especially by a certain Julius, who was a very powerful figure in Cyrene and remained the opponent of Synesius for the rest of his life. Perhaps, too, officers in command of the imperial troops in the province resented his opinion of them. For a time, at least, his enemies had the best of the argument: Synesius surprised even his own brother by embarking unexpectedly for Athens in obedience to mysterious warnings sent in dreams that many people were bent on doing him harm if he did not at once leave Cyrene.[35] In another letter, he wrote that he found in Athens nothing but the ancient sites, the mere desiccated skin of the city which once had lived. One might have expected a more gentle comment from one so attached to a Cyrene that was also shorn of its ancient glories.

Whatever the cause of this unexpected trip and however

[34] *Epist.* 95. Lacombrade (73) assumes from this letter that Synesius was a member of a provincial council and that these activities took place there, but he does not cite any passages bearing on the matter. In an earlier paper (above, chap. 6, p. 161) the present writer stated his belief that they took place in the *curia* of Cyrene and that still seems probable to him. The texts do not make the matter entirely clear. As ambassador to Arcadius, he says, he is sent by Cyrene, a Greek city; *De Regno* 2 (Terzaghi 3). But, writing at a later time, he says that dreams helped him to manage public affairs "in the best interests of the cities"; *De Insomniis* 9 (Terzaghi 14). In Hymn 3 (Terzaghi 1), he speaks of bearing his μστέρα πάτραν on his shoulders at the time of his embassy and prays God to preserve what he had gained for the Libyans. Synesius seems to have thought of himself as envoy from Cyrene but also to have felt that the benefits which resulted from his mission redounded to the welfare of the province as a whole.

[35] For the opposition of Julius, see *Epist.* 50, 95. *Epist.* 54 and 136 inform us of the visit of Synesius to Athens. The connection between this trip and the enmity of Julius is suggested by Lacombrade (74).

vigorous the opposition of Julius, Synesius soon returned to Cyrene and apparently carried a vote in the *curia* in favor of the measures he desired: in 399, we find him in Constantinople as envoy from Cyrene and in that capacity advocating, in a formal address before Arcadius, that the Emperor should abandon his life of luxurious and hieratic seclusion, that he should assume real control of his government and real command of his armies, that the barbarians should be excluded from the government and from the armies, that provincial governors should be chosen on a basis of merit only, that the Emperor should learn to know his dominions by travel and by listening to the requests of missions sent to his court, and that he should enrich the cities and his subjects in general by curbing extravagance and reducing taxation.[36]

It will not be possible to discuss many interesting aspects of this famous speech: we are concerned with Christianity and the barbarian invasions, so that it is the attitude of Synesius toward the barbarians that must occupy us. Only a few years before, an earlier orator, Pacatus, had praised Theodosius the Great, the father of Arcadius before whom Synesius spoke:

> Dicamne ego receptos servitum Gothos castris tuis militem, terris sufficere cultorem? . . . quaecumque natio barbarorum robore

[36] For the vote in the *curia* of Cyrene, see above, n. 34. For the chronology of the stay of Synesius in Constantinople, for the interpretation of the *De Providentia,* etc., see Otto Seeck, "Studien zu Synesios" (above, chap. 6, n. 8 442–60, a study which remains authoritative on these points, although, with Lacombrade, we do not believe that Seeck was always correct in the date suggested by him for the letters of Synesius. We have already referred (above n. 11) to Lacombrade's recent translation of this speech, and an excellent English version is included in FitzGerald's *Essays and Hymns,* cited in the same note In connection with this speech, special reference should be made to J. R. Asmus "Synesius und Dio Chrysostomus," *BZ* 9 (1900) 85–151.

ferocia numero gravis umquam nobis fuit, aut boni consulit ut
quiescat aut laetatur quasi amica, si serviat . . .[37]

Synesius painted an entirely different picture:[38] Gothic generals seated in the consistory, large Gothic contingents in
the Roman armies, Gothic slaves in quantities. The situation
was ripe for the wolves — generals, soldiers and slaves together — to fall upon the sheep. Indeed, parts of the Empire
(Synesius was referring to Tribigild in Asia Minor and
Alaric in Epirus) were already inflamed by such movements.
The Emperor should therefore purge his council and his
armies of the barbarians while he could still do so.

It was not merely that Pacatus and Synesius looked upon
public affairs from different points of view, but that the
situation had deteriorated with startling speed during the
decade between the two orations. When Pacatus spoke in
389, all the elements of danger which disturbed Synesius
were already in existence, but they remained inactive, kept
down by the firmness of Theodosius. Three years later,
though, in January 395, Theodosius died, and the dam broke
in the East. In that very month, Alaric led his Goths against
Constantinople. The praetorian prefect Rufinus, humbling
himself by going to the Gothic camp dressed as a German,
persuaded Alaric to withdraw, but he withdrew only to
plunder Macedonia, Thessaly, Greece, and Epirus. Saved
once by Rufinus and another time by the perhaps deliberate
laxity of Stilicho, Alaric had, at the time Synesius spoke,
been bought off temporarily by receiving the appointment
of *magister militum per Illyricum*, a position which put him

[37] See above, chap. 6, n. 4. For the date of this panegyric (A.D. 389) see
Hanslik, *RE* XVIII 2058.
[38] *De Regno* 11, 14, 15.

in the happy situation of maintaining himself and his people at public expense while playing off one half of the Empire against the other.

To return, however, to 395, the Huns raided Thrace in January and in the summer broke through the Caspian Gates, crossed Armenia, besieged Antioch, and ravaged Asia Minor. Later in this same eventful year, Rufinus was hewn to pieces in the presence of the emperor Arcadius by the soldiers of Gainas, a Gothic general who had been instigated by Stilicho to commit the murder. The *praepositus sacri cubiculi*, the eunuch Eutropius, succeeding to the power of Rufinus though not to his office, undertook a campaign against the Huns and, to vary this series of disasters, drove those still formidable enemies back across the Caucasus. In this he was helped by Tribigild, another Gothic officer. But Tribigild, feeling himself insufficiently recompensed by Eutropius, revolted and campaigned with varying, but on the whole increasing, success in Asia Minor, much helped by slaves who fled to him and by Germanic soldiers in the Roman armies who deserted to him, but seriously endangered at times by the resistance of the local population. In the meantime, Gainas had been appointed commander in chief of the forces of the Empire in the East (*comes et magister utriusque militiae*). Not only had he used his power to strengthen his position by bringing many more Goths into the Empire and by increasing the number of Gothic officers in the imperial armies, but he had been so conspicuously unsuccessful in fighting Tribigild that he was suspected of being in collusion with the rebel.[39]

[39] Since Synesius himself is our major authority for the later phases of th

With the crisis, though, came the reaction. Not only Synesius in Cyrenaica, but a powerful party in the capital, with support throughout the Empire, had come to feel that it was imperative to expel the barbarian masses from the Roman armies, and the barbarian leaders from positions of civil and military command. This party came into power with the fall of Eutropius in 399, and Aurelian, one of the leaders of the movement, took office as praetorian prefect of the East. The speech of his supporter Synesius, the envoy from Cyrene, was evidently the official declaration of policy of the new government, the first dramatic step in the reaction that, for all the immediate difficulties that it caused, was to save the Empire in the East and make possible its preservation for a millennium.

Aurelian now proceeded to put into effect the policies advocated in the oration of Synesius: he reduced taxes, including those of Cyrene; he encouraged education and learning; he beautified and enlarged the cities of the Empire; he selected capable and upright officials. Synesius, in compensation for his services, was relieved of his curial obligations.[40] In view of the policy announced by Synesius, it is entirely possible that Aurelian also took measures designed

---

revolt of Gainas, it is worth mentioning that we have excellent independent authority for the statement that Tribigild was much helped by slaves who escaped to join his forces (Zosimus 5.13.4) and by Teutonic soldiers in the Roman armies who deserted to him (Zosimus 5.17.1f), and much hindered by the resistance of local forces (Zosimus 5.15f); that Gainas strengthened his position by bringing in more Goths and appointing more Gothic officers (Socrates 6.6.4; Sozomen 8.4.1; Joh. Antiochenus, *Frag.* 190); that he was suspected of being in collusion with Tribigild (Zosimus 5.13–18; Eunapius, *Frags.* 75, 76; Joh. Antiochenus, *Frag.* 190; Socrates 6.6.5; Sozomen 8.4.2; Philostorgus 11.8).

[40] *De Providentia* 1.12.18; *Epist.* 100. Relief from curial obligations for at least two years was the normal reward for a *curialis* who had undertaken the expense of serving as an envoy to the Court. *Digest* 50.7.8, 9; *Paratitlon* of Gothofridus to *Cod. Theod.* 12.12, and the laws there cited; cf. above, chap. 6, n. 2.

to increase the Roman levies, to reduce the barbarian forces in the Roman armies, and to replace the barbarian officers by Roman ones. In fact, Synesius tells us that Aurelian was suspected by Gainas of doing these things, and it is difficult to suppose that the suspicion was unjustified.[41]

Gainas, then, was suspicious. He gave one puff, and the fine new administration fell like a house of cards. Whatever his relations with Tribigild may have been before, he now openly accepted the latter's support and marched upon Constantinople. Arriving at Chalcedon, just across the Bosporus, he refused to negotiate with any one except Emperor Arcadius in person. The helpless monarch, anxious to save his capital, crossed the strait. It was agreed that Caesarius, the brother of Aurelian but his political rival, should be made praetorian prefect and that Gainas should occupy Constantinople with his troops, as *magister militum praesentalis*.

The bayonet seems not to have come into use until the seventeenth century, but, if the reader will pardon the anachronism, Gainas soon learnt the truth of Napoleon's saying that the one thing one cannot do with bayonets is sit on them. He and his army were in Constantinople: there was no resistance to them, but he could not think of any way to make real use of his position. Nearly a century later, Theodoric put into practice the ideal of Ataulf: a state in which a German king and army would control and protect a civilized, Roman administration and society. Gaiseric, midway in time between Gainas and Theodoric, used the magnificent position of Carthage to found a pirate state

[41] *De Providentia* 1.15.

Gainas, in the even finer position of Constantinople and in possession of the heart of the Empire, was probably prevented by that very fact from conceiving the idea of setting up a kingdom hostile to the Empire and was incapable of understanding the ideal of Ataulf and Theodoric — to say nothing of realizing it. The closest comparison is perhaps with his contemporary Alaric, who could ravage Greece and the Balkans, march up and down Italy, sack Rome, but, lacking Africa, could not even provision his own troops. Gainas, to be sure, was better off than that: if Constantinople itself was to be provisioned (and Arcadius had no Ravenna in which to take refuge while leaving Rome to starve), then Gainas and his Goths would be fed.

What then? They were clumsy barbarians in a hostile, highly civilized city. Hated, tricked, tormented, no doubt murdered in back alleys whenever opportunity offered, they probably underwent much the experience which befell the Germans during their occupation of Italy during the last war. More, the situation was envenomed by religion: the inhabitants of Constantinople were fanatically orthodox, the barbarians were Arians. John Chrysostom had already assigned them a church in which to hold services in Gothic; he had even preached there himself, making use of an interpreter. These services, though, were of course orthodox. The Goths, supported by Caesarius, requested the use of a church within the city walls in which they might hold Arian services. This would be a pollution of the sacred city, and St. Chrysostom opposed them face to face in the presence of Arcadius. Though the demand was dropped — or at least, not pushed to a conclusion — yet the injection of religion into the already tense situation stimulated the public to the highest pitch of excitement. The inevitable comet appeared in the heavens.

The Goths became subject to panics, believing that hostile soldiers were being secretly introduced into Constantinople. At one moment, they would threaten to burn or sack the city; at another, they would flee from intangible but terrifying enemies. Matters reached such a point that Gainas determined to evacuate the capital. With his family and a large part of his army, he encamped some miles outside the walls and attempted to dominate the city from there.

Shortly afterwards, on July 12, 400, while another contingent of Gothic forces was evacuating the capital, a riot broke out at one of the gates between the soldiers and the townspeople. The citizens succeeded in seizing the gates and in holding them against both the Goths within and those without. Inside the city, they hunted the hapless barbarians, now in utter panic, through the streets. Many of them were slain as they fled, but a great part of them laid down their arms and took refuge in their church. The infuriated mob, apparently encouraged by Arcadius, set the building on fire, and the wretched suppliants were burnt.

Gainas and his surviving followers, after an unsuccessful attempt to cross the Hellespont to Asia Minor, withdrew across the Danube. Here he was defeated and killed by Uldin, a chieftain of the Huns, who sent his head to Constantinople. It was paraded through the streets on a pike on January 3, 401.

The Empire in the East had not seen the last of the barbarians, nor even of the Goths. Not so many years later, the great patrician, Aspar, himself of mixed Gothic and Alan blood, supported by a large Gothic following, occupied a position comparable to that which Stilicho had held, even succeeding in procuring the elevation of his son Patricius to the rank of Caesar. About the same time, Theodoric the Amal and Theodoric Strabo, both Gothic chieftains, ravaged Thrace and the Balkans and more than once threatened the capital. Never, though, were these or any other barbarian leaders able fully to restore the position which Gainas had failed to maintain. The emperors were always able to play off their dangerously powerful supporters against each other or to build up new forces to hold them in check. The crisis of the East was over; the defeat of Gainas was as decisive as the Sicilian Vespers.

Aurelian was recalled and replaced Caesarius as praetorian prefect, but only after a considerable interval, in 402. Seeck is surely right in supposing that the final overthrow of Caesarius was due to the weakening of the position of Stilicho by Alaric's invasion of Italy;[42] it may be, also, that the position of Caesarius was shaken not only because of the lessened influence of Stilicho, but because, with Gainas dead and Alaric definitely committed to an Italian war, there was less need for a conciliatory policy toward the remaining barbarians.

This new reversal of fortune brought the long mission of Synesius to a successful conclusion: the benefits which Aurelian had conferred and Caesarius had revoked were reaffirmed. The envoy, however, took French leave of his bene-

[42] In *RE* II 1150. His account of these events in his *Geschichte des Untergangs der antiken Welt* (V 314–26; above, chap. 6, n. 20) is one of the clearest to be found.

factors: during the great earthquake of 402, he fled in terror to a ship bound for Alexandria and sailed without seeing his friends, except for one, to whom he shouted and waved from a distance.[43]

It is entirely certain from the *De Regno,* the *De Providentia* and Hymn 3 that Synesius grasped the full significance of these events. We should, perhaps, take special note of two passages, because of their bearing on his future. In *De Providentia* 18, Synesius tells us that God revealed to the philosopher (himself) that the tyranny would not last long and that the giants (the barbarians) would be cast out whenever "those now in power shall attempt to introduce innovations in our religious rites . . ." and that Typho (Caesarius) himself would fall shortly afterwards. The other passage is in Hymn 3 (Terzaghi 1). Synesius tells us that while he was in Thrace, he

> visited as many temples as were builded for Thy holy ceremonies . . . I supplicated the gods that labour, even as many as hold the fruitful plain of Thrace, and those who on the other side rule the Chalcedonian pastures, whom Thou, O King, hast crowned with Thy annunciating beams, to be Thy sacred ministers. The blessed ones have indeed taken to them my supplications, they have engaged in many labours with me.

Now, in spite of the references to "gods" and "temples," so typical of the hymns of Synesius, this hymn was written when Synesius was already a Christian bishop.[44] The "temples" therefore must have been Christian churches and the "gods" their patron saints — to say nothing of the fact that

[43] *Epist.* 61.
[44] *Contra,* Lacombrade 177. See, however, in the same hymn, "Behold now also in Thy Libya, in Thy august priesthood, a soul feeble and exhausted, one given up to holy prayers to Thee . . ."

open worship in pagan temples in Constantinople would have been quite impossible at that time. What are our passages, then, other than clear recognition by Synesius that the orthodox Christian Church had proved the most effective force of resistance against the barbarians, the necessary support, therefore, of that classicism, that Hellenism to which his life was dedicated?

After stopping briefly at Alexandria, Synesius proceeded to Cyrene, presumably to give an account of his mission.[45] There, too, he remained for a short time only, returning once more to Alexandria, this time for a longer visit — an important one, since it was during this stay that he married. Theophilus, the formidable bishop of Alexandria, officiated at the ceremony.[46] Vasiliev believes that Synesius had already become a Christian at this time, and FitzGerald envisages this as a possibility.[47] It seems much more probable that it was his wife who was a Christian, not, as yet, Synesius; that Theophilus, destroyer of the Serapeum though he was, would himself marry a Christian woman to a pagan provided that the pagan was Synesius — Synesius, one of the most prominent citizens of Cyrenaica; Synesius, the friend of courtiers, cabinet ministers, and generals, of governors and prefects; Synesius, the admired philosopher, scientist, and writer; above all, Synesius, the favored disciple of Hypatia. Such a convert justified a little subtlety and a little time; in a few years we shall meet the Patriarch angling again.

[45] Lacombrade 131–36. He rightly identifies *Epist.* 4 as Synesius' exuberant account of this voyage.

[46] *Epist.* 105.

[47] A. A. Vasiliev, *Histoire de l'Empire Byzantin* (Paris 1932) I 117; Fitz-Gerald, *Letters,* 31. Cf. below, n. 66.

A son was born of Synesius' marriage while he was still
in Alexandria, but in 405 we find him back in Cyrenaica
with his wife and child. The barbarian tribes from the desert
were attacking as usual, and he personally led the defense of
his estate against them, scouting at dawn, conducting patrols
at night, thankful for archers from a neighboring town to
defend access to wells and stream. We find him assembling
weapons, criticizing inadequate leaders, praising good ones,
urging his brother to resist.[48] The war seems not to have
been continuous, but rather a series of yearly raids at harvest
time. Perhaps, as Seeck thinks,[49] the barbarians were encouraged by the ineptitude of the Roman leaders who con-
ducted operations after the expulsion of the German officers
from the army. Certainly there is much in the letters of
Synesius, anti-German though he was, to support this view,
but we also find him praising some of the officers and even
praising barbarian troops when under capable leaders able
to keep them in hand.[50] It may be, also, as we have already
suggested, that the nomadic tribes were beginning to acquire greater mobility through the use of the camel, being
able to attack more unexpectedly and in greater force than
had formerly been possible, and to retreat more rapidly and,
if necessary, to more remote oases. Whatever the explanation, the desert tribes seem to have ravaged the countryside
every year, reducing the landowners to taking refuge in their
fortified villas, capturing at least some of these and some of

[48] For these wars, see *Epist.* 40, 57, 59, 61, 62, 89, 94, 95, 107, 108, 130, 132,
133, 134; *Constitutio; Catastasis. Epist.* 104, 113, 122, and 124, also having to
do with the barbarian wars, seem to belong to the period preceding the embassy
of Synesius; see above, nn. 30 and 32.
[49] (Above, n. 42) 326f and notes. See also Stein I 363.
[50] *Epist.* 62, 78, 94, 110, 130, 132, 133; *Constitutio; Catastasis.*

the smaller towns, and at times besieging even major cities. On one occasion, Synesius speaks not only of the desperate state of Cyrenaica, but of danger to Alexandria itself.[51]

The spasmodic nature of the war, though, left Synesius at least some time to continue his letters and his literary work. We find him sending three completed compositions, the *Dio,* the *De Insomniis* and the essay addressed to Count Paeonius on the gift of an astrolabe, to Hypatia for her approval, the two former being hitherto unpublished works and the third having been written during the stay of Synesius in Constantinople.[52] It is to this period, too, that, following Lacombrade, we ascribe the letters to his brother, describing the education of the latter's son and telling of the birth of two more sons of his own, twins, and also one telling his brother of the dismissal of the rascally trainer in athletics.[53] Nevertheless, he complains that the wars interfere with his writing and even with his beloved hunting.[54]

War and politics, though, were soon to cause him far greater hardships than these. His property near Cyrene was occupied by the barbarians, and they used his house — no

---

[51] *Catastasis* 1569.

[52] *Epist.* 154. "My essay concerning the Gift," referred to in *Epist.* 154, was undoubtedly his letter to Paeonius on the gift of an astrolabe, which is an essay in the form of a letter. Hercher did not print it in his edition of the letters, but FitzGerald has given the translation at the end of the volume of letters, and Terzaghi prints it in the *Opuscula.*

[53] *Epist.* 53, 111, 32, 18. FitzGerald translates the word ἐγεννησάμην in *Epist.* 18 as "born." Lacombrade (137) translates it as "engendrés." That is, according to Lacombrade, the eldest son was begotten and born in Alexandria, but the twins, begotten in Alexandria, were born in Cyrenaica. This makes *Epist.* 18 not inconsistent with *Epist.* 132, in which Synesius writes that it will be hard for him to leave his "wife and child" before going into battle, and with *Epist.* 108, again a letter written on the eve of a battle, in which Synesius recommends his "children" to his brother. The point is a very small one, but it has some bearing on the length of the stay of Synesius in Alexandria.

[54] *Epist.* 61, 130, 134.

doubt a great fortified villa such as we see in the magnificent mosaics at the Bardo in Tunis — as "a base whence to menace Cyrene."[55] Not only that. His political enemies succeeded in driving him away from Cyrene itself: "I mourn over the famous site of Cyrene, in the past the abode of the Carneadae and of the Aristippi, but now of the Joannes and the Julii. In their society I cannot live with pleasure, and so I live away from it with pleasure."[56] In another letter, we find him indignantly repelling his brother's attempt to reconcile him with Julius.[57] We may suppose, with Lacombrade,[58] that he withdrew to Ptolemais, the capital and the metropolitan see of the province. His withdrawal, though, proved to be no retirement: his prestige and his services made it impossible for him to leave the field to his opponents even if he wished to — which one may doubt. The next reasonably certain date in his life is his election as Bishop of Ptolemais, in the summer of 410.[59]

We have already written of the paramount importance of the bishop to the people of his city at the beginning of the fourth century, especially as their defender against oppressive officials and against the barbarians. It is evident that Synesius was chosen precisely because he had shown himself such a staunch opponent of the barbarians, such a courageous defender of the local interests against oppression by corrupt and grasping officials, both civil and military, such an effec-

---

[55] *Epist.* 95.
[56] *Epist.* 50.
[57] *Epist.* 95.
[58] 207.
[59] For this date, see Lacombrade 209–12. FitzGerald also accepts it, but without analysis: *Letters,* 44. Von Campenhausen gives the same date, but only as an approximation; *RE* IV A 1363. We may, however, accept Lacombrade's demonstration as conclusive.

tive advocate of Cyrene and of the province before the Throne itself. As for personal benefactions, Synesius seems to have been a generous master to his slaves and a generous friend to his equals, and above all a liberal and public-spirited citizen.[60]

These were obvious reasons for selecting Synesius as bishop, and the fact that he was known to be generous and public-spirited was a good reason for supposing that he would accept the position. He must, further, have been swayed by his experiences in Constantinople, by the fact that the orthodox Christian Church had proved to be the crystallizing element around which grew the forces of resistance to Gainas and his barbarians. There were, though, four obstacles. Synesius had achieved a nice balance of life between public service, literature and philosophy, and sports — especially hunting. He very genuinely felt that the chase and outdoor life were indispensable to his well-being. In a letter to his brother — one which he asked his brother to make public and especially to bring to the attention of Theophilus — [61] he wrote of his love of arms, horses, dogs, and hunting but said that he would resign himself to giving them up "if it is the will of God." Second, though he detested lawsuits and quarrels, he would nevertheless do his best to perform the administrative duties of bishop so long as strength was given him to do so.[62] Third, he was a mar-

[60] As to slaves, see *Dio* 13; *Epist.* 32, 145. As to friends, see especially *Epist.* 134. As to public life, see especially *Calvitii Encomium* 13; *Epist.* 57, 100.

[61] *Epist.* 105. Our whole discussion of the obstacles to the consecration of Synesius is based on this most extraordinary letter, except when we have indicated other sources. It should be noted that, since Ptolemais was the metropolitan see of the Pentapolis, Theophilus, the patriarch of Alexandria, would be the immediate superior of the new bishop, and that it would be his duty to decide whether or not to confirm the election and to consecrate him.

[62] Cf. *Epist.* 11, written on his acceptance of the charge.

ried man — indeed, as he points out, he had been married
by Theophilus himself — and had no intention of living
apart from his wife: "I will not be separated from her, nor
shall I associate with her surreptitiously like an adulterer
. . . I shall desire and pray to have many virtuous children."
Finally, and most serious of all, there were grave theological
difficulties:

> I can never persuade myself that the soul is of more recent origin
> than the body. Never would I admit that the world and the parts
> which make it up must perish. This resurrection, which is an
> object of common belief, is nothing for me but a sacred and
> mysterious allegory, and I am far from sharing the views of the
> vulgar crowd thereon . . . Just as the eye would be injured by
> an excess of light, and just as darkness is more helpful to those
> of weak eyesight, even so do I consider that the false may be
> beneficial to the populace, and the truth injurious to those not
> strong enough to gaze steadfastly on the radiance of real being.
> If the laws of the priesthood that obtain with us permit these
> views to me, I can take over the holy office on condition that I
> may prosecute philosophy at home and spread legends abroad,
> so that if I teach no doctrine, at all events I undo no teaching,
> and allow men to remain in their already acquired convictions
> . . . No, if I am called to the priesthood, I declare before God
> and man that I refuse to preach dogmas in which I do not be-
> lieve. Truth is an attribute of God, and I wish in all things to
> be blameless before Him.[63]

In short, Synesius was still a Neo-Platonist in many of his
convictions and would not agree to preach any doctrines inconsistent with them.

The struggle was not an easy one. It lasted for more than

---

[63] It will be noted that in this letter, Synesius writes of the Christians as "us."
He must therefore have become a catechumen by the time he wrote it. The
church historians state positively that he was not baptized until after his election;
Evagrius *Hist. Eccl.* 1.15; Nikephoros Kallistos *Hist. Eccl.* 14.55; Photius *Bibl.
Can.* 26. All these are cited by von Campenhausen (above, n. 59).

six months, while Synesius, presumably in Alexandria, tried to secure some declaration that would allow him to reconcile acceptance of the episcopate "with my school of thought and sect." [64] He realized that he could not refuse the episcopate and still return to the Pentapolis; he thought of going to Greece. In fact, though, he was consecrated bishop, probably some time during the first three months of 411. [65]

It has been argued that Synesius did not give way either in the matter of separating from his wife or in his theological position, [66] but this view has not been generally accepted, and Lacombrade, his most recent biographer, shares the opinion that Synesius yielded to Theophilus, "humain, trop humain, le coeur gros d'amertume mais éperdu de bonne volonté." He takes Epistle 11, written by Synesius to the elders of the Church of Ptolemais directly after his consecration, to be an expression of this attitude. [67] Epistle 11 is indeed an expression of the new bishop's attitude, but that attitude seems not one of a man who has either been converted as to the theological points at issue or who has sacrificed his moral position:

> I was unable, for all my strength, to prevail against you and to decline the bishopric, and this in spite of all my machinations;

[64] *Epist.* 96.

[65] *Ibid.* For the date see above, n. 59.

[66] Crawford (above, n. 17) 238–53; A. F. Villemain, *Tableau de l'éloquence chrétienne au IVe siècle* (Paris 1861) 218; H. Koch, "Synesius von Cyrene bei seiner Wahl und Weihe," *Hist. Jahrb.* 23 (1902) 751ff; U. von Wilamowitz-Moellendorff, "Die Hymnen des Proklos und Synesios," *Sitzungsb. der kgl. preuss. Akad. der Wiss.* (Jahrg. 1907) 280f, 286; Bury's Gibbon (6th ed., London 1913) II 325 n. 118. Vasiliev (above, n. 47) writes of Synesius as converted to Christianity as early as the time of his marriage. In another passage (II 156) he remarks that Synesius, though converted to Christianity, married to a Christian, and consecrated bishop of Ptolemais, "se sentait probablement plus paien que chrétien." This seems to imply that Vasiliev believed Synesius to have maintained his reserves.

[67] 224–28.

> nor is it to your will that I have now yielded. Rather was it a
> divine force which brought about the delay then, as it has caused
> my acceptance now . . . If I am not forsaken by God, I shall
> then know that this office of Priesthood is not a decline from
> the realms of philosophy, but, on the contrary, a step upwards
> to them.

The delay, in short, has proved useful, and apparently in the
sense that Synesius had wished: he believed it would be possible to "prosecute philosophy at home and spread legends
abroad," to reconcile the acceptance of the episcopate "with
my school of thought and sect." The matter becomes clearer
when we read Epistle 13. In that letter, Synesius informs
Peter, the Elder, that he has just sent a carrier to Peter "with
the Paschal letters, announcing the date of the holy festival
. . . so that the night which precedes the day in question may
also be consecrated to the mystery of the Resurrection" (τὸ
ἀναστάσιμον . . . μυστήριον). In the same letter, he refers
to this festival as "an old ancestral custom of the Church"
(ἔθος ἀρχαῖον καὶ πάτριον). He concludes, "If I can say none
of the things you are accustomed to hear, there must be for-
giveness for me and blame to yourselves, for instead of choosing one deep in the knowledge of the scriptures, you have
selected one who is ignorant of them." (His profession of
ignorance was of course merely a polite excuse for his refusal
to deliver an Easter sermon: he had been discussing the theological point with Theophilus for more than six months.)
Is not this the very language one might expect from a Synesius who had in the end obtained the theological concessions
which he required of Theophilus? And is it not on one of
the very points concerning which he had made his reserva-

tions? Synesius was upset by the material requirements of his office, but there is no passage that we have been able to find in his writings that is not consistent with the theological reservations which he made in his letter to his brother.

On the other hand, though we have no proof, there is reason to believe that he did separate from his wife. That, with the possible exception of Hymn 8, he never mentioned her after he became bishop is scarcely a convincing argument, because he mentioned her only three times in all the works and letters that have come down to us. First, when he was about to go into battle, he wrote to his brother that he would find it difficult to leave his wife and child.[68] Second, as we have just seen, he wrote that he could not agree to become bishop if that should entail separation from his wife. Third, he mentioned his wife in Hymn 8. The question, for all practical purposes, turns solely on whether Hymn 8 was written before or after Synesius became bishop and, if written after, whether it implies that he had separated from his wife. We have seen that Synesius had three sons, one born in Alexandria and the other two, twins, born in Cyrenaica. We shall see that one of the three died very shortly after the consecration of Synesius. In the hymn, Synesius appears to refer to his two sons. Since he was never in the position of having only two sons until after one of the three had died, this seems to date the hymn to a time subsequent to his consecration. There is a possibility, if one is willing to make a not unplausible emendation of the text, that Synesius is not referring to two sons, but to two sisters,

[68] *Epist.* 132, cited above, n. 53.

but it is not the traditional reading, and we must consider
the hymn at least as likely to have been written after the
consecration as before it.[69] The relevant passage is:

> . . . the partner of my marriage bed, O King, keep Thou from
> illness and harm, united to me, of one mind with me; preserve
> my wife in ignorance of clandestine associates. May she maintain
> a holy couch, unsullied, pious, inaccessible to unlawful desires.

(It will be noted that the word ἐρίηρον which FitzGerald
has translated "united to me" can as well mean "faithful" —
and even "united to me" does not necessarily imply physical
union.) The passage has been interpreted as evidence that
Synesius was "époux heureux et père comblé" at the time he
wrote it.[70] To me, on the contrary, it seems to show a man
separated from his wife against his will and hoping that she
will remain faithful to the marriage which has been so ar-
bitrarily and indecently terminated. If this understanding
of the hymn be correct, then Synesius did separate from his
wife.

However all this may be, the fact that the objections were
made and maintained either for the rest of the good bishop's
life or at the very least for more than six months — this
shows that Synesius, though a deeply religious man, was not
moved to accept the office because of any burning zeal for
the orthodox theology. Rather, he became bishop for reasons
of patriotism, out of a sense of duty. As Wilamowitz well

---

[69] The text is: Γνωτάν τε, συνωρίδα / τεκέων τε φυλάσσοις. Wilamowitz (281;
above, n. 66) proposes a Doric Γνωτᾶν and takes the passage to refer to a pair
of sisters and a pair of children, a reading which would still support the
argument in our text. Lacombrade, however (16ff), printing a comma after
συνωρίδα, understands a pair of sisters and an undefined number of children.
If this be correct, though, then τεκέων seems difficult to accept. Terzaghi, after
hesitation, has definitely rejected the emendation to Γνωτᾶν; *Hymni*, p. 259.

[70] Lacombrade 180.

says, "Der an Besitz, Ansehen und Mut erste Notable der Provinz, fand in dem Bischofsamt die Stelle, von der aus er seine Heimat verteidigen konnte." [71]

Synesius was now entering upon the last years of his life. They were marked by a bitter political struggle; by the varying, occasionally almost desperate, fortunes of war; by conscientious but often distasteful performance of the duties of his episcopal office; by deep personal sorrows; by ill-health.

At the time of his return as bishop, the state of the province appears to have been more favorable than it had been for many years. Gennadius, the civil governor, had given the Pentapolis a mild yet capable administration; the *dux,* Anysius, had proved a brilliant officer and had brought the campaign with the barbarians to a successful close, at least for the time being. Unfortunately, Gennadius was about to be replaced by Andronicus, a man for whom Synesius had done some favors, but one of whom he had the poorest possible opinion, one who, though a Cyrenaican by birth, had been hostile to the interests of Ptolemais in the past. Now, even before arriving in the province, he was instigating an unjustified prosecution of Gennadius, the departing governor, for embezzlement of public funds. Synesius wrote to his friend Troilus at Constantinople, requesting him to intervene with the praetorian prefect Anthemius to secure the revocation of the appointment, partly on the ground that such a man as Andronicus would make a bad governor, partly on the ground that, as a native of Cyrenaica, he could not legally administer the province, since Anthemius him-

---

[71] (Above, n. 66) v. 280. This passage is quoted with approval by von Campenhausen (above, n. 59).

self had caused a new law to be promulgated forbidding that any province should be governed by one of its own natives. More, he had bought his office.[72]

When Andronicus arrived, he fully justified the fears of Synesius. He proved a merciless tax-gatherer, scourging and torturing the *curiales,* bullying them into selling estates to his supporters, oppressing his personal enemies. He was, in short, just such a governor as Synesius had inveighed against in his address to Arcadius.[73]

Synesius, the *curialis* and ambassador, had denounced such oppression before the emperor; Synesius, the bishop, fought Andronicus both at court and on the spot. He now tried to secure the recall of the Governor through another friend, Anastasius, the tutor of the children of Arcadius. In Cyrenaica, he boldly supported the victims, he went to comfort his friend Leucippus, when the latter was subjected to torture by the Governor in the full glare of the African noon.[74] This act provoked the Governor to blasphemy, and Synesius was quick to seize his advantage and to draw up a formal excommunication of his enemy. Lacombrade points out that in this matter Synesius may have gone rather beyond the letter of the law.[75] However that may be, the step checked Andronicus, though not permanently. The Governor at once

---

[72] *Epist.* 73, 72, 58; Cf. *Cod. Iust.* 1.41.1.

[73] *De Regno* 21.

[74] *Epist.* 73, 79. Cf. *Epist.* 46, 118.

[75] 239 n. 55. Synesius, though, states that Andronicus nailed to the church door "edicts of his own" denying the right of sanctuary to his victims and threatening any priests who might afford them sanctuary. Synesius is evidently claiming that the decrees of Andronicus are more extensive or more drastic in penalty than anything authorized by the imperial law. Further, he accuses Andronicus of blasphemy for having called out three times "that no one shall be torn from the hands of Andronicus, not even should he be embracing the foot of Christ Himself." See *Epist.* 57 and 58 for Synesius' account.

promised to moderate his conduct, and Synesius, yielding to the unanimous recommendation of his clergy, suspended publication of the decree of excommunication. But the leopard did not change its spots: Magnus, the son of a man of senatorial rank, but himself a *curialis,* died in consequence of a scourging inflicted by order of Andronicus. Synesius now published his decree of excommunication:

> Andronicus of Berenice let no man call a Christian . . . Let the precincts of no house of God be open to Andronicus and his associates . . . Let every sanctuary and enclosure be shut in their faces . . . I exhort therefore every private individual and ruler not to be under the same roof with them, nor to be seated at the same table, particularly priests, for these shall neither speak to them while living, nor join in their funeral processions when dead. Furthermore, if any one shall flout the authority of this church on the ground that it represents a small town only, and shall receive those who have been excommunicated by it, for that he need not obey that which is without wealth, let such a one know that he is creating a schism in the Church which Christ wishes to be one. Such a man, whether he be deacon, presbyter, or bishop, shall share the fate of Andronicus at our hands, and neither shall we give him our right hand, nor ever eat at the same table with him, and far be it from us to hold communion in the holy mysteries with those desiring to take part with Andronicus and Thoas.[76]

It will be noted that this formula called for the support not only of priests, deacons, and bishops, but also of private persons and, expressly, rulers.

The weapon, destined to become so powerful, proved effec-

---

[76] See *Epist.* 72 for the delay, the story of Magnus, and the publication of the decree. For his curial rank, see above, chap. 6, p. 178 and n. 87. *Epist.* 57 seems to be a public denunciation of Andronicus, coupled with an offer of Synesius either to resign as bishop or to accept a coadjutor. *Epist.* 58 is the formal decree of excommunication.

tive against Andronicus. Perhaps, too, the appeals of Synesius
to his friends in Constantinople had something to do with
the result, and maybe Julius, the old enemy of Synesius, had
his share in the matter, since he also was an opponent of the
Governor. At any rate, the last we hear of Andronicus is in
a letter from Synesius to Theophilus of Alexandria.[77] He
writes that the misfortunes of the wretched man have been
such that

> the Church . . . now . . . pities him for that his experiences
> have exceeded the measure of her malediction. On his account
> we have incurred the displeasure of those now in power . . .
>
> So we have snatched him from the fell tribunal here, and
> have in other respects greatly mitigated his sufferings. If your
> sacred person judges that this man is worthy of any interest, I
> shall welcome this as a signal proof that God has not yet entirely
> abandoned him.

It is evident that Synesius had actually removed Andronicus
from the custody of the civilian authorities, who were trying
him for his misdeeds, and sent him to Theophilus, leaving
it to the latter, apparently, to release him from the excommunication which Synesius had pronounced against him and
to protect him from further prosecution. Perhaps Synesius,
who had borne the brunt of the struggle, did not wish to
leave the prestige of success to the lay authorities and especially not to his old antagonist, Julius, but even if such motives may have entered into his action, we are, one feels, justified in supposing that the mercy of which he spoke was
the principal reason for it. When we consider some of his

---

[77] *Epist.* 90. Anastasius in Constantinople certainly supported Andronicus at
one time, but there is some reason to suppose that he may have changed sides
later; above, chap. 6, n. 92. For the enmity between Julius and Andronicus, see
Epist. 79.

other actions as bishop, we shall see that moderation, reason-
ableness, and mercy were characteristic of them.

It is unexpected to see a provincial bishop daring at this
early date to excommunicate an imperial governor; interesting to find that the excommunication proved effective; startling to see the victorious bishop dare to remove the disgraced
governor from the custody of the lay court. Fascinating, too,
from a slightly different point of view, to hear this same
bishop, in his denunciation of the upstart, Andronicus, refer
to his own descent from "Eurysthenes who settled the Dorians in Sparta."⁷⁸ It is, though, no less important to realize
that the struggle between the two men really had nothing to
do with the Church. Synesius had been compelled to accept
the episcopal office because the people felt him to be their
natural protector against invasion and oppression. Andronicus represented the tyrannical bureaucracy that was attempting to enrich its members no doubt, but also to preserve the
Empire at the cost of the curial class. Synesius was defending
that class (to which he himself belonged) because he felt it
to be the true representative of the classical tradition, of the
old life of the πόλις and the *municipium*. In the course of
this basically lay quarrel, Synesius saw an opportunity to use
ecclesiastical weapons against his opponent: he did not hesi-
tate to use them — indeed, we have seen that he wished to
proceed to extremes more quickly than his clergy would
allow — and with devastating effectiveness.

One final period of desperate warfare darkened the last
years of Synesius. Anysius, the successful general, had been
replaced not long after Synesius had returned to Ptolemais

⁷⁸ *Epist.* 57.

as bishop. He seems to have been followed by Innocentius, a well-intentioned but ineffective commander. Synesius, bishop though he was, stood watch upon the walls of Ptolemais, placed pickets at night, prepared (so he said) at one moment to flee across the sea, at another to die beside the altar of his church. What he did do in fact was to send an extremely dramatic appeal to one of his friends with a request that the latter should have the desperate situation brought to the attention of the imperial council. It was quite possibly in response to the appeal of Synesius that a new commander, Marcellinus, was dispatched to help the beleaguered provincials. If so, Synesius had performed a last and very great service for the Pentapolis: Marcellinus completely routed the enemy and restored peace throughout the region.[79]

Through war and peace, political reverses and political success, Synesius continued to perform his purely ecclesiastical duties. We have noticed that he forebore from giving theological instruction in connection with the celebration of Easter; when some Eunomian missionaries became active in his see, he appears to have consulted St. Isidore of Pelusium, probably an old friend from Alexandrian days, before decreeing that they should be expelled. And even then he insisted that they were not to be plundered, but should be allowed to take back across the frontier all property they had brought with them. He composed disputed episcopal elections; he settled quarrels between bishops concerning

[79] *Epist.* 57, 62. For the contention that Marcellinus was general (*dux*), not governor (*praeses*), see above, chap. 6, and cf. Lacombrade 230 (n. 7) and 234. *Contra,* however, Otto Seeck, "Studien zu Synesios" (as above, chap. 6, n. 8); Wilhelm Ensslin in *RE* XIV 1444.

property; he healed quarrels between priests — in reporting some of these to Theophilus, his ecclesiastical superior, he expressly refrained from mentioning names and requested Theophilus, if the latter should guess the identity of the priests involved, still to refrain from naming them in his reply, since Synesius wished to rebuke them in private only. He encouraged the election of a worthy candidate as bishop and requested Theophilus to consecrate him; he urged that a technical defect should not be used as a reason for unseating a bishop who had held his office for many years, one beloved by his congregation; he treated with personal kindness and respect — though not recognizing him as a bishop in church — a bishop who had been expelled from his see for having sided with St. John Chrysostom against Theophilus, and referred to Chrysostom with marked respect even when writing to Theophilus himself; he suggested that this bishop and others in similar situations should return to their sees, now that peace had been restored in the Church, and that they should not be accorded episcopal honors if they chose not to return. He founded a monastery — Neo-Platonist or Christian, he was still devoted to the life of contemplation; it may well be that he hoped to be allowed to resign his charge and to retire there. In short, he was inclined to avoid theological disputes and in all matters of practical administration to advocate neither unnecessarily drastic measures nor weakness nor evasion, but rational, moderate, humane courses of action. He was, we believe, a highly unorthodox Christian, but an exceptionally good one.[80]

[80] For Synesius and the Eunomians, see *Epist.* 5; Isidore of Pelusium *Epist.* 1.241; Lacombrade 259. For other aspects of his episcopal activities, see *Epist.* 12, 13, 45, 66, 67, 76, 121, 126, 128.

The last years of his life, then, were successful so far as external matters were concerned. He performed his ecclesiastical duties well, at the sacrifice of his affections and his favorite pastimes, but not at the sacrifice of his principles. Politically, he was very conspicuously successful; he seems to have had much to do with bringing the war against the barbarians to a successful conclusion.[81] On the other hand, this period was a time of suffering and great sorrow for him. We have seen that, in all probability, he accepted, though sadly, separation from his wife. All three of his sons, of whom he had such hopes, died during the years of his episcopate. One of them, indeed, died just before he arrived in Ptolemais after his consecration.[82] He lost the friendship of Anastasius[83] and that of Hypatia herself.[84] Further, he was in ill-health.[85] He seems to have survived Theophilus, who died on October 15, 412, but probably by very little, since we have no letters addressed to the new patriarch, Cyril.[86] Let us quote his last, sad letter to Hypatia:

> I salute you, and I beg of you to salute your most happy comrades for me, august Mistress. I have long been reproaching you that I am not deemed worthy of a letter, but now I know that I

[81] The wars against the desert tribes were certainly not permanently ended by the victory of Marcellinus. We find Anastasius reorganizing the defense of Cyrenaica; Joh. Antiochenus, *Frag.* 216. Justinian, too, constructed fortresses in the country and walls at Arsinoe that are still imposing; Procopius *De Aedif.* 6.4.2. But at least we hear no more of raids and wars during the brief period that remained of the life of Synesius. *Contra,* von Campenhausen thinks it probable that Synesius died in these wars, shortly after the composition of the *Catastasis*; (above, n. 59) 1364. The chronology of Lacombrade seems to us more probable.

[82] *Epist.* 10, 16, 57, 81, 126.
[83] *Epist.* 46; cf. above, n. 77.
[84] *Epist.* 10, 16.
[85] *Epist.* 15, 16.
[86] See Lacombrade (251f) for an acute and convincing analysis of *Epist.* 12, from which he deduces that Synesius survived Theophilus.

am despised by you all for no wrongdoing on my part, but because I am unfortunate in many things, in as many as a man can be. If I could only have had letters from you and learnt how you were all faring — I am sure you are happy and enjoying good fortune — I should have been relieved, in that case, of half my own trouble, in rejoicing at your happiness. But now your silence has been added to the sum of my sorrows. I have lost my children, my friends, and the goodwill of every one. The greatest loss of all, however, is the absence of your divine spirit. I had hoped that this would always remain to me, to conquer both the caprices of fortune and the evil turns of fate.[87]

One thing, at least, Synesius was spared: there is no reason whatever to believe that he survived to hear of the horrid death of Hypatia in 415 at the hands of the fanatical Christian mob of Alexandria.

Such was the life of Synesius. Why have we coupled him with Rutilius Namatianus and Paulinus of Nola? Why have we chosen, to illustrate this chapter (see plate IV), a gorgon's head of white marble, once part of an old Doric temple at Cyrene and later incorporated into a Byzantine fountain? Rutilius, it seems to us, felt clearly the incompatibility of classical civilization and the Christian religion. We have tried to support our belief that, fiercely loyal to Rome and the old way of life, he felt deep within himself that Rome was destined to perish and the new religion to triumph. But even if Rutilius whole-heartedly believed that it was Rome that would survive, he certainly did not believe that considerable elements of classicism would survive precisely through the Christian Church. Paulinus, also, the favored pupil of Ausonius, felt the two paths to be incompatible, and, on becoming converted to an active Christianity, chose asceticism

[87] *Epist.* 10.

and renounced his literary friends, his political prospects and his civic responsibilities. Yet force of circumstances compelled him, like Synesius — and at just about the same time — to accept consecration as bishop and to do his best to protect his people — and, in doing so, no doubt to preserve elements of the classical life against the barbarian tide. But even in this emergency, he remained a pacifist and, when it became necessary for him actually to face the barbarians in person, fulfilled his boast.

> nos crucis invictae signum et confessio munit,
> armatique deo mentem non quaerimus arma
> corporis . . .[88]

Synesius, the contemporary of them both, made a different and more prophetic choice than either. Even after he had become bishop of Ptolemais, he still kept watch against the enemy, he still set out pickets at night. One feels that he found it difficult not to take, any longer, a direct part in the fighting. He still praised and encouraged successful generals and appealed to the consistory for help when the military situation appeared desperate. Nor did his assumption of the office of bishop appear to him inconsistent with political activity: the great event in local politics after his consecration as bishop was the overthrow of Andronicus — it is an extraordinary combination of the old and the new to find Synesius boasting of his descent from Eurysthenes in the very address in which he announces the excommunication of the Governor. Both before and after his conversion, Synesius remained without sympathy for fanaticism; both before and after, he attached real importance to style in writing. As

[88] Paulinus *Carmen* 26.106ff.

a young man, he wrote to Hypatia to ask whether she thought his writings worthy of Greek ears.[89] As a bishop, he warned that God attached no importance to inspired diction or "literary pettiness": οὐδὲν μέλει τῷ θεῷ θεοφορήτου λέξεως. πνεῦμα θεῖον ὑπερορᾷ μικρολογίαν συγγραφικήν.[90] But his own diction is certainly not inelegant in this very passage. It was as bishop, too, that he wrote to Theophilus, complimenting him on the style of a Paschal letter.[91] Once more, it was in a report to Theophilus that Synesius apologized for using a Latinism.[92]

In short, Synesius, both before and after his conversion, was not only a classical figure, but perhaps more truly so than most of his contemporaries — at least, than those of his contemporaries that we know about. Though Rutilius felt it his duty to return to his native Gaul, Rome was the unquestioned center of his interests; Paulinus lived in Gaul, Spain, and Italy without, so far as we can see, any sense of being more at home in one of these regions than another — if he preferred Nola, it was only because the tomb of St. Felix was there. To Synesius, Constantinople was exile;[93] Athens indifferent;[94] even Alexandria and Hypatia could not draw him away, though they tempted him, from Cyrene.[95] Cyrene and Cyrenaica were his life; he lived for his πόλις as truly as any Greek of the high classical era, and, as truly as any of them, stood for and represented in himself

---

[89] *Epist.* 154.
[90] Homily 1.
[91] *Epist.* 9.
[92] *Epist.* 67.
[93] Hymn 3.1600; *De Insomniis* 9.
[94] *Epist.* 136.
[95] *Epist.* 124.

the classical interest in balance and beauty, in moderation and good sense.

In character and interests, then, Synesius, though he lived as late as the fifth century after Christ, was the embodiment of classical Cyrene. And it was his very devotion to the classical spirit that led him, in spite of intellectual and personal difficulties, to grasp at the Christian Church as the only possible supporter of civilization, classical or otherwise, in the time in which he lived. Rutilius and Paulinus of Nola had each of them understood that Christianity was incompatible with classical civilization in its pure form, and each took his stand accordingly, the one rejecting Christianity and the other his classical past. Synesius did neither: he deliberately took the old Doric acroterion and, painfully for himself, transformed it into the Byzantine fountain, from which the spring of classicism continued to refresh the eminently Christian State, which, in turn, protected and developed civilization for another thousand years.

Postscript

Ignorance of Dutch has unfortunately prevented me from reading a comparatively recent article about Synesius: "Synesios vom Cyrene, liberator, mysticus, bisschop," by A. J. Visser. This appeared in *Nederlandsch Archief voor Kerchengeschiedenis* 39 (1952).

An interesting and balanced study of one of the important works of Synesius is *Il "De Providentia" di Sinesio di Cirene, Studio critico e traduzione* (Padua 1959), by Salvatore Nicolosi. The author puts a healthy emphasis on the tendency of Synesius to exaggerate, to see himself and his friends as angels, his opponents as devils. (Cf. above, chapter 6 n. 80, and also n. 32 above.) This, though, is a tendency common to all men. It was indeed marked in Synesius, but perhaps not so much more strongly marked in him than in the rest of us. Let us remember his intervention on behalf of his old and bitter enemy Andronicus, his patience when his admired and beloved Hypatia turned away from him.

On page 244 above, I pointed out that the "temples" visited by Synesius when he was in Constantinople must have been Christian churches, and the "gods" their patron saints. Yet in a passage immediately following, I doubted that Synesius had become a Christian at the time of his marriage by Theophilos, bishop of Alexandria, to a Christian woman. This although, as I mentioned, Vasiliev supposed him to have been a Christian at this time and FitzGerald thought it a possibility. I did not go into my reasons at that point, but they were, of course, the theological objections raised by Synesius to the Christian religion just before his consecration as bishop of Ptolemais. These (see above, p. 250) were considerable: he did not believe that the soul was of more recent origin than the body. Nor that the world was destined to perish. Nor in the resurrection except as "a sacred and mysterious allegory."

Yet there is indeed good reason to believe that Synesius was already a catechumen when he was in Constantinople. Henri Irénée Marrou, in his interesting lecture, "Synesius of Cyrene and Alexandrian Neoplatonism," published (pages 126–50) in *The Conflict Between Paganism and Christianity,* already referred to on p. 203 above, calls our attention to another passage in Hymn 3 (Terzaghi 1), the hymn quoted by me concerning the visits made by Synesius to the churches in Constantinople: "Now at last, let my suppliant soul bear the seal of the Father." The expression used is σφραγῖδα πατρός, and Marrou rightly points out that it is a technical one for Christian baptism. Synesius, then, was a catechumen at this time. In view, though, of the persistence of his theological doubts, we may suppose that he remained in this state until very shortly before his consecration as bishop of Ptolemais.

CHAPTER X

TWO REVIEWS

A: Rome and the City of God: An Essay on the Constitutional Relationships of Empire and Church in the Fourth Century (KARL FREDERICK MORRISON)

R ENDER therefore unto Caesar the things which are Caesar's; and unto God the things that are God's." This quotation, with which Professor Morrison ends his essay, was spoken by a Jew to Jews, but the attitude of the Roman State to the Jews was entirely consistent with it. The author points out that the concepts *gens, populus,* and *civitas* were familiar in Roman law as legal corporations which, by virtue of their separate ethnic or national characters, were entitled to live according to their own laws and customs so long as their practices did not conflict with the *utilitas publica.*

The early Church, he continues, was clearly conscious of its Jewish origin, claimed similar privileges for itself, and after the edict of Galerius, obtained recognition of its claim.

Yet the emperor still had an important part in the definition of faith and in the trial and deposition of bishops. He

The first review is reprinted from *Speculum* 40 (1965) 360–62; the second, from *Speculum* 35 (1960) 638–47. The books reviewed were published respectively in 1964 as part 1 of vol. 54 (n.s.) of the Transactions of the American Philosophical Society and in 1959 (ed. Eugene F. Rice, Jr.) by the Cornell University Press.

frequently called synods and councils to decide these matters, and they gathered under his patronage or that of his representatives. But, although the emperor confirmed and enforced the decisions of such gatherings, or, rejecting them upon appeal, submitted the issues anew to competent ecclesiastical bodies for readjudication, yet "he did not frame or promulgate them . . . the imperial power supplemented the juridical organs of the Church, without itself being one of them or altering them in any way." (One is reminded of the trial of Christ before Caiaphas and Pilate.)

The emperor would of course have his own opinion of what was the true faith — and perhaps of which dogma was the more consistent with the interests of the Empire. If he was interested primarily in politics, or if he was blinded by intolerance, he would have many ways of bringing pressure to bear on synods and councils to render decisions favorable to his views. The position contained at least the germ of caesaropapism.

The second half of this study is devoted to an analysis of the situation from the theological point of view as seen by Saints Athanasius, Hilary, and Ambrose. The interminable vicissitudes of the contest between St. Athanasius and the Arians illustrate clearly both the role which Athanasius felt the emperor might properly assume, and also the exercise of improper pressure, which the saint resisted with all his might, feeling that Constantius "infringed ecclesiastical order and mingled Roman sovereignty with the constitution of the Church, introducing the Arian heresy into the Church of God."

St. Hilary emphasizes especially the second of these points, considering the Emperor not merely the abettor of the Arians but the fomentor of the Arians, Antichrist himself. Professor Morrison amusingly points out that St. Hilary waited to use this wild language until Constantius was safely dead.

He also remarks: "Had Constantius undertaken the support of the Homoousians, Athanasius and Hilary might have regarded his efforts with the same favor which orthodox bishops later showed to orthodox emperors in their attempts to stamp out heresy. But Constantius fostered the Arians, and the Fathers, not being able to reject the Roman Empire, were forced to emphasize the distinction between the Empire and the Church . . ." That, one feels, comes unpleasantly close to the root of the matter. Said Bishop Warburton, "Orthodoxy, my Lord, is my doxy; heterodoxy is another man's doxy." In an age that knew no tolerance, those that disagreed with the doxy of the government took the lofty position that it should not bring pressure upon them in support of its doxy; those who agreed with the doxy of the government were very willing to accept its pressure on their opponents.

St. Ambrose at any rate accepted the help of the State in religious matters or opposed its authority according to whether the ruler opposed or favored the Arians. He was probably the instigator of Gratian's decree against the Arians; he certainly welcomed it.[1] He was jubilant when Gratian restored to the Catholics a basilica which had been assigned to the Arians;[2] he was outraged when the empress Justina endeavored to have two basilicas assigned to the Arians.[3] He

[1] Dudden (above, chap. 7, n. 1) I 191f.
[2] *Ibid*.
[3] Dudden I 271–80.

was the protagonist in the great struggle concerning the Altar of Victory.

But he went further still: as bishop, he was the proper guide for the conscience of Christian emperors. Valentinian II, a mere catechumen, should not presume to assign basilicas to the Arians or to restore the Altar of Victory to the senate if Ambrose, the bishop, told him that it was wrong to do so. It was for Ambrose, the bishop, not for Theodosius, the emperor, to decide whether the Christians should be compelled to rebuild the synagogue which they had destroyed at Callinicum. With more propriety from our point of view, Ambrose excluded the emperor Maximus from communion because of the murder of Gratian, the emperor Theodosius because of the Massacre of Thessalonica.

The circle had come full swing: if Constantius had threatened caesaropapism, St. Ambrose was the prototype of theocracy. *Pace* Morrison, one feels that St. Ambrose at least, among the Fathers of the fourth century, showed some indications of being willing to retain for the Church a penny or two that might properly have been rendered unto Caesar.

It seems probable, though, that this trend might have been reversed in the west — it never really developed in the east — except for the fact that the emperors in the west gave way before too long to kings at once Arian and barbarian, rulers too weak to resist their Catholic subjects, led, as these were, by a comparatively educated Catholic clergy. It would be ungenerous to impute insincerity to Theodoric when he wrote, with the pen of Cassiodorus, "religionem imperare non possumus, quia nemo cogitur ut credat invitus," [4] but

---

[4] Cass. *Var.* 2.27.

it would be stupid not to recognize that when, at the end of his life, he did persecute the Catholic Church, he undermined one of the two pillars (the other being the Gothic army) on which Gothic rule in Italy was based. Clovis, too, made a curious comment on his own conversion to Catholicism when he said, "It irketh me sore that these Arians hold a part of Gaul. Let us go forth, then, and with God's aid bring the land under our sway." [5]

If the weakness of the barbarian kings strengthened the position of the Catholic clergy, the distance of the emperors was no less a factor in strengthening the position of the popes. Vigilius could not oppose Justinian and the Three Chapters with the impunity enjoyed by Gelasius in his opposition to Anastasius and the *Henotikon*.[6]

Morrison makes good use of his sources; it is a pleasure to find the too often neglected Theodosian Code among them. He has given us a clear, interesting, and excellently written essay. It is to be hoped that he will carry his story further.

B: *Medieval and Renaissance Studies*
(THEODOR E. MOMMSEN)

If Theodor E. Mommsen did not possess the exuberantly fertile genius of his grandfather, he did have an excep-

[5] Gregory of Tours, *Hist. Franc.* 2.27 (MGH, *Script. rer. Merov.*, I 99): "Valde molestum fero, quod hi Arriani partem teneant Galliarum. Eamus cum Dei adiutorium, et superatis redegamus terram in ditione nostra." English text from Dalton's translation.

[6] For Gelasius, cf. Peter Charanis, *Church and State in the Later Roman Empire* (University of Wisconsin Press, Madison 1939) 19–39. This book, though written with perhaps more sympathy for the imperial point of view than Morrison's essay, may be usefully compared with it, since Charanis' work deals with a later but in many ways similar controversy.

tionally penetrating and clear mind, utter sincerity, and a deep earnestness of purpose — by no means incompatible with an alert, pleasantly astringent sense of humor. It might have been expected that these qualities, combined as they were in him with excellent training and great erudition, would have enriched us with a major work from his hand. If the circumstances of his life have disappointed us of this, we must be the more grateful to Eugene F. Rice for having gathered together fourteen of Mommsen's major studies and offered them to us in this beautifully printed and illustrated volume. Rice truly remarks that these papers, viewed as a whole, strikingly bring out "both the coherence and the variety of his scholarship."

The opening study treats of the negotiations leading to the marriage between the sister of Frederick the Fair of Habsburg and Duke Charles of Calabria, the son of Robert the Wise. These were a contest in astuteness, Frederick wishing to acquire at least theoretical recognition of imperial authority over the Guelf lands and towns in Italy, the Angevin determined to avoid that, yet wishing to make certain that Frederick would not support his rival, Peter, the Aragonese king of Sicily. The second paper, dealing with much the same period, analyzes the rise to power of Castruccio Castracani, and his relations with Louis of Bavaria. Here again, it is the German ruler who seems to have been overreached. Mommsen makes his point admirably clear:

> The fall of the Hohenstaufen had removed the peninsula's supreme source of law . . . Yet ultimately every political authority had to be legitimized in law, however fictitious in origin . . . The Guelfs turned to the Papacy; more specifically, the Guelf

communes appealed to customary law . . . The Guelfs, then, could consider themselves "conservatives." The case was very different for rulers like Castruccio, who had arisen out of noth- ing . . . In most cases, they had used republican forms to rise to power in their own communes. But once on top they inevitably tried to secure their authority with other than democratic guar- antees, in principle always revocable . . . We see him [Castruc- cio] after each forward step in his career turn immediately to the German king in order to obtain legal sanction for what he had already acquired in fact. By studying the royal grants . . . we can follow his rapid rise to power, but in estimating their real significance we must recognize that in none of them was Castruccio given anything he did not already possess.

Conversely, to return to the first essay, Frederick of Habs- burg had hoped to obtain at least titular recognition of im- perial supremacy by appointing his brother-in-law, Duke Charles of Calabria, "imperial vicar for all areas in Italy which were Guelf in the time of Henry VII." But King Robert, holding his kingdom as a papal fief, and leader of the Guelf party in Italy, could not acknowledge the imperial authority in Italy. In the very document in which he an- nounced the marriage of his son to Frederick's sister, he called Frederick "ducem Austrie Alemanie regem illustrem," and in another, written before the marriage but after it had been arranged, he referred to Henry VII as "se Romanorum regem dicentis."

The third paper publishes a bull of Pope Julius II, a copy of which was found — Mommsen is too modest to say that he found it himself — in the Scheide Collection of the library of Princeton University. The text is preceded by an explana- tion of the circumstances which led to its promulgation. In his successful efforts to bring the Helvetian Federation into the Holy League (an alliance nominally directed against Alfonso d'Este, duke of Ferrara, and the Bentivoglio family of Bologna, but actually against Louis XII), the Pope used both the carrot and the stick. The carrot was, of course, money; this bull was the stick. By excommunicating the French sent by Louis XII (but not, as Mommsen points out, Louis XII himself, who remained "charissimus in Christo filius noster Ludovicus Francorum rex christianissimus") to help the enemies of the League, and excommunicating in advance any others, "presertim Helvetiis et Suetensibus prefatis," who might join these enemies or their helpers — by this excommunication, Julius both brought into line his rather hesitant allies and made it difficult for the very Catholic Swiss to enter the war on the French side. Since the last thing these professional soldiers desired was to remain without pay from either side, this stick proved effective in persuading them to be content with somewhat fewer carrots than they would otherwise have insisted on receiving.

The last essay in this series reviews the sources from which we hear of the destruction of the Parthenon during the siege of the Acropolis by the Venetian army in 1687. It is only too well known that a bomb from a mortar penetrated the roof, and set off a store of powder that had been put in the Parthenon by the Turks, thus reducing to ruins perhaps the most perfect building of antiquity — or, indeed, of any other time. It has, though, been a matter of controversy whether this was accidental or deliberate. The question is primarily one of differing witnesses, some of whom speak of the disaster in rather general terms as if it were the result of a haphazard shot, while others tell us that a deserter from the besieged army informed the besiegers of the existence of the powder magazine and that they thereupon specifically concentrated their fire on the Parthenon. Mommsen inclines to believe this testimony, giving his reasons, in spite of its rejection by Ranke and others, and is certain that in any case the destruction of the Parthenon cannot be called " 'an unfortunate accident.' " He feels that "all the buildings on the Acropolis" had become "military objectives," that "Although the Venetians regretted the ruin of the Parthenon, they were highly pleased by this quick success of their arms; they felt no need for apology when they announced the news of the conquest of Athens in the *Reporti di Venezia* and other official and semi-official publications which were sent all over Europe."

Those who feel otherwise must remember that an officer has an overriding duty to his soldiers not to expose their lives uselessly or longer than necessary. Further, that our own country, though it has not been the first to use methods of undiscriminating destruction in warfare, has not been among the less effective users of such methods. The fault is not that of the soldiers, but that of a society which tolerates war, or at least tolerates the use of such methods in war. The destruction of the Parthenon was a deplorable event, but it is not to be unqualifiedly condemned by, of all the people who have lived on earth, our generation. It is interesting to notice that this essay was first published in 1941.

The next seven studies are devoted to Petrarch. Petrarchan study was, as F. G. Marcham reminds us in his introduction to the present volume, the center of Mommsen's scholarly interests. The series starts, fittingly, with a sketch of the life and work of the poet, originally printed as an introduction to Anna Maria Armi's translation of Petrarch's *Sonnets and Songs,* published by the Pantheon Press in 1946. It is a well-balanced and sensitive introduction to these poems; it is not primarily an analysis of Petrarch's poetic art.

In the next paper Mommsen identifies a hitherto unrecognized representation — he points out that a portrait is not intended — of the coronation of Petrarch as poet laureate on the Capitol in 1341. This is found, most appropriately, in a manuscript, dated 1418, of his *De Viribus Illustribus.* It is of special interest because earlier in date than other known representations of him as laureate, and as showing that in the early part of the fifteenth century it was still remembered that the laurel crown "consecrated in him 'the great poet and the great historian.'" We are thus reminded that, though we remember Petrarch today primarily for his Italian poetry and as one of the founders of the Italian language, he himself considered his Latin epic, *Africa,* his greatest title to fame, and his contemporaries "found his principal merit in his Latin writings, not in his Italian poetry." The relevant page of the codex is beautifully reproduced.

John Addington Symonds in his famous article on the Renaissance in *The Encyclopaedia Britannica* (11th ed.) wrote: "Petrarch first opened a new method of scholarship, and revealed what we denote as humanism . . . It roused a desire to reappropriate the whole abandoned provinces of mundane energy, and a hope to emulate antiquity in works of living loveliness and vigour." It is not surprising to learn that Petrarch himself was conscious of such desires, but it is interesting to be shown in his own words how clearly he was aware of them, what he thought of classical antiquity, of the succeeding ages through his own time, what he foresaw for the future.

This Mommsen does in his next essay, "Petrarch on the Dark Ages." He reminds us that Petrarch "stated in his *Secretum* that he had confined his work *De Viribus Illustribus* to the time 'from Romulus to Titus.'" That he wrote, "Quid est enim aliud omnis historia quam Romana laus?" Again, referring to Charlemagne, "Carolum regem quem magni cognomine equare Pompeio et Alexandro audent." And, writing of his own times, "Nolui autem pro tam paucis nominibus claris, tam procul tantasque per tenebras stilum ferre: ideoque vel materiae vel labori parcens, longe ante hoc saeculum historiae limitem statui et defixi." Also, addressing his own poem, *Africa*:

> . . . Michi degere vitam.
> Impositum varia rerum turbante procella.
> At tibi fortassis, si — quod mens sperat et optat —
> Es post me victura diu, meliora supersunt
> Secula: non omnes veniet Letheus in annos
> Iste sopor! Poterunt discussis forte tenebris
> Ad purum priscumque iubar remeare nepotes.

Tantasque per tenebras! *discussis forte tenebris*! The Dark Ages! *O Speculum tenebrarum*! [It will be remembered that this review was printed in *Speculum*.]

In "Petrarch and the Decoration of the *Sala Virorum Illustrium* in Padua," Mommsen has undertaken a task of somewhat different nature. With the aid of an illuminated manuscript in the State Library of Darmstadt, a translation of Petrarch's *De Viribus Illustribus,* he establishes the original appearance of the hall (the present *Sala dei Giganti*) as built by Petrarch's friend and patron, Francesco il Vecchio da Carrara. Following Julius von Schlosser, the discoverer of the Darmstadt codex, Mommsen feels that the illuminations of this manuscript are undoubtedly taken from the original decorations of the hall. He shows how very closely they follow the text of Petrarch, and draws attention to the fact that many of the Roman scenes show identifiable buildings as they actually existed at about his time. Further, he notices that all those identifiable are either classical or at least incorporate visible remains of classical structures. Indeed, he is inclined to believe, with the sixteenth-century humanist Marcantonio Michiel, that Petrarch (and Lombardo, according to the Venetian) supplied the subject-matter of these pictures. In fact Mommsen goes further, and feels that the selection of Roman backgrounds and perhaps even the particular monuments shown were due to the advice of Petrarch. If so, it is the more amusing " 'that costumes as well as the architecture' " — except of course the identifiable classical buildings, and even they, as we have seen, were shown as they appeared at the time — " 'are decidedly those of the fourteenth century, not those of ancient Rome.' " In conclusion, the article mentions other great halls similarly decorated and notes that in none of them, with a single exception, were the characters selected taken solely from Roman history. This paper gains very greatly from the number and excellence of the illustrations.

Not unconnected with the study on the *Sala Virorum*

Illustrium is the following one, "Petrarch and the Choice of Hercules." Following Panofsky, Mommsen points out that the conception of Virtue personified was not acceptable to Christian theology, though personification of the various virtues was allowable, as is shown by the many medieval representations of the cardinal and other virtues. It may be for this reason that Petrarch did not mention the choice of Hercules in his life of that hero. As Cicero tells us — we quote Cicero and not Xenophon because, as Mommsen reminds us, Petrarch did not know Greek, and so, though he cited Xenophon as one of the sources of the story, he really knew it only through Cicero — "Herculem illum, quem hominum fama beneficiorum memor in concilio caelestium collocavit . . ." Fame among men, though, was no part of the reward promised to the Christian. Yet Petrarch did mention the tale in a later work. In his *De Vita Solitaria*, begun in 1346, he wrote that when Hercules "in bivio" (Mommsen permits himself an interesting and learned digression concerning Petrarch's insertion of this phrase into the tale) chose the path of virtue, it led him "non ad humanae modo gloriae verticem, sed in opinionem divinitatis." The essay ends in emphasizing the importance attached by Petrarch to *virtus*, that quality which enabled the truly illustrious man to shape his own destiny and "to achieve true fame through great deeds." In his earlier essay, "Petrarch on the Dark Ages," Mommsen wrote: "It would be highly gratifying to our sense of the logical if we were able to prove conclusively that this gravitation towards ancient Rome originated in and resulted directly from Petrarch's coronation which made him a *civis Romanus* both legally and ideally.

The material at our disposal, however, is too scanty to show this with absolute certainty." The coronation took place in 1341. Is not the fact that Petrarch did not mention the choice of Hercules in his life of that hero, probably written, Mommsen tells us, in 1337 or shortly afterwards, but did mention it twice and did refer to *virtus* as the path to mundane glory in his *De Vita Solitaria*, begun in 1346 — is not this at least a little further evidence in support of Mommsen's hypothesis?

One of the glories of Cornell University is the Petrarch Collection left to the library by Willard Fiske. Nor is this collection allowed to stagnate: a recent addition is a manuscript of Petrarch's will, bought not many years ago. The will had never been translated into English, and Mommsen undertook the task, using the recently acquired manuscript but of course collating it with others. *Petrarch's Testament* was sadly, but appropriately enough for a Petrarchan, Mommsen's last book.[7] It is from that book that the next study is taken: "The Last Will: a Personal Document of Petrarch's Old Age." It is a perspicacious analysis, sympathetic but frank, of the provisions of the will, and of the light they cast upon Petrarch's mentality and character, his circumstances, and his friends. The tactful consideration shown in the bequests made to those friends, his understanding of painting — he possessed a Simone Martini and a Giotto and spoke most highly of Giotto's work, both in the will itself and elsewhere — his touches of vanity, even a charming and gentle humor. Mommsen especially calls our

[7] Edited and translated, with an introduction, by Theodor E. Mommsen (Cornell University Press 1957).

attention to the delightful remark with which Petrarch accompanied the bequest of a silver and gilded goblet to his old friend Lombardo della Seta: "Let him drink water from it, which he drinks with pleasure — indeed with much greater pleasure than he drinks wine."

Mommsen is struck by the fact that the will makes no disposition of Petrarch's books, an omission the more surprising not only because these surely formed a very substantial part of his estate (at least enough, if they were to be mortgaged or sold, to pay for building a small chapel at Arquà, a project that was never realized), but because he had shown great interest in the disposition both of his own library and in that of Boccaccio. Indeed, he had at one time assembled his library in the house in Venice which the Republic had provided for him in return for his agreement to leave his books as the foundation for a public library there. Mommsen explains the silence of the will by supposing that, at the time he drew it, Petrarch still felt bound by this agreement. He seems, however, later to have taken his books to Arquà and later still to Padua, and in the end they were dispersed.

The section of the volume dealing with Petrarchan studies concludes with "Rudolph Agricola's Life of Petrarch." It is not necessary here to discuss the fate and influence of that work, to bring out, as Mommsen very ably does, both its good qualities and its defects. We may, however, close our review of this section by quoting a remark of Agricola's which Mommsen also found worthy of quotation:

It is glorious to have deserved praise on account of some achievement, and the glory of whatever has been excellently done remains; but it is most glorious to create for oneself those things for which one is praised . . . To such a glory, it seems to me, nobody is more entitled than Francesco Petrarca, to whom all the erudition of our era is owed.

The last section of the volume turns to an entirely different period, the first quarter of the fifth century after Christ. For reasons of convenience, we shall open our review of this section with the second of the three essays in this section, "Aponius and Orosius on the Significance of the Epiphany." Mentioning that the original significance of January 6th as the date chosen by large sections of the Church for the celebration of the birth of Christ had largely died out — not, however, in Jerusalem — Mommsen points out that the Roman Church, strongly supported by St. Augustine, selected that date to celebrate the Epiphany, the revelation of Christ specifically to the Gentiles as symbolized by His adoration by the three Magi. To the eastern Churches, however, and to the Church in many of the most important parts of the West, January 6th had come to be the day for the commemoration of the baptism of Jesus and of the institution of the sacrament of baptism, the Epiphany by the revelation of Jesus to mankind as Christ, the Son of the Father. This, indeed, is still true in the eastern Churches. The paper continues with proof that Aponius, probably a Syrian writing in Rome between 410 and 415, still regarded the Epiphany as referring to and commemorating the birth of Christ in the flesh, and that to Orosius the Epiphany was still the commemoration of our Lord's baptism and of the institution of the sacrament of baptism; to neither of them was it the commemoration of the revelation of Christ to the Magi. This, it is pointed out, has direct bearing, since Orosius was a Spanish priest, on the date of the introduction into Spain of the usage followed by him, a matter which has apparently been the subject of some difference of opinion. Orosius was, as is shown by a passage which Mommsen quotes, quite aware of the view held so strongly by his teacher, St. Augustine, and by the Roman Church, but ventured, though in very respectful terms, to assert his belief in the importance of commemorating our Lord's baptism on 6 January, the Epiphany.

Differing on the meaning of the Epiphany, Aponius and Orosius were united in feeling that, as Christ was to bring spiritual peace to His followers, so His coming was also to mark the advent of physical peace and that Augustus and the Roman Empire were instruments selected by God for the latter purpose.

In the following article, "Orosius and Augustine," Mommsen develops further the thought that Orosius, like many Christian writers of his time, following Eusebius, believed that, though the world always had been, and still was, filled with sorrows and wars, pestilences, horrid crimes, and evil of every kind, yet it had become more peaceful and conditions less appalling with the advent of Christianity and that the improvement would continue as the new religion spread and took deeper root. Pointing out that the *Seven Books of Histories Against the Pagans* had been undertaken at the request of St. Augustine and had been published only after having been submitted to him by the author for his approval, Mommsen nevertheless quite rightly feels that St. Augustine did not share the belief of Orosius that Christianity brought increasing political peace and material progress. Both agreed that the calamities of their era did not exceed those of the pagan past, and both agreed that God controlled human history, but at this point Augustine ceased to follow. Drawing attention to the fact that even on the one occasion when Augustine expressed in sharp terms his disagreement with a belief held by Orosius, he did not mention his opponent by name, Mommsen sees sufficiently clear evidence of disapproval expressed in the whole substance of Augustine's *City of God*. He sees it, too, in the casual manner in which Augustine treated the coincidence between the birth of Jesus and the universal and peaceful reign of Augustus, a coincidence which Orosius considered of the greatest importance as proof of the Divine plan; in the fact that in those parts of *The City of God* written after the publication of Orosius' history, Augustine nowhere referred to his former pupil — indeed, the only time after the publication of the *Histories* that Augustine mentioned Orosius at all was at the end of his life, and then, considering their former relationship, in very cool terms, "a certain Spanish priest, Orosius." For all this, however much Augustine may have disapproved of the foundation on which the work of Orosius was based, it was, Mommsen reminds us, the *Seven Books of Histories Against the Pagans* that received the endorsement of the Papacy, so that the historians of the Middle Ages, in accepting Orosius' interpretation of history, supposed themselves to be following the theories of St. Augustine.

The true belief of St. Augustine concerning the meaning of history is admirably set forth in the one essay we have still to consider, "St. Augustine and the Christian Idea of

Progress: the Background of *The City of God*." *The City of God*, of course, was written, as Orosius' history had been, to refute the pagan contention that Rome had been treated more favorably while the old pagan rites had been followed than it had been since official observance of these rites had been suppressed by the Christians, and that therefore Christianity was a false religion, at least for patriotic Roman citizens. As we have just seen, Orosius maintained precisely the contrary, and in consequence came to precisely the opposite conclusion, believing that the world — and "Rome" included the whole world so far as concerned Orosius, Augustine, and even those pagans against whom they were writing — had become more peaceful and more prosperous with the advent of Christianity and that progress would be continuous as the new religion spread — at least until those last, dreadful days that would witness the coming of the Antichrist. To St. Augustine, both beliefs were false, and both dangerous to Christianity. The world had always been evil, it was evil, it would continue to be evil. Nor were there cycles of good times and evil ones, golden and iron ages. (Mommsen points out that Augustine in this argument, though nominally opposing the pagan philosophers, was probably directly concerned with opposing Origen. He might, one feels, also have pointed out that this aspect of Augustine's argument, this opposition to all cyclical theories of history, was not inconsistent with the Eusebian and Orosian conception of Christian progress; even the conception of a spiral in time, according to which there would always be ups and downs in history, but each down would be a little less low than the last, and each up a little higher than the preceding one — even this would be inconsistent with a progress caused by the advent of Christianity, and destined by the very nature of its cause to increase until the coming of the Antichrist.) "To Augustine, then, history takes its course, not in cycles, but along a line. That line has a most definite beginning, the Creation, and a most definite end, the Last Judgement . . . From Augustine's conception of the course of history it follows that every particular event that takes place in time, every human life and human action, is a unique phenomenon which happens under the auspices of Divine Providence and must therefore have a definite meaning." How should this be reconciled with the material evils of which the world is full, and always has been, and always will be until the end of time? Very simply: material evil also serves the purposes of God, and has no other importance to Him. Apart from the Divine purpose served by their material prosperity or their material suffering, it is nothing to God, and should be nothing to the true Christian, whether or not in this world the wicked prosper and the righteous suffer in the material sense.

"Lest, however, any emperor shall become a Christian in order to merit the blessed felicity of Constantine, — when everyone ought to be a Christian for the sake of the eternal life — God took away Jovian far sooner than Julian, and He allowed Gratian to be slain by the sword of a tyrant." "There are still wars, wars among nations for supremacy, wars among sects, wars among Jews, pagans, Christians, heretics, and these wars are becoming more frequent. When man learns that in himself he is nothing and that he has no help from himself, then arms in himself are broken in pieces, then wars in himself are ended." (Mommsen reminds us that St. Augustine held firmly to these views in spite of the direct criticism of St. Jerome.) The purpose of God in permitting these material evils was so to allot material suffering and material prosperity as to allow the citizens of the City of God to achieve salvation by giving them such admixtures of good and evil fortune as might best be used by them for the increase of their spiritual welfare. All the foregoing quotations from St. Augustine[8] appear in Mommsen's article. One wishes that he had also quoted a passage from the *Sermones*,[9] one given by Karl Löwith at the beginning of his book, *Meaning in History*.[10] That Mommsen knew this book is certain: he quotes it in notes 37 and 43 of the essay under review:

> Thus the world is like an oilpress: under pressure. If you are the dregs of the oil you are carried away through the sewer; if you are genuine oil you will remain in the vessel. But to be under pressure is inevitable. Observe the dregs, observe the oil. Pressure takes place ever in the world, as for instance, through famine, war, want, inflation, indigence, mortality, rape, avarice; such are the pressures on the poor and the worries of the states: we have evidence of them . . . We have found men who grumble under these pressures and who say: "how bad are these Christian times!" . . . Thus speak the dregs of the oil which run away through the sewer; their color is black because they blaspheme: they lack splendour. The oil has splendour. For here another sort of man is under the same pressure and friction which polishes him, for is it not the very friction which refines him?

[8] From *The City of God,* except the last, which is from his *Ennaration on Psalm xlv.13–xlvi.9.*
[9] Ed. Denis, 24.11.
[10] University of Chicago Press 1949.

It is remarkable that in a series of papers written in English by an author to whom English was not native there should be, so far as the reviewer can see, no grammatical errors. The only misprint noticed is "inbar" for *iubar* on p. 127, n. 80. There are a few — remarkably few — unidiomatic expressions, and there is, but again only very seldom, a clumsiness that is unfortunately by no means restricted to the English of the foreign-born.

Full justice has been done to the author by Rice. The format of the volume is pleasant, the paper and the printing are excellent. A delightful photograph of Mommsen with some of his pupils is used as a frontispiece, and there are illustrations for two essays for the proper understanding of which they are really needed. In the first of these studies, "An Early Representation of Petrarch as Poet Laureate," there is only a single illustration, but it is a full-page one and of fine quality, and no others are needed, particularly in view of the various versions of an actual portrait of Petrarch that are given in the many illustrations, also very good, in the other article, "Petrarch and the Decoration of the *Sala Virorum Illustrium* in Padua." There is no index, but that is scarcely necessary in a book consisting of short essays on varied subjects. Following a preface by Rice, there is an introduction in the form of a short biographical sketch by Marcham; at the end of the volume, there is a complete and welcome bibliography. We may be grateful to Professor Rice and to Cornell University for having produced at once a work of genuine intrinsic interest and a most fitting memorial to a distinguished scholar.

INDEX

INDEX

296 Index

Caelianus, 3, 5, 34
Caesar, Caesars, 218, 269; Gaius (Caligula), 61; Julius, 117, 135; Patricius, 243
Caesarius, 162, 168, 240–241, 243–244
Caesaropapism, 270, 272
Caiaphas, 270
Calabria, 219. *See also* Charles, duke of Calabria
Callinicum, 272
Calvitii Encomium, 231
Cambyses, 105–107
Camel, 104–105, 108, 134–138, 140–143, 231–232, 246. *See also* Austoriani; Laguantan; Nomads; Sahara
Campania, 92
Campbell, A. H., 3
Campenhausen, von, 248, 250, 262
Canius, 61
Canossa, 181
Capitol, the, 27, 278
Capraria, 211, 215–216
Capua, 116, 124, 199
Carneadae, 248
Carthage, Carthaginians, 105, 108–109, 126, 160, 201, 240. *See also* Cyrenaica, economic connections of
Caspar, E., 66–67
Caspian Gates, 238
Cassiodorus, 31–32, 55, 80–81, 102, 148; and trial of Basilius and Praetextatus, 33, 40–41; and Boethius, 61–63, 81, 89–90, 93; on *iud. quinq.,* 3, 5, 35, 40–41; influence on monasteries and *scriptoria,* 203–204
Castor and Pollux, 134
Castorius, 32
Castruccio Castracani, 274–275
Catabathmus, *see* Solum
Catholic, Catholics, 47, 64–65, 71, 73, 102, 271–273; and Boethius, 47–48, 53, 86–87, 97. *See also* Church
Cato the Younger, 135
Catullus, 133–134
Caucasus, 185, 239
Cedrenus, 14
Cerberus, 126
Cerealis, 112
Cessi, Roberto, 74–76
Chalcedon, 20, 240, 244

Chamoux, François, *see* Cyrenaica, recent works on
Charanis, Peter, 273
Charlemagne, 38, 279
Charles, duke of Calabria, 274–275
Charles V, 59
Chierici, Gino, 202
Chosroes, 132
Christ (*Christus*), 178, 180–181, 192, 195–196, 256–257, 270, 284–286
Christian, Christians, 272, 288. *See also* Christianity; Church
Christianity, 209, 216, 285–289; and barbarians, 196–198, 203, 220, 230, 236; and classical civilization, 192, 203–204, 213–215, 218–221, 263; and Paulinus of Nola, 188–190, 192, 205, 266; and Rutilius Namatianus, 210–215, 266; and Synesius, 229, 250–253
Chronikon Paschale, 12–15, 19–20
Chrysostom, St. John, 241, 261
Church, the, 64, 169, 178, 181–182, 257, 261; and St. Ambrose, 272; and Andronicus, 182, 258–259; and barbarians, 196, 220, 222, 245, 249, 272–273; and Boethius, 48; and classical civilization, 219–220, 222, 245, 263, 266; relationship to emperors and empire, 269–273; as directing force in Europe, 219, 273; and Honorius, 210; and January 6th, 284–285; as Jewish sect, 219, 269; reunification of, 57; autonomous position under Roman law, 269, 271; and senatorial aristocracy, 220, 222; and Synesius, 244–245, 249, 266; and Theodoric, 99, 102, 272–273. *See also* Catholic, Christianity
Cicero, 91, 281
Cimitile, 198, 202
Cinyps, 108
Circe, 211, 215
Cirta, 160
City, the, *see* Rome
City of God, The, 198, 213, 218, 286–289
Civitas, and Roman law, 269
Clarissimus, clarissimi, clarissimate, *see Vir clarissimus*

Index

Index